The Democrats Must Lead

The
DEMOCRATS
Must Lead

The Case for a Progressive Democratic Party

edited by
JAMES MacGREGOR BURNS
WILLIAM CROTTY
LOIS LOVELACE DUKE
LAWRENCE D. LONGLEY

WESTVIEW PRESS
Boulder ■ San Francisco ■ Oxford

Copyright © 1992 by Westview Press, Inc., except for Chapter 13, which is © James A. Nathan

Published in 1992 in the United States of America by Westview Press, Inc., 5500 Central Avenue, Boulder, Colorado 80301-2847, and in the United Kingdom by Westview Press, 36 Lonsdale Road, Summertown, Oxford OX2 7EW

Library of Congress Cataloging-in-Publication Data
The Democrats must lead : the case for a progressive Democratic Party
  / edited by James MacGregor Burns . . . [et al.].
    p. cm.
  Includes index.
  ISBN 0-8133-1569-7 — ISBN 0-8133-1570-0 (pb)
  1. Democratic Party (U.S.). 2. United States—Politics and
government—1989–   . I. Burns, James MacGregor.
JK2317 1992c
324.2736—dc20   92-11444
                                                                              CIP

Printed and bound in the United States of America

The paper used in this publication meets the requirements
of the American National Standard for Permanence of Paper
for Printed Library Materials Z39.48-1984.

10   9   8   7   6   5   4   3   2   1

Contents

PART THREE
A Politics of Substance

Preface

This is an unusual book. It is a book with a message, and a liberal one at that. Our belief is that the time has come to offer a viable liberal alternative to the Republicans and the conservative excesses of the last quarter of a century. And the political party to do this is the Democratic party: The Democrats must lead.

This book represents the views of leading academicians and political figures. Though relatively brief, it is intended to be clear in focus and argument and outspokenly liberal in orientation. In these regards, it is not a typical academic treatise—highly qualified in argument, somewhat dull in presentation, and limited in its appeal to a mainly professional audience. On the contrary, this presentation is advocacy oriented, direct, and aimed at a broad audience.

Each contribution makes a self-contained argument, which in turn is based on the most relevant of contemporary data and analyses as well as on the personal experience and knowledge of the particular author. Taken together, the chapters reemphasize the basic theme of the book: that the Democrats can win by appealing to a liberal constituency with liberal issues. The country needs a vibrant political alternative. The only party that can provide this alternative is the Democratic party.

The indictment of Republican rule is massive: economic mismanagement, tax restructuring to benefit the wealthy, official corruption and exploitation of public office, a politics of racial division, environmental neglect, a disregard for civil rights and an intolerance for the concerns of minorities, recessions, joblessness, Savings and Loan bailouts, homelessness, an educational system in disarray, military build-ups, a series of undeclared wars, urban decay, out-of-control deficits, exploding medical costs in a limited-coverage health care system, and two constitutional crises —the Watergate of Richard M. Nixon and the Irangate of Ronald Reagan and George Bush.

Conservatism is an ideology of privilege, exploitation, and excess. Its time has passed. The country is looking for an informed and compassionate leadership willing to address the nation's fundamental needs and politically skilled enough to do something about them. The Democratic party can provide that alternative.

This book thus represents a call to arms by authors who share a commitment to a liberal political agenda and a rejuvenated, more combative Democratic party. It is a statement of the nation's political and social needs. It is a call for the Democrats to lead and to represent those who need representation. A Democratic party that addresses the country's real problems can win. This book is an effort to return the Democratic party to its roots. That is our purpose.

The chapters herein were developed under the auspices of the Political Scientists for a Progressive Democratic Party. The group was formed several years ago under the direction of James MacGregor Burns. Its intention, above all, is to offer policy alternatives and an ongoing source of ideas (representative of the liberal community in academics) to the political party most likely to act upon them—the Democratic party. But it hopes, as well, to provide options in a debate long dominated by conservatives and characterized by the sterility and class bias of a politics of privilege.

There are choices to be made. Liberals must reassert themselves; they must offer voters reasonable and attractive policy positions. The proposals contained within this book are meant to contribute to both these ends.

As editors, we are grateful to Jennifer Knerr and Amy Eisenberg of Westview Press, who have been supportive of and involved in this project since its inception; to Jane Raese, the book's project editor; and to Chris Arden, its copyeditor. We wish to thank a number of people who have contributed to the final result: Joel Tabin at Northwestern University; Marianne Blair at Clemson University; the Faculty Secretarial Office at Williams College; and, especially, Vicki Koessl at Lawrence University, who assumed and discharged with skill the considerable responsibilities of producing the book's final camera-ready typescript.

James MacGregor Burns
William Crotty
Lois Lovelace Duke
Lawrence D. Longley

PART ONE

A Party That Can Lead/
A Party That Should Lead

1

JAMES MacGREGOR BURNS

The Democrats Must Lead— But How?

What does it take to lead? Realistic grasp of party heritage and party potential. Political sense of concrete problems and realities. Above all, moral purpose and conviction. In sum, thoughtful, practical, and principled leadership on the part of men and women at every level of the Democratic party.

But first the Democrats must take psychological leadership—of themselves. Party debate during 1991 consisted mainly of pessimistic talk about Democratic changes in 1992, bleak poll results, abject failures of Democratic party leaders in Congress to carry the fight to President Bush, and divisive debates among Democrats as to the best strategy for 1992 and the rest of the 1990s.

It was not a Republican but a Democrat, for example, who most sharply castigated the party for its failings. The party, he said, was torn between the Twin Peaks of the American political psyche: greed and guilt. The Democratic party had lost the capacity to be morally indignant. It did not dare to lose, because losing was seen as a character flaw. These were the words not of a young Turk sitting on the sidelines but of the head of the Virginia Democratic party. One Democratic aspirant to the White House early in 1992, with fine impartiality, called the politics of both parties "brain-dead."[1]

The media lost no opportunity to savage the Democrats as divided, irresolute, and weak—in short, as political wimps. The announced presidential aspirants were rated about C-plus in quality. Senate and House Democrats were called trimmers, opportunists; they were seen as utterly lacking in creative leadership. The party as a whole was pictured as a weak clone of the GOP. Meg Greenfield castigated the party's "big guys" for not

"I beg your pardon," said Alice, "but which of you is the Democrat?"

Drawing by Handelsman; © 1991. Reprinted by permission of The New Yorker Magazine, Inc., December 16, 1991, p. 42.

daring to run against Bush, leaving the fight to the "second-tier" aspirants.[2] And cartoonists had a field day; one pictured Alice-in-(political) Wonderland confronting Tweedle Dee and Tweedle Dum and asking, "But who's the Democrat?"

HOW DEMOCRATS WIN—AS PROGRESSIVES

As usual, the ideological war among Democrats—though a bit muted during an election year—is almost as intense as the attacks from reactionary Republicans. When conservative Democrats—or "centrists" and "mainstreamers" as they prefer to be called—challenge the progressive Democrat wing of the party, they rarely attack progressivism itself. To do that would be to attack the best of the party legacy. No, from their pulpit—the Democratic Leadership Council—comes the argument that the party has lost five of the last six presidential elections primarily because its candidates were too liberal, too out of touch with the voters, too radical especially on "social issues."

Hence the best strategy, the centrists contend, is to choose presidential nominees representing the widest consensus in the party, candidates who are moderate and "reasonable," candidates always willing to negotiate and compromise with the opposition, even Republicans. That is the way to win.

Historically the opposite has been true. "Let's look at the record"—the historical record, that is—but we must start at the party's beginning, in order to understand the whole rich party heritage and the almost two centuries of lessons our earlier Democratic leaders have taught us.

In 1800 Thomas Jefferson and James Madison and their zealous supporters made a strong appeal to the people with their attacks on John Adams's elitism and heavy defense-spending taxes, as well as on Federalist violations of Bill of Rights liberties. They won with this kind of "progressive" attack. Granted, many domestic policies were left to the states to formulate and carry out; but Jefferson, under the "new federalism," was no passive president. He and James Gallatin framed new fiscal policies, he and his supporters in Congress carried through the Louisiana Purchase, and he dispatched historic expeditions to the West. The Jeffersonian momentum carried over to the Madison and Monroe presidencies. At both the national and state levels the early Jeffersonians were often bold activists.

No one ever accused Andrew Jackson of standpattism. His attack on the elites of the day doubtless would be condemned today as "negative campaigning," but in office he quickly established himself as a tribune of the people. Against conservative and respectable advice from fellow Democrats, he attacked the "Nullifiers" during his first term and Nicholas Biddle's bank during his second. The Jacksonian impetus carried over to Martin Van Buren's election victory in 1836 and to his administration as well.

The Democrats won in 1844 with an activist candidate, James K. Polk, who had old Andy Jackson's support. They won again in 1852 and 1856 with candidates who supported the Compromise of 1850, but the party fell apart in the face of the rising conflict over slavery. There was no Jefferson nor Jackson to lead the party in a bold and principled direction. The Democracy was at its nadir from the Civil War to Woodrow Wilson's election in 1912. Whereas the Republican party frankly spoke and acted for the burgeoning high-tariff corporate interests, the Democrats failed to offer clear alternatives, except on the corruption issue. Woodrow Wilson, however, took progressive positions on domestic issues in both his campaigns.

After another period of centrism and defeat in the 1920s the Democratic party entered a new era of leadership under FDR and Harry Truman, and then again, during the rising civil rights crisis, under JFK and LBJ. A fresh and exciting presidential candidate, Jimmy Carter, won in 1976, but his administration appeared to end up on dead center. Then it was the GOP's turn. Under Ronald Reagan's Hollywood-style but committed conservative leadership, the Republicans broke the "Goldwater jinx," won power on a boldly rightwing platform, and—for a time, at least—governed as conservatives, until they bogged down in their own Washington quagmire. Bush won as a conservative in 1988.

Looking back on this historical record, one takes it for granted. Of course progressives like Jefferson and Jackson, Wilson and FDR, Kennedy and Johnson, would win by holding to the left. But that outcome was not so obvious at the time. None of these leaders took the stands they did without powerful opposition from within the Democratic party. FDR, for example, faced an open rebellion by Al Smith and a host of outspoken conservatives in 1936. He "won big" that year—and, more important, established the New Deal so solidly in national programs and policy that the core of the New Deal would never again be in jeopardy, even under Republicans. The leaders, at every level from the grassroots up, made a choice, took progressive action, and achieved practical and lasting results.

PATTERNS OF SUCCESS AND FAILURE

History does not always repeat itself. Progressive Democrats do not always win; George McGovern lost against Nixon in 1972, at a time when Watergate crimes were still proving helpful to the Nixon Republicans before turning into their downfall. But the pattern of Democratic party history is clear. Progressives—by whatever name—usually won, and when they won, they won a government, they won at least the moral right to act. Moderate Democrats like Buchanan and Cleveland won office but had relatively little impact on public policy.

Recent experience in this century followed that pattern. After World War II, for example, it was Harry Truman's turn toward a strongly progressive stance during his 1948 campaign that, most historians agree, helped him win his "miracle victory" over Thomas E. Dewey. Adlai Stevenson ran two moderate campaigns against Eisenhower, in the "flaccid '50s," and lost twice. Kennedy conducted a cautiously progressive campaign in 1960, moved toward progressivism during his three years in office, would almost certainly have run as a progressive in 1964 had he lived, and doubtless would have defeated Goldwater as soundly as Lyndon Johnson did. LBJ "won big" in 1964 as an outspoken progressive. Hubert Humphrey ran a moderate-liberal campaign against Nixon in 1968, especially on the Vietnam issue; Walter Mondale ran the same kind of campaign against Reagan in 1984, as did Michael Dukakis against George Bush in 1988. All three of these fine, attractive candidates lost.

In view of the historical record, both long run and recent, why are some Democrats and their supporters in the media telling us that we can win only with a moderate, centrist Democrat in 1992 and thereafter? Because it's different now, some say. The question is, what are people thinking; how will they vote, *today?* So let us look at that record, too.

According to Harris polls published in July 1991 (polls conducted during the post-Gulf War height of Bush's popularity), almost three-quarters of voters saw the Republican party as no longer frugal in government spending. By a more than 2 to 1 ratio they perceived the GOP as racking up the biggest deficits in American history. By almost 3 to 1 they viewed the Republicans as working too much to "protect the interests of the rich and big business." They blamed the GOP far more than the Democrats for the S&L scandal. On abortion rights they saw the GOP as "too closely tied to those who would deny women the right to choose in the case of abortion," and by a wide margin they felt that the Democrats would handle abortion rights better. And on another sensitive issue—affirmative action—whites by a large margin believed that Democrats were "fairer."

A 56 to 38 majority, as Louis Harris summed it up, viewed the Democrats as correct on such issues as "abortion, environment, education, health, children, the elderly, and even taxes and spending." So—again— why is the party being told to go "centrist"?

WHAT DO WE WIN WHEN WE WIN?

Perhaps, in some sports, winning is "everything." Not so in politics. Through elections politicians win *positions*. But do they win *power*—to carry out their campaign pledges, to do all the good things they promised, to really, actually, help people, to offer them real opportunity, to bring about tangible improvements in their lives? In short, does winning mean not just taking over offices but gaining a *government?*

Toward this end, progressive Democrats must do more than preen themselves on their fine policies and benevolent plans. They must face some major political problems confronting the party.

One is the failure to reach the voters in recent elections. Sixty percent of the voters, Louis Harris reported, criticized Democrats for not being able to "come up with real solutions to today's problems." Seventy-five percent believed that the party has chosen "poor candidates for president" for a long time. For progressives who believe that they do have solutions, such voters' attitudes are lethal.

Obviously progressives must learn to communicate better with the electorate. Professors Betty Glad and Lois Lovelace Duke offer valuable advice on the specifics of this issue in later pages. But the question transcends tactics. The voters want to feel a sense of commitment, of follow-through, of tenacity on the part of leaders. And the question of whether progressive leaders can actually deliver on their promises may turn on two other questions.

One concerns the capacity of the party itself. Conventional wisdom now has it that both of the two major parties—and especially the Democrats—have become disorganized, underfinanced, largely impotent organizations. Yet we continue to rely on parties to choose candidates, mobilize voters, indoctrinate the citizenry, and provide a kind of "party team" to run the government. In this volume Professor Samuel Patterson reminds us of the stronger leadership structures that have come into being in Congress. But the whole party needs refurbishing, such that at the least it can renew its ancient function of propagandizing and mobilizing the potential Democratic vote. Professor Kay Lawson, a close student of parties abroad as well as at home, directly confronts the crisis of the party system.

The Democrats, however, cannot mobilize the national electorate and control the government if they are unable to govern themselves. In the last half-century the Democrats as a national organization have lost that capacity. Who's to blame? Not only the usual suspects such as television and faulty campaign finance. Even more devastating has been the rise of national and state primaries that have destroyed the main function of parties—recruiting and electing their candidates and empowering and holding them responsible in office. We must restore the national convention, democratically chosen, as the place to make the top party decisions, including the drafting of candidates when feasible and necessary. Restoring the national midterm issues convention—to debate policy, not just politicians, and to strengthen and democratize the national organization of the party—would be a strong step toward effective conventions. Democrats must learn that a participatory party and a strongly led party are not necessarily antithetical—as a number of state parties have demonstrated. Lawrence D. Longley, himself a party activist at the state and national levels, explores below the severe problems and the great potentials of national party renewal.

Another harsh test for Democrats is the governmental system itself. The worst obstacle for progressives over time has been neither GOP conservatism nor Democratic centrism but, rather, a government so fragmented that the party could not carry out its program. Even FDR, the master politician, was frustrated and defeated by "checks and balances" during his second term. Can a constitutional system devised in the eighteenth century meet the tremendous burdens of the twenty-first? William Kreml deals with this enduring governmental problem in this volume.

In facing all these problems, committed leadership is indispensable. Making the party work, making the government produce, is not the kind of job you put into the hands of middle-of-the-road trimmers, incessant compromisers, behind-the-scenes brokers, consensus-at-any-price deal makers. Governor Mario Cuomo, during the last election year of 1990, mused over precisely these problems in an interview with a prominent historian.

It wasn't the *ideas* that lost in the recent presidential elections, Cuomo observed. "The *philosophy* didn't lose." He personally liked the centrists in the party, he said, "but this Democratic Leadership Council is a joke to me." Why? "The proposition that you must move away from what we're saying because the other side is beating us is wrong. Who's right, them or us? *Winning* is not the measure."[3] The governor in effect was calling for moral, principled leadership.

BEING TRUE TO OURSELVES

And moral, principled leadership remains the ultimate, the crucial test for Democrats. Here the enemy is not so much Republicans or conservative Democrats—the "enemy is us." Let's face it: For too long Democrats have been living off the fifty-year-old ideas of the New Deal. Surely it's high time for fresh ideas, new departures, far more bold and innovative policymaking. Even after those fifty years, Democrats have not yet fully realized FDR's dream of freedom from want and freedom from fear. And during those fifty years they have compromised far too much—with Republican presidents, with Southern reactionaries in both parties, with "bipartisan" foreign policies that left us with Vietnam and other disasters. If the Democrats wish to govern, William Crotty insists, they must learn how to oppose—that is, to offer clear and principled alternatives to GOP-ism.

The harshest moral test facing Democrats is posed in this volume by Professor Mileur—whether we can rid ourselves of our coalition with a Dixie party bloc that over the years has tarnished our image, perverted our policies, and lessened our chances of electoral victory. More recently the Dixie bloc has thwarted congressional Democrats in overriding Reagan and Bush vetoes of desperately needed legislation. Some contributors to this volume might prefer a different approach than Mileur's: They might wish only to jettison the "solid South" while seeking to hold onto at least Texas and Florida, perhaps also trying to mobilize black-white voter coalitions even in the Deep South, at least over the long run. But would these alternatives still mean compromising even with "outer-rim" Southern politicos to a degree that would impair the party's moral standing?

This moral standing presupposes, however, that progressive Democrats are prepared to deal with the intertwined problems of poverty and racism, and that they will do so on the basis of both progressive principles and political reality. Progressives are constantly taken to task for overempha-sizing issues of poverty, joblessness, family structure, (black) welfare dependency, homelessness—in short, for repeatedly forcing Democratic "national candidates into the suicidal position of defending minority rights against majority values."[4] Some of us had thought that protecting minorities was what the Democratic party, as a grand coalition of minorities, was all about. Charles Hamilton's brilliant analysis of the "realistic" compromises of the Democratic party during the last six decades shows that they have not been in fact realistic but rather self-defeating in crucial social areas.

Still, the critics are right when they say that the party needs fresh, innovative policies to win back millions of potential Democratic voters who have deserted the party on "social" issues. Stewart Burns and I have urged enactment of one such policy in our recently published *A People's Charter*—and here we speak of a policy replacing "affirmative action" policies with "real opportunity" programs that would be addressed to the concrete needs and aspirations of individuals, not group categories.[5] Carrying out real opportunity, as we define it, would be the most revolu-tionary and effective policy innovation of the late twentieth century. Other progressive Democrats will and must come up with their own new departures and bold innovations, especially in the many potential post-cold war initiatives that James A. Nathan lays out in example after example.

CONCLUSION

Probably the supreme moral challenge to Democrats concerns the place of women in the party, as Mary Lou Kendrigan spells out in convincing detail. A supreme political opportunity is also at stake. Women's widening economic base across the nation in jobs and income, their slow but constantly increasing election victories, their intensifying militance and assertiveness—these factors can draw hundreds of thousands of activists into the party. And women's concerns with human relationships and rights can bring the qualities of nurturing and sharing to a political system long dominated by macho competitiveness and brokerage. But artificial obstacles stand in women's way—especially such obstacles as the "party" primaries, which, given their voracious demand for huge amounts of campaign money, put special burdens on women holding lesser access to big money. This is another reason to call for stronger party organizations that can recruit women and help them burst through the Democratic party's own "glass ceiling." And it is another example of how moral leadership can nourish practical politics—that is Democratic party victories.

Combining moral principle with intellectual realism and political practicality—that is how Democrats must lead.

NOTES

1. Bill Clinton, quoted in the *Berkshire Eagle*, January 7, 1992, p. A3.

2. *Newsweek*, September 16, 1991, p. 72.

3. Interview of Mario Cuomo by William Leuchtenburg, *American Heritage* (December 1990), p. 66.

4. Thomas Byrne Edsall with Mary D. Edsall, *Chain Reaction: The Impact of Race, Rights, and Taxes on American Politics* (New York: W. W. Norton, 1991), as reviewed by David Oshinsky, *New York Times Book Review*, October 20, 1991, p. 1.

5. James MacGregor Burns and Stewart Burns, *A People's Charter* (New York: Alfred A. Knopf, 1991), ch. 14.

2

KAY LAWSON

Why We Still Need
Real Political Parties

WHAT IS A "REAL POLITICAL PARTY"?

Scholars have as many definitions of party as there are parties. Some have gone so far as to declare that any organization that calls itself a party is a party.[1] Others argue that no clear definition is possible, that mere interest groups can slip in and out of partyhood with such ease and frequency that there is no good way to tell them apart: Yael Yishai gives us the "interest parties" of Israel as an example.[2] For still others, myself among them, the line is very clear: A party is an organization that nominates candidates to stand for election to public office. Any group that does this becomes, unambiguously, a party. When it stops nominating candidates, it stops being a party.

However, this simple and, I think, useful definition is not what I mean here by the term "real political party." Here, I use the word "real" in the good, strong, popular sense of "the very epitome of what the thing ought to be." The term implies not only an ideal but also a set of qualities upon which there is reasonably wide agreement.

Reasonably wide agreement, not unanimity. For some, I acknowledge, the very notion of an "ideal" political party is an oxymoron. We have become so accustomed to disliking our parties that we can no longer imagine what one we might admire would resemble.[3] Nevertheless, the idea of a "real" political party sets our tribal memories astir. Wasn't there a time . . . didn't Van Buren say . . . what was it that Lincoln suggested . . . I seem to recall that during the Great Depression Roosevelt. . . .[4]

Existentialists all, we define the good by the act that is pleasing to ourselves. A party is judged by the acts it performs. Realists all, we recognize that no organization acts unselfishly. Parties are organizations for acquiring control over powerful offices of government, and they act accordingly. Even when they have no hope of placing their own members in such control, they seek to influence the behavior of those who win elections. However, citizens all, we nevertheless look for parties whose selfish acts at the same time serve our own larger social purposes. Parties that work only for themselves may be real enough in their own evaluations, and in those of scholars intent on studying them regardless of their social usefulness—but they are not sufficiently real to the citizens who need them to do more.

It is no wonder, then, that parties in the United States today have little or no reality for most American citizens. Elite organizations that work only for themselves and fellow elites, they appear to most voters to serve no larger societal functions, or else to serve them so poorly that they no longer merit support. If forced by an inquiring pollster to think about them, we rank political parties at the bottom of any list of public institutions; and normally we don't pay them any attention at all. For that matter, we choose our candidates on the basis of incumbency, media personality, or issue stance rather than on what party labels they wear.[5]

What could political parties do in order to become real again? (The cynic interrupts, and offers to answer for the citizen trapped in a seemingly endless recession: "'Get me a job.'") And, indeed, the idea of Tammany as a "real political party" has its appeal. William Riordon, in his widely read and humorous interviews of New York District Leader George Washington Plunkitt, taught many of us to think of the machine boss, even when motivated by the basest greed and engaged in the rawest expropriation of public moneys, as somehow a rather appealing figure, the "realistic" agent of a personalized democracy.[6] The voter gets a low-paying job, the boss gets the vote and with it access to all that power can buy. Textbook after textbook has accepted the idea that the machine, actually an instrument of oppressive criminality, was a useful if makeshift means of assimilating new citizens into "democracy" and that our most reasonable response to it might well be one of nostalgia for the good old days when that's how politics was done. (The careful scholarship of David Mayhew, who notes that very few cities ever actually had machines of any kind, has largely been ignored.)[7] Nevertheless, the facts are that the United States never had extensive machine politics, and that what it did have, none of us should reasonably want back. Parties that buy our votes with one-on-one material payoffs are not viable alternatives today, and cannot be the real political parties we seek.

The functions of real political parties go back longer in time than to turn-of-the-century machinations. They go back to the very origins of parties themselves. The modern political party came into being as a way to solve the problems raised for candidates by an expanding suffrage. As soon as it became impossible for the candidates to secure election—or reelection—by personally persuading the few persons of one's own elevated class who had the vote, some kind of vote-gathering organization became necessary. Furthermore, that organization had to find grounds on which to appeal to a larger and more economically heterogeneous electorate (racial and sexual heterogeneity came later, much later). In other words, it needed candidates *and* issues that would have a wider appeal. The originators of party naively believed that voters would follow their lead only for good reason. They lacked the mass communication technology and skills for persuading voters that bad reasons—or no reasons at all—could make a fair substitute. Although their own motive, the conquest of power, was the same as any party politician's today, they had a different view of what would motivate the voter: They believed they had to either buy the vote (a practice that began long before Tammany but became less and less feasible the more the suffrage expanded) or offer to use that power on behalf of the voters' own interests. Parties became the agencies that made democracy possible because they believed their own fortunes depended on playing the democratic game with some minimal level of rectitude.

In the beginning, then (and it was a beginning that lasted well into the twentieth century), parties were organizations that did not seek to motivate voters solely through materialistic horsetrading; nor did they have the capacity to do so, lacking today's sloganistic media blitz. Instead, parties promised to perform specific functions—and voters who took the job seriously evaluated them on the basis of the quality of that performance. These functions, all of which made pragmatic good sense to vote-seeking organizations with limited funds and skills but all of which were also of great use to budding democracies, were the following:

First, parties *aggregated interests, formulated issues, and proposed programs.* They discovered the concerns of a significant body of voters, worked out necessary compromises, and wrote platforms incorporating this work.

Second, parties *recruited and trained candidates* who would support their programs. Training actually came first; working for and in the party was the best way to learn the delicate arts of competitive politics as well as to demonstrate one's aptitude for public office.

Third, parties *structured the vote.* It was they who gave life and meaning to elections. They did so by making their own nominations and allowing those selected to wear the label of the party—a label that had a consistent meaning, or at least one that changed only gradually over time. They did so by conducting campaigns for their candidates, raising the necessary funds, training volunteers, and canvassing door to door. They helped with registration and they got out the vote. In fact, their constant preparations gave substance to the coming election—specifically, by helping citizens decide to vote, and how.

Fourth, parties *provided a means of holding elected officials accountable.* If elected officials did not carry out the party's program, or the party's program once carried out did not produce the desired results, voters had the option of looking elsewhere—and activists had the option of choosing other candidates. For the voters who were not active party members this function was performed by the parties together, not one by one: It was in their diversity, in the choice that they collectively made possible, that the noninvolved voters' hope of holding elected officials accountable lay. Those with the time and interest could, however, join and become active in a particular party, and there combine with like-minded others to utilize the organization as an instrument of accountability.

THE PERVERSION OF PARTIES

Do not American parties perform the same four functions today? Is it not, indeed, upon them that we depend for the performance of these tasks? The answers are: no and no, with one minor exception.

Although it makes sense when speaking of "real political parties" to begin with interest aggregation, because that is where the political process ideally begins and rebegins, in order to understand what has happened to our parties today we need to consider first how candidates are recruited—because that is where the political process begins today.

American parties today do not look for candidates to support their programs. Instead, they accept as their candidates whoever has been able to rally the strength to extract the nominations. A party's nomination is no longer its own to bestow. Primary elections ensure that the candidate who can gather the most funds and/or the candidate who is an incumbent running for reelection (and normally the two attributes are found in combination) will normally win the party's nomination without any help from the party whatsoever—and, indeed sometimes against the wishes of the party's active membership and leaders. Furthermore, in the vast majority of American elections, political parties are prevented from presenting candidates at all: More than 85 percent of municipal elections are, by law, nonpartisan. (There are, of course, vastly more city elections than state and national elections—some 19,000 per year in California, for example.) In these elections, the parties may not even make nominations; and in some states, they do not even have the right to endorse or repudiate any of the self-nominated candidates for city office.[8]

It is also less and less likely today that the candidates will have learned the art of politics by taking an active part in party life. Party activism is now rewarded, if at all, more by the opportunities it provides to have firsthand contact with candidates than by any chance to become one. Would-be candidates spend their time more effectively working with wealthy and powerful nonparty persons or groups than by bothering with intraparty activism. It is true that the candidate, having gained the nomination, may well benefit from training in a party-sponsored school for candidates; but that, of course, is a clear case of putting the cart before the horse (in this case, a horse that is already off and running). Today's parties do not perform the second function on our list.

And because they do not perform the second, they do not perform the first. Parties do not aggregate interests, formulate issues, and then propose programs that take stands on those issues that will appeal to a significant body of voters. The situation may look like that, at least in elections at the level of state and nation, but that is not what is going on. At the level of the states, where platforms are often written separately from the conventions, an effort may or may not be made to find out and aggregate the points of view of party members or the public; but even if made, that effort will almost always be limited to issues that have already been determined to be "important"—because either powerful interests or the media (normally both, the second in this case responding to the former) have declared them so and, furthermore, have determined the terms of the debate to be held on them. Ideas that might be excellent and clearly consistent with the party's broad philosophy of government (if one may still be discerned), but that seem likely to lower the income of a bloc of major contributors if ever implemented, are unlikely to gain a fair hearing. The same may be said for those ideas that might require extensive voter education. Proposals explaining a political agenda in detail, even when every detail is easy to understand, are similarly excluded. As the purpose is always to take as many of the votes of the massive number of nonpartisans as well as of the other party's putative supporters as possible, in addition to those of one's own supporters, the rush to the center would break the back—or least the patience—of any animal more sensitive to strain than the American electorate. The final result would be an excellent document, entirely lacking in controversy, almost impossible to implement, and eminently unread.

At any rate, it doesn't matter. The program that *will* eventually matter, at least a little bit, will not be the party's program; it will be the program of the candidate, which may or may not agree with that of the party. As we have already seen, getting the nomination does not depend on concurrence with the party program (an absence of linkage that is true at the national level as well), although the attention given the national party's platform is considerably greater and is part of the work of the nominating convention. "Do you agree with the platform?" a reporter asked President Jimmy Carter after the 1980 Democratic convention. "I agree with most of it," the party's nominee affably replied. How nice someone thought to ask.

With the third function, we come to our minor exceptions. Today's political parties do perform some part of the job of structuring the vote. They do not do so, however, via the meaningfulness of the party label. Inasmuch as they no longer control their own nominations, their labels are now associated only with the transient programs of those who have become their candidates, programs as deliberately substanceless as their own. However, both our major parties have become particularly adept at fund-raising (each in its own way), and even if they have lost control over the choice of candidates for whom the money is being raised, they can sometimes play favorites to useful effect. They help with the task of canvassing, if not door to door, at least sometimes phone to phone. They work very hard indeed on voter registration and getting out the vote. They do all this guided not by their own programs or their own convictions but by the wishes of the candidates and by the candidates' and their own powerful professional advisers, political consultants whose concern for electoral victory far outweighs any passing dreams of principled formulation of issues with distinctive substantive content—and very often has little to do with issues at all. But our parties do help structure the vote. Even though today they share that role more than ever with the media, with the candidates' personal organizations, and with independently spending Political Action Committees (which now spend over $20 million per presidential election year independent of contributions to candidates or parties), it must be granted that they are reasonably efficient electoral machines.[9]

As for the fourth function, surely little need be said. The only force that holds U.S. elected officials accountable is the force that is needed to open a wallet. Parties' wallets are now worth opening, but parties themselves have nothing substantive to which to hold the successful bearers of their name accountable. Candidates are chosen and elected whose loyalty to—or even familiarity with—the party platform is minimal at best. The ability of presidents to distance themselves from their own parties is obvious, but we sometimes imagine we see a measure of party discipline in Congress. To persuade ourselves of this, however, we must consent to a very diluted idea of what constitutes a party. Once inside Congress, those miscellaneous victors who succeeded in wresting the label away from one party or the other and using it to win public office may dutifully call themselves "Democrats" or "Republicans" and may even sometimes cobble together a program of sorts; but that program need have little in common with the program of the party organization that exists outside Congress. Furthermore, the other determinants of congressional votes—constituency pressure, personal friendships, personal convictions, and, above all, campaign donor pressure—are at least as likely to prevail should differences arise.

THE EVER-SWIFTER DESCENT OF THE PARTIES— AND THEIR COMPLICITY THEREWITH

Because our parties no longer perform most of the functions a democratic society requires from its parties, their place in the affections of the American people drops lower and lower. This is apparent when any question about them is put to the people directly. Their dissatisfaction with the parties is not compensated for by a conviction that other institutions are working well, as is apparent not only in opinion polls regarding those institutions but also in the increased demand for alternative democratic reforms in the political process and in the decreasing interest of the public at large in any form of political activity whatsoever. Yet the parties themselves appear unconcerned about this decline, even to the point of deliberately fostering it—a phenomenon that is not so surprising as it may seem at first. Let us look at each of these factors in turn.

The first significant study of the declining popularity of the parties was made by Jack Dennis in 1975.[10] Bringing together his own work with that of others, Dennis pointed out such discoveries as the following:

- More than 66 percent of Americans thought that party labels should not be on the ballot.
- Eighty-five percent said that parties create conflict.
- Seventy-eight percent believed that parties confused rather than clarified the issues of the day.
- Only 26 percent believed that parties knew how to make the government responsible to citizens.
- Only 32 percent believed that parties did what they promised.
- Only 35 percent believed that parties wanted to know what citizens thought.
- Only 40 percent thought it mattered whether one party or another won an election.

In the seventeen years since Dennis published his study, the situation has not improved. Howard Reiter combined his own calculations with those of other authors to show that between 1974 and 1980 the number of those who believed that "parties help government pay attention to what people think" had fallen by four percentage points, to 18 percent, whereas the number who believed that "parties are only interested in people's votes, but not in their opinions," had risen during the same period by one point to 59 percent.[11] More recent figures confirm the pattern: Asked to give a letter grade to the performance of the two parties in the 1988 presidential campaign, a national sample gave both parties an average grade of C.[12] Other studies suggest that any improvement made by the parties in distinguishing themselves from each other in the voters' minds (a form of improvement that some studies suggested did take place to some extent during the Reagan years) had largely disappeared by 1990 and 1991, when a full 25 percent saw no difference between the parties in "keeping the country prosperous," 30 percent saw none in their ability to keep the nation out of war, and, most significant of all, 41 percent saw none in their ability to handle "the nation's most important problem" (whatever that might have been in their own minds).[13]

Dissatisfaction with the parties cannot be dismissed on the grounds that Americans are satisfied in general with their political system, even if they think the parties are largely worthless. The continuing decline in voter turnout is one index, and it is worthwhile to note not only that voting in presidential elections has dropped to the 50 percent level but also that a mere 33 percent of the voting-age population voted in the midterm elections of 1990 (only Maine, Minnesota, Montana, and Alaska were able to turn out more than 50 percent of those eligible to vote).[14] However, as nonvoting itself is sometimes ascribed to contentment, it is important to go beyond that possibly ambiguous signal. It is not difficult to do so. In October 1990, 66 percent of Americans said they were "dissatisfied with the way things are going in the United States at this time," 68 percent disapproved "of the way Congress is handling its job," and 54 percent were dissatisfied with the performance of the president.[15]

Yet another index of dissatisfaction is the growing interest in alternative means of democratizing our political system. There is now remarkably strong support for the devices of direct democracy, despite growing awareness of their deficiencies as a means of basing public policy on public will.[16] Asked "Should we trust our elected officials to make public decisions on all issues, or should the voters have a direct say on some issues?" a national sample favored giving voters a direct say by 76 percent (only 18 percent were opposed; 6 percent did not know). More specifically,

a strong majority (57 percent) supported the idea of a national initiative—that is, a constitutional amendment permitting citizens to gather
signatures for a proposed law to be placed on the ballot at the succeeding
general election and to become law if a majority approved. Only one-fourth
were opposed (18 percent were not sure). Fully two-thirds said they believed
the Constitution should be changed to permit the recall of members of
Congress, whereas 55 percent specified that it should allow recall of the
president.[17]

Support for other reforms is also indicative of popular distress with the
performance of our weak-partied political system. Term limits have been
adopted in California to ensure that state legislators will not serve more than
two consecutive terms in office, and the idea has recently been proposed for
members of Congress as well. And the proposals for reforming campaign
finance appear as endless as the resistance of the legislators whose votes
would be needed for their success—but whose pockets always need more
relining than the reforms would be likely to permit.

Yet there is little if any evidence that the parties are interested in making
changes that would put themselves back in the ring as leading agencies in
the democratic process. Another illustration from California is particularly
apt. Parties are as weak in California as they are anywhere in the nation,
and weaker than in most states.[18] Voting rates have been dropping, and
ardent efforts by both parties to increase registration have had little payoff
in terms of turnout. Recently, a body of antiparty law was successfully
challenged as unconstitutional by a multipartisan reform group, the
Committee for Party Renewal. The 1988 ruling of the U.S. Supreme Court
in the case, *Eu* v. *San Francisco County Democrats*, gave the parties of
California the right both to issue endorsements in primary elections and to
set their own rules and regulations on important matters hitherto closely
controlled by law. California's parties now have unambiguous opportunities
to strengthen their ability to carry out several of the key functions identified
earlier, becoming more responsive to their membership in the endorsement
of candidates, in the writing of the state party platform, in the selection of
delegates to the party's national convention, and in all party activities.

However, both major state parties have been extremely reluctant to take
advantage of these opportunities. The Republicans have made no changes
whatsoever, and the Democrats have instituted a method of endorsing
primary contestants that greatly advantages incumbents and keeps final
control at the highest echelons of the party. Neither party has made any
other changes in internal rules that could be termed party-strengthening. The
Democratic party rejected by a 2 to 1 vote a proposal to change to a mixed-
delegate-selection system that would have had the undeniably party-building

effect of giving California Democrats a strong say in the party's selection of its presidential candidate. (Half of California's delegates would have been picked in March caucuses—rather than all, as at present, at a June primary that takes place well after the national nominee has been clearly identified in other, earlier primaries.) The national Democratic party actively campaigned, along with the present state party leadership, for the rejection of this plan, even while acknowledging that the proposal did not contradict national party rules and that the state party did have the right to make the change if it wished. The opponents of the plan argued that it would be too expensive and time-consuming, although evidence presented from other states suggested that the cost would have been minimal and that the party-building effects would have justified the time required. But what the plan *would* have done is give local party activists a much stronger say in candidate selection.[19]

A further example from California of a party insisting on maintaining its own weakness is the refusal (at present writing) of the state Democratic party to support a second lawsuit that, if successful, will give California's parties the right to issue endorsements in local elections. This despite the fact that nothing contributes more to the weakness of parties—or is more patently unconstitutional—than refusing them their First Amendment right of free speech in local elections, as is presently the law in California.[20]

Why should the parties in the nation's most populous state—or in any state—be so eager to maintain themselves as agencies incapable of performing the functions of responsive intermediary between people and the state? The answer is not hard to find. Our current parties are not impersonal organizations; they are elite organizations operating on behalf of themselves and fellow elites. As such, they seek power; and our electoral system gives that power not to those who win the support of a majority of the electorate but to those who win a plurality of the vote. So long as victory is won, by however small a percentage of the potential electorate, the fewer who take part in politics the better for the parties. With the advent of mass communication, the parties do not need mass participation to win and do not want it. It is helpful to have a stable and docile work force that can be convoked when needed to carry out, for no pay, the tedious jobs of registration and getting out the vote. But beyond that it is very difficult to know what to do with activists, especially those who are concerned about social problems. It is hard to keep them from expecting to play a role in issue formulation and candidate recruitment, and hard to keep them from figuring out ways to hold representatives accountable to a broader public than that represented by the most powerful PACs. The tears our parties' leaders occasionally weep over declining public support and loss of membership should suggest to us that donkey and elephant might both well be replaced by crocodile.

WHY WE STILL NEED REAL PARTIES

If the political parties of the United States have degenerated into mere fund-raising electoral machines working on behalf of candidates who represent ever more narrow interests, with no need for or interest in serving as responsive intermediaries between people and the state, and if the general public is at the same time contemptuous and disinterested, is there any point in trying to change the situation, and if so, how?

The first question is easier to answer than the second. The point in trying to do something to change the parties is that the status quo provides us with a set of conditions that should be intolerable to any citizenry committed to its own democratic governance. The parties have become the tool—and merely one among many that are stronger—of persons much more interested in taking power for personal advantage than in resolving the problems from which we as a nation suffer. A report that documented our deficiencies in child care, education, race relations, health care, treating the AIDS epidemic, caring for the aged poor, and addressing the problem of abuse of women and children would contain enough human suffering to break the heart of any sensitive reader, yet would leave out as much as it included. As of 1990, by conservative official estimate, nearly 7 million job-seekers were unable to find employment.[21] Nearly 1.5 million violent crimes are committed per year, in addition to nearly 11 million crimes against property.[22] Every year 1.25 million persons are admitted to alcohol treatment centers.[23] There are nearly 400,000 cocaine addicts in New York City alone.[24] Demands for shelter by homeless families are increasing at the rate of approximately 20 percent per year.[25] And the list goes on. We are a nation in desperate crisis, as most of our potential electorate is well aware, all too often from firsthand experience. Nonvoting cannot be construed as a sign of contentment in today's America; it is much more likely a silent scream of despair.

Furthermore, the continuing inability of our political system to treat these problems effectively is rife with the danger that democracy itself will be cast casually aside by those who do continue to vote, and who are clearly becoming ever more prepared to accept any form of leadership that seems to promise succor. We have already gone a very long way in that direction by so drastically overextending the powers of the presidency in recent years. Lacking the methods and arenas that real parties might provide us for articulating our problems, for exploring practicable political solutions, and for placing men and women in office who are dedicated to enacting those solutions, we now sign over all power to those we do not know and who do not know us; we call them "leaders" and keep them in office so faithfully that it is no wonder they lose all interest in knowing what precisely we would have them do.

Sometimes, of course, we become so overwhelmed by the immensity of a particular problem that we feel we must "do something." But normally we can think of nothing better to do than write a check on behalf of the appropriate single interest group that, even if it works hard on the problem in question (an assumption that is not always well founded), is very likely to do so by refusing the degree of compromise with other interests that is essential to produce a national agenda composed of interconnected and harmonized policies moving steadily in a consistent direction. Yes, we still need real political parties. Is there any way, however, to get them? Certainly there is little point in asking them to please reform themselves. Citizens must use the weapons they have at their command, to serve their own purposes. And what weapons are those? We have, above all, the possibility of using our intelligences to recognize not only the seriousness of the situation but also our own responsibility for effecting change. We have the vote, and we might learn to use it—and to withhold it—more wisely, refusing to support any party that does not offer to take at least a few steps in the direction of responsible performance of the functions that parties have always been expected to perform in democracies. Voting for a minor party that has no chance of victory can send a stronger message for change to the major parties than accepting, year after year, the dreary burden of deciding which of two barely distinguishable evils is the lesser.

However, these are weak arms against the arsenals accumulated by the major parties over the years in the battle for power. The real weapons are inside the major parties. All we really have to do is go in and take them. Thus far the major parties have contented themselves with merely discouraging our participation; they have not closed their gates altogether. They are open to us, and if we dared to enter them as citizens bent on restoring them to democratic usefulness, we could no doubt succeed in turning them back into agents of our will. Such an effort is within the realm of the possible and, given our current predicament, may be the only way to recreate our democracy.

CONCLUSION

As a Democrat, I believe that my party is the one that is the most likely to adopt and carry out a program that addresses our desperately serious social problems. I believe it is the party that is most likely to reduce defense expenditures in this time of lessened international tension and to increase the tax burdens of the rich in order to secure the funds to carry out the program of a Progressive Democratic party.

The argument normally made against adopting such a program is that we are immersed in an era of deep conservatism and that a Progressive Democratic party will lose elections. However, the main reason Americans have become so conservative is that the Republicans have found strong spokespersons for conservatism, whereas the Democrats have utterly failed to modernize and defend the tenets of progressive liberalism. A lost election or two may be the price that has to be paid in order to transform the Democratic party back into a party whose victories are worth celebrating. Certainly the current strategy of out-Republicanizing the Republicans has not proved effective.

Be that as it may, I do not expect to see the Democratic party change of its own accord into the party demanded by the nation's current plight and by its own history. Indeed, it will become such a party only when I and others who think as I do take an active part in its deliberations, day after day. Although I believe that party renewal is possible, and that the Democratic party can be transformed into a real political party, a Progressive Democratic party, I no longer believe that somebody else is going to do the job. It is time for us to take responsibility for our own affairs—or else to be honest and stop calling the United States a democracy. Now is the time to go to the aid of our party.

NOTES

1. Thomas Hodgkin, *African Political Parties* (London: Penguin, 1961), p. 16.
2. Yael Yishai, "Interest Parties: The Thin Line Between Groups and Parties in the Israeli Electoral Process," in Kay Lawson, ed., *How Political Parties Work: Perspectives from Within* (New York: Praeger, 1992).
3. The American habit of disliking parties began even before the institution had been well established. "There is nothing," said our first vice-president, John Adams, "I dread so much as the division of the Republic into two great parties, each

under its leader. . . . This . . . is to be feared as the greatest political evil under the Constitution."

4. For what Van Buren said, see Richard Hofstadter, *The Idea of a Party System* (Berkeley: University of California Press, 1969), pp. 223-231.

5. As of the midterm elections of 1990, incumbency reelection rates had reached 96.9 percent in the Senate and 96.0 percent in the House. Only fifteen House incumbents and one incumbent Senator were defeated for reelection. See *Congressional Quarterly Almanac*, 1990, pp. 903-906.

6. William T. Riordon, *Plunkitt of Tammany Hall* (New York: E. P. Dutton, 1963).

7. David Mayhew, *Placing Parties in American Politics: Organization, Electoral Settings, and Government Activity in the Twentieth Century* (Princeton, N.J.: Princeton University Press, 1986).

8. In one of the more recent examples, a Superior Court judge in San Francisco issued a restraining order on November 27, 1991, against the Democratic Party of San Francisco, barring it from endorsing Mayor Art Agnos for reelection. See Richard Winger, "Democratic Party Muzzled," *Ballot Access News* (newsletter privately published in San Francisco), December 9, 1991, p. 3.

9. For figures on PAC independent expenditures, see *Statistical Abstract of the United States 1990* (U.S. Department of Commerce: Bureau of the Census, 1990), p. 267.

10. Jack Dennis, "Trends in Public Support for the American Party System," *British Journal of Political Science* 5 (April 1975): 187-230.

11. Howard Reiter, *Parties and Elections in Corporate America* (New York: St. Martin's, 1987); Warren E. Miller, Arthur H. Miller, and Edward J. Schneider, *American National Election Studies Data Sourcebook, 1952-1978* (Cambridge: Harvard University Press, 1980). It should be noted that, with regard to believing that the parties care about people's opinions, the 1980 figure was actually an improvement over that of 1978—62 percent.

12. *The People, The Press and Politics 1990* (Los Angeles: Times-Mirror Center for the People and the Press), November 16, 1990.

13. *Gallup Poll Monthly*, September 1990, no. 300, p. 32, and May 1991, no. 308, p. 36.

14. *Congressional Quarterly Almanac*, vol. 46, 1990.

15. *Gallup Poll Monthly*, October 1990, no. 302, pp. 34-40.

16. Thomas E. Cronin, *Direct Democracy: The Politics of Initiative, Referendum, and Recall* (Cambridge, Mass.: Harvard University Press, 1989).

17. Ibid., pp. 80, 174, and 132.

18. Kay Lawson, "How State Laws Undermine Parties," in A. James Reichley, ed., *Elections American Style* (Washington, D.C.: Brookings Institution, 1987).

19. Kay Lawson, "Questions Raised by Recent Attempts at Local Party Reform," paper presented at the Workshop on Political Organizations and Parties, Annual Meeting of the American Political Science Association, Washington, D.C., August 28, 1991.

20. Winger, "Democratic Party Muzzled," p. 3.

21. *Statistical Abstract of the United States 1990*, p. 381.

22. Ibid., p. 170.

23. *State Resources Annual* (Washington, D.C.: National Association of State Alcohol and Drug Abuse Directors, August 1990), p. 25.

24. Katherine McFate, "Failing to Meet the Demand for Drug Treatment," *Focus* (Joint Center for Political and Economic Studies), November/December 1990, p. 4.

25. *Status Report on Hunger and Homelessness in America's Cities, 1990* (Washington, D.C.: U.S. Conference of Mayors, December 1990), p. 23.

3

LAWRENCE D. LONGLEY

The National
Democratic Party
Can Lead

National political party organizations in the United States have long been derided as inherently weak and lacking political authority—and even as somewhat electorally irrelevant. In a political system in which elections are conducted exclusively on the state and local levels—congressional contests and presidential campaigns for state-by-state blocs of electoral votes being no exception—national party organizations have, at best, a weak claim of electoral centrality. In a separation-of-powers constitutional system in which the political bases of presidents and congressional leaders are independently developed and retained through skills of individual political entrepreneurship, national parties are limited further in role and purpose. Finally, in a federal political system, national parties suffer in comparison with the electorally directly engaged state parties. For all of these reasons, national political party organizations have traditionally been seen not as summits of power in American politics but as side-show arenas for the playing out of personal, parochial, and localized political intrigue. As implied by the title of the classic study of the two parties' national committees published nearly thirty years ago, what is most characteristic of national party organizations is "politics without power."[1]

A major source of weakness of the national parties, it has been traditionally argued, lies in their sharply decentralized composition. As E. E. Schattschneider pithily wrote in 1942, "Decentralization of power is by all odds the most important single characteristic of the American major party. . . . The American major party is . . . a loose confederation of state and local bosses for limited purposes."[2] Echoing these views, V. O. Key, Jr., argued twenty-two years later, in 1964:

> Federalism in our formal governmental machinery includes a national element independent of the states, but in our party organization, the independent national element is missing. Party structure is more nearly confederative than federal in nature. . . . Federalism in government tends to encourage confederation in the party's government.[3]

Cornelius P. Cotter and Bernard C. Hennessy, in their famous study of the party national committees, found that this decentralization—especially of national committee membership selection—determined the national party organization's limited role:

> Except for occasional meetings—largely for show and newsmaking purposes—the national committees may be thought of not so much as groups, but as lists of people who have obtained their national committee memberships through organizational processes wholly separate in each state.[4]

The national committees, composed as they are of state politicians pursuing local agendas, historically have been seen as lacking stomach and incentive for competing with their party's president or congressional leaders for national political leadership. Rather, the national parties traditionally have been subservient to others—to the president of that party if in office, to the nominee for the presidency once determined, or otherwise to congressional leaders. As Frank J. Sorauf wrote some years ago in the third edition of his best-selling textbook *Party Politics in America:*

> The party organization . . . remains decentralized. It is a victim of the triumph nationally of the party in government: the *president* in his party, the *congressional* group in the opposition party. It suffers also from the jealousies of powerful state and local organizations and from the fact that those lower levels of organization control both the recruitment of party activists and the payment of rewards for organizational service.[5]

This perceived weakness of the national parties—including that of the national Democratic party—was long seen as having profound policy and ideological consequences. The domination of the national Democratic party by presidential and congressional officeholders was equated to a domination of the Democratic party by conservative forces especially present, in the context of the 1950s and 1960s, in a seniority-dominated Congress. This domination of party by officeholders inherently favored the status quo, rather than reflecting the more liberal and progressive currents of the time. In this view, a weak national Democratic party inhibited political and policy innovation; conversely, a stronger and more independent national party organization could be a potential engine of progressive reform.

Much of the story of the national Democratic party in the 1950s and into the 1960s is one of half-hearted efforts to loosen somewhat the debilitating stranglehold of officeholders on the national party, efforts strenuously backed by liberals and progressives and resisted with equal strength by many powerful national and congressional leaders. In 1956, following that year's disastrous presidential campaign, Democratic National Committee (DNC) Chairman Paul Butler formed the Democratic Advisory Council, a quasi-independent national party structure for national policy articulation made up of senior party leaders, only to find his term as party chairman dominated by resulting controversy. Democratic congressional leaders in particular reacted with hostility to the creation of a party organization competing with their policy prerogatives and domains. Butler left the party chairmanship in 1961, following the presidential election of John F. Kennedy, and the Democratic Advisory Council was quickly dismantled.[6]

The national Democratic party did little better as an independent entity in the 1960s during the presidencies of Kennedy and Lyndon Johnson. Neither president was the least bit interested in seeing the national party take on any policy-articulating role that might compete with presidential policy priorities. By the end of the 1960s, national Democratic party organizations in many ways had hit their low ebb as the tensions of the Vietnam War and domestic political upheaval made the national party—and the DNC in particular—a battleground for competing political interests: arenas of conflict deciding little, however, beyond symbolic victories of one faction over another.

This context is the starting place for a consideration of the events of the past twenty years, which, it will be argued, have finally given promise that the national Democratic party *can* lead, that it *can* play a meaningful role in electoral politics, both nationally and locally. What is more, it will be asserted, the national Democratic party can lead *substantively*—in terms of a progressive policy program relevant to the major issues and problems of the day.

In the next section, this account of the evolution of the national Democratic party will be continued into the 1970s through a consideration of the stymied Democratic Charter Movement of 1972 to 1974. This will be followed by an examination of the gradual institutionalization of both national parties—first the Republican organizations in the 1970s and then the Democratic entities in the early 1980s and into the 1990s. The status of the

national parties as of the early 1990s, especially that of the Democratic
National Committee, will be considered. Discussion will then turn to the
possible impact of the DNC, particularly that of its individual members, on
the presidential politics of 1992. Finally, this chapter will conclude with a
consideration of the opportunities for progressives resulting from the
contemporary revitalization of the national Democratic party. As the
national Democratic party can lead, so progressives, using the national
Democratic party as a channel for innovative ideas and ideals, can also lead.

THE PARTY CHARTER MOVEMENT, 1972-1974

In the early 1970s, a party reform movement emerged within the national
Democratic party devoted to the reconstitution and revitalization of the
national party. This loose group of intellectuals and progressive activists—prominent among them Professor James MacGregor Burns and, in a
far lesser role, the author of this chapter—came to be known as the
Democratic Charter Movement. The original impetus for this reform effort
came from the realization that the national Democratic party had no formal
written constitution or set of bylaws. Throughout its long existence, it had
operated on the basis of various understandings (not always, however,
understood by everyone), resolutions adopted by national conventions (often
haphazardly and late in convention sessions), and case-by-case actions taken
by the National Committee that provided in various ways for its own governance. In light of the internal party upheavals in the 1968 and 1972 election
periods, such a lack of generally available structural definition and statement
of rules, procedures, and lines of authority seemed to accord undue power
to political insiders at the cost of insurgents. Thus, the initial goal of the
party reform movement was a simple one (and in these terms relatively
uncontroversial): to write a party constitution (or charter) that would outline
the structures and procedures of the national party.

Soon, however, many of those in the party Charter Movement began to
define a more ambitious goal: utilization of the occasion of the creation of
a National Democratic Party Charter to strengthen the political independence
of the national Democratic party and its officers. As their thinking evolved
through a flurry of position papers and draft documents during 1973, what
party reformers envisioned was a Democratic Charter that would enshrine
national Democratic party organization, especially the Democratic National
Committee, as a relatively independent "central office." This national party
element would be able to articulate and promote national policy initiatives

and political strategies while remaining insulated from undue influence by congressional leaders, the party's nominee for president, or even the party's president. Party officers, and possibly National Committee members, for example, would be elected for a four-year term at some point removed from the presidential election cycle—perhaps at a midterm date—and would be expected to serve through the election year events, independent and fair to all yet actively engaged in the policy debates of the day. Under this conception, the national party would not be the handmaiden of elected officials, presidential nominee, or president but, rather, would have its own basis independent of the political passions and personal ambitions of officeholders and candidates. In short, the national Democratic party would speak for the continuing ideological (and presumably progressive) values and ideals of the party, and provide much-needed programmatic continuity.

The vision of the thinkers of the Democratic Charter Movement, then, called for the creation of a policy-oriented, progressive, and independent national Democratic party—one led at the national center by an independent organizational core of party strategists and policy-articulating leaders. In many ways, this conception of national party leadership corresponds to the model of the institutionalized national party. According to this construct, political parties become institutionalized through "the development of the national party headquarters as agencies that have sufficient autonomy to enable them to define and pursue their own programs with assurance that their continued existence does not depend upon the whim of a presidential candidate or party."[7] Events in the real political world, however, would stymie this process of party institutionalization—at least in the 1970s.

Congressional leaders in general, along with many traditional party leaders, were appalled at the proposals of the Democratic Charter activists. An ideologically charged and independent central party element, they feared, would become a prime target for McCarthy, McGovern, and antiwar activists who, once ensconced in national party positions, would be free to turn the party organization to their own extreme ends. The electoral consequences of such a development to Democratic officeholders or candidates might be disastrous if voters were bombarded with competing claims as to what the Democratic party stood for—claims consisting, on the one hand, of statements from a possible runaway national party and, on the other, of disclaimers from local congressional candidates burdened with party policy pronouncements antithetical to constituency or candidate. Efforts were set in motion to blunt the more sweeping goals of the Charter Movement.

Clearly, some manner of a written charter for the party would have to be adopted; the lack of any formal party constitution or bylaws seemed indefensible. In order to produce a "responsible" document, a Democratic Party Charter Commission was created, headed by former North Carolina Governor (and more recently U.S. Senator) Terry Sanford. By requirement of the 1972 Democratic Convention, the work of this commission would itself be subject to review and approval at a special midterm Democratic National Party Convention, which was mandated to be held in 1974.

The work of the Democratic Charter Commission was marked by controversy and divisiveness as leaders of the Charter Movement fought to keep their potentially far-reaching proposals from being diluted and, in many cases, discarded by the party regulars amply represented on the commission. The final meeting of the commission, in mid-August 1974, disintegrated into "bitterness and confusion . . . when blacks and liberal members walked out to protest what one of them called 'the Sunday afternoon massacre' of many of their long-sought reforms."[8]

The official approval of the national Democratic Charter would, however, rest with the special 1974 mini-convention of the Democratic party—the first such gathering in U.S. history. By the time the 1,600 delegates, together with (not by accident) more than 800 public and party officials, gathered from December 6 to 8, 1974, in Kansas City, most of the fight had gone out of the Charter Movement and innovation out of the proposed charter text. The final draft document prepared for the convention delegates, "The Common Thread: A Democratic Party Charter," embodied few of the sweeping ideas and proposals that had been designed to establish an independent and programmatic national Democratic party. Rather, the mini-convention, ironically called the "1974 Conference on Democratic Party Organization and Policy," was asked to approve a charter sharply limiting any new political and policy independence of the national party organization. Instead of institutionalizing the national party, the Democratic Party Charter, as eventually approved with remarkably little dissent in Kansas City, essentially legitimized existing party practice. The Democratic Charter Movement had ended by producing not a lion but at most a rather diminutive mouse. It would not be for another decade and more that some, but by no means most, of the goals of the party charter leaders in the early 1970s would be realized gradually through a slow and partial institutionalization of the national Democratic party.

THE GRADUAL INSTITUTIONALIZATION OF THE NATIONAL DEMOCRATIC PARTY IN THE 1980s AND 1990s

The stymieing of the Democratic Charter Movement in the early 1970s did not end the process of institutionalization of the national Democratic party. Instead of being advanced at one time through one reform vehicle, however, it would progress instead slowly over nearly two decades, the 1980s and early 1990s. A major stimulus for this gradual growth of Democratic party structure, authority, purpose, and resources came not from within the Democratic party, but from outside. This was the dramatic growth of the capabilities of national *Republican* party organizations in the late 1960s and 1970s under two innovative Republican National Committee (RNC) party chairmen, Ray C. Bliss (1965-1969) and, to an even greater extent, William E. Brock (1977-1981). These developments included major expansions of the staff size of the Republican National Committee and of allied congressional campaign committees, technical support services for candidates, finances, and independence from domination by state parties and political leaders.[9]

What occurred within the national Republican party during these years—and eventually in the Democratic party in the 1980s during the DNC leadership of Charles T. Manatt (1981-1985) and Paul G. Kirk, Jr. (1985-1989)—was a significant degree of party institutionalization, marked by the recruitment of greater numbers of full-time staff, a clarification of the division of labor among staff structures, a heightened degree of general professionalism in organizational activities, and a significantly expanded budget.[10] Paul S. Herrnson has defined the concept of party institutionalization and applied it most fully to the national parties: "The institutionalization of the national party organizations refers to their becoming fiscally solvent, organizationally stable, and larger and more diversified in their staffing; it also refers to their adoption of professional-bureaucratic decisionmaking procedures."[11]

Table 3.1 summarizes the staff growth of the two national party committees for the twenty-year span from 1972 to 1991. At the beginning of this period, the RNC and DNC were equal in staff personnel, each only minimally staffed with about 30 persons—considerably fewer than the number of staffers typically commanded by even a medium-sized city mayor! Four years later, however, the number of RNC staff personnel had leaped sharply upward to 200, and by 1980 the staff resources of the RNC had surged more than tenfold over the comparable figure eight years earlier. By 1984, total RNC staff personnel topped 600 persons, *twenty* times its 1972 size! Meanwhile, the Democratic National Committee continued at minimal levels of three dozen or so staffers until the early 1980s, when the DNC staff increased threefold in the period between 1980 and 1984, about eight years later than the far greater Republican staff expansion.

What is particularly evident in Table 3.1 is the dramatic difference in Republican and Democratic National Committee staff totals at every point

TABLE 3.1 Democratic and Republican National Committee Staff, 1972-1991

	1972	1976	1980	1984	1988	1990	1991[a]
DNC	30	30	40	130	160	130	113
RNC	30	200	350	600	425	400	335
RNC/DNC Staff Ratio	1.0	6.7	8.8	4.6	2.7	3.1	3.0[a]

[a] As of mid-November 1991.

Sources: For 1972-1984 data: Paul S. Herrnson, *Party Campaigning in the 1980s* (Cambridge, Mass.: Harvard University Press, 1988), p. 39. For 1988 and 1990 data: Herrnson, "Reemergent National Party Organizations," in L. Sandy Maisel, ed., *The Parties Respond: Changes in the American Party System* (Boulder: Westview Press, 1990), p. 51; Herrnson, "Parties and Congressional Elections: Out of the Eighties and Into the Nineties," paper presented at the Annual Meeting of the American Political Science Association, Washington, D.C., 1991; and Herrnson, "National Party Organizations and the Postreform Congress," in Roger H. Davidson, ed., *The Postreform Congress* (New York: St. Martin's Press, 1992), p. 53. The 1991 data were based on estimates provided by the Democratic and Republican National Committees in mid-November 1991, and are first reported here. The RNC/DNC staff ratios were specially calculated for this table.

after 1972, with RNC staff sizes being between 2.7 and 8.8 times greater than comparable DNC personnel resources. This massive staff advantage of the Republican National Committee over the Democratic National Committee has continued: As of late 1991, the RNC had a staff of 335 persons, whereas DNC had a staff of but 113—a Republican staff advantage of 3 to 1.

Of course, it is possible that the persistent personnel disadvantage of the DNC might be offset somewhat by the staff members employed by its allied congressional campaign committees, commonly known as the "Hill committees." After all, one might reason, recurrent Democratic majorities in House and Senate should be able to support staff resources for the election of fellow congressional partisans greater than those of the minority Republicans, perhaps rebalancing the Republican National Committee staff advantage.

Table 3.2 disproves this theory. The figures reported there for the combined national committee and Hill committee partisan staffs reflect at best a slight narrowing—but by no means an elimination—of the substantial

TABLE 3.2 Total Democratic and Republican National Party Staff, 1972-1991, Combining Staff of National Committees and Party House and Senate Campaign Committees

	1972	1976	1980	1984	1988	1990	1991[a]
Democratic	39	41	86	207	290	255	193
Republican	40	214	420	820	593	611	506
Rep./Dem. Staff Ratio	1.0	5.2	4.9	4.0	2.0	2.4	2.6[a]

[a] As of mid-November 1991. The breakdown of staff by national party organization is as follows: DNC (Democratic National Committee), 113; DCCC (Democratic Congressional [House] Campaign Committee), 50; DSCC (Democratic Senatorial Campaign Committee), 30; RNC (Republican National Committee), 335; NRCC (National Republican Congressional [House] Committee), 88; and NRSC (National Republican Senatorial Committee), 83.

Sources: For 1972-1984 data: Paul S. Herrnson, *Party Campaigning in the 1980s* (Cambridge, Mass.: Harvard University Press, 1988), p. 39. For 1988 and 1990 data: Herrnson, "Reemergent National Party Organizations," in L. Sandy Maisel, ed., *The Parties Respond: Changes in the American Party System* (Boulder: Westview Press, 1990), p. 51; Herrnson, "Parties and Congressional Elections: Out of the Eighties and Into the Nineties," paper presented at the Annual Meeting of the American Political Science Association, Washington, D.C., 1991; and Herrnson, "National Party Organizations and the Postreform Congress," in Roger H. Davidson, ed., *The Postreform Congress* (New York: St. Martin's Press, 1992), p. 53. The 1991 data were based on estimates provided by the Democratic and Republican National Committees and by each of the parties' House and Senate campaign committees in mid-November 1991, and are first reported here. The Rep./Dem. staff ratios were specially calculated for this table.

Republican National Committee staff-size advantage, with the combined total Republican/Democratic partisan staff ratios after 1972 ranging from 5.2 (in 1976) to 2.0 (in 1988). As of late 1991, the combined Democratic national partisan staff totaled 193 persons and was greatly exceeded more than two and a half times by the combined Republican national partisan staff total of 506.

In short, Republican National Committee staff resources soared from the early 1970s through the mid-1980s. To a lesser degree, Democratic National Committee staff totals increased, but starting only in the early 1980s. In addition, total national Democratic partisan staff—DNC in combination with the Democratic Hill committees—have been outnumbered consistently by counterpart Republican national partisan staff by a factor of at least 2 to 1—and often much more.

Staff resources, of course, do not determine electoral outcomes. Money, the "mother's milk" of politics, plays an even greater role than staff in determining the level of candidate services available from the national parties—as well as the extent of direct financial support for those candidates.

Table 3.3 summarizes Republican and Democratic national committee receipts for the fifteen-year period from 1976 to 1991. Here again one can observe a persistent and sizable financial edge for the RNC over the DNC, ranging up to an astonishing high of about 5 to 1. Since 1976, only in the presidential election years of 1984 and 1988 (when receipts for both national committees were swollen by some degree of "flow-through" of presidential campaign funds) has the money received by the DNC totaled as much as *one-third* that raised by the RNC. Looking at late 1991 financial data, we find that the RNC's financial advantage over the DNC was more than 5 to 1. Even if we consider the combined total of direct campaign funds ("hard money") and party-building, noncampaign receipts ("soft money"), the 1991 Republican National Committee financial advantage is considerable—in the range of 4.5 to 1.

Once again, one might speculate that Democratic money available through the efforts of that party's congressional campaign committees might substantially offset the RNC financial advantage over the DNC. Table 3.4, however, shows that this is not the case. Since 1976, the total receipts of Republican national party organizations (the RNC, the National Republican Congressional [House] Committee, and the National Republican Senatorial Committee) have run between *3.7 and 6.7 times* the total receipts of the counterpart Democratic national organizations (the DNC, the Democratic Congressional [House] Campaign Committee, and the Democratic Senatorial Campaign Committee). In the first six months of 1991, for example, national Democratic partisan receipts of $9.6 million were dwarfed 4.3 to 1 by the comparable Republican fund-raising total of $40.8 million. For the same six-month period, the party receipts combining "hard" and "soft" money reflected a continuing Republican domination over the supply of "mother's milk": Whereas Republican national partisan entities raised a total of $51.6 million, the Democratic national party organizations gathered but $12.9 million, a Republican advantage of 4 to 1.

The data provided in Tables 3.1 through 3.4 have illustrated a number of important trends in the gradual institutionalization of the national political parties over the past two decades. To summarize, these trends include

TABLE 3.3 Democratic and Republican National Committee Receipts, 1976-1991 (in millions)

	1976	1978	1980	1982	1984	1986	1988	1989	1990	1991[a]
DNC	$13.1	$11.3	$15.4	$16.5	$46.6	$17.2	$52.3	$6.8	$14.5	$3.3
RNC	29.1	34.2	77.8	84.1	105.9	83.8	91.0	30.6	68.7	17.6
RNC/DNC Receipts Ratio	2.2	3.0	5.1	5.1	2.3	4.9	1.7	4.5	4.7	5.3[a]

[a] The 1991 figures apply to the first six months of 1991 and—as with all the other figures in this table—cover only "hard money" receipts (funds available for direct campaign use). First six-month national committee receipts *combining* hard money with "soft money" receipts (funds limited to party-building, noncampaign use) were (in millions): DNC, $5.3; RNC, $23.9. The RNC/DNC receipts ratio was 4.5. Subsequently, the DNC reported year-to-date combined receipts (as of November 15, 1991) of $10.2 million; still far behind the *six*-month RNC total of $23.9 million.

Sources: For 1976-1988 data: Paul S. Herrnson, "Reemergent National Party Organizations," in L. Sandy Maisel, ed., *The Parties Respond: Changes in the American Party System* (Boulder: Westview Press, 1990), p. 49; and Herrnson "National Party Organizations and the Postreform Congress," in Roger H. Davidson, ed., *The Postreform Congress* (New York: St. Martin's Press, 1992), p. 50. For 1989 data: Richard L. Berke, "Contributions to Democrats Lagging," *New York Times*, February 2, 1990, p. A12. For 1990 data: Herrnson, "Parties and Congressional Elections: Out of the Eighties and Into the Nineties," paper presented at the Annual Meeting of the American Political Science Association, Washington, D.C., 1991. For 1991 data: Federal Election Commission figures (for six-month data for both political parties), Finance Division of the DNC, and Report of DNC Chairman Ronald H. Brown to the Executive Committee of the Democratic National Committee, Chicago, Ill., November 21, 1991 (for Democratic Party receipts figures through November 15, 1991). The 1976 to mid-1991 figures are based on Federal Election Commission data; mid-1991 and November 15, 1991, national committee receipts figures are first reported here. The RNC/DNC receipts ratios were specially calculated for this table.

TABLE 3.4 Total Democratic and Republican National Party Receipts, 1976-1991 (in millions), Combining Receipts of National Committees and Party House and Senate Campaign Committees

	1976	1978	1980	1982	1984	1986	1988	1989	1990	1991[a]
Democratic	$15.0	$14.4	$20.2	$28.6	$65.9	$42.9	$81.1	$18.9	$41.1	$9.6
Republican	43.1	59.2	120.4	191.0	245.9	209.7	191.4	80.2	167.6	40.8
Rep./Dem. Receipts Ratio	2.9	4.1	6.0	6.7	3.7	4.9	2.4	4.2	4.1	4.3[a]

[a] The 1991 figures are for the first six months of 1991 and—as with all the other figures in this table—cover only "hard money" receipts (see Table 3.3 for definition). Hard money receipts for the first six months of 1991 by national party organizations (in millions) were: DNC, $3.3; DCCC, $3.1; DSCC, $3.2; RNC, $17.6; NRCC, $7.5; NRSC, $15.7. (See Table 3.2 for identification of party organizations.) *Total* party receipts combining "hard" and "soft" money for the first six months of 1991 (in millions) were: DNC, $5.3; DCCC, $4.3; DSCC, $3.3; combined *Democratic* national partisan total receipts, $12.9; RNC, $23.9; NRCC, $9.2; NRSC, $18.5; combined *Republican* national partisan total receipts, $51.6. The Rep./Dem. receipts ratio for the first six months of 1991 receipts of the national committee *and* House and Senate campaign committees (combining hard and soft money) was 4.0.

Sources: For 1976-1988 data: Paul S. Herrnson, "Reemergent National Party Organizations," in L. Sandy Maisel, ed., *The Parties Respond: Changes in the American Party System* (Boulder: Westview Press, 1990), p. 49; and Herrnson "National Party Organizations and the Postreform Congress," in Roger H. Davidson, ed., *The Postreform Congress* (New York: St. Martin's Press, 1992), p. 50. For 1989 data: Richard L. Berke, "Contributions to Democrats Lagging," *New York Times*, February 2, 1990, p. A12. For 1990 data: Herrnson, "Parties and Congressional Elections: Out of the Eighties and Into the Nineties," paper presented at the Annual Meeting of the American Political Science Association, Washington, D.C., 1991. For 1991 data: Federal Election Commission figures (for six-month data for both political parties), Finance Division of the DNC, and Report of DNC Chairman Ronald H. Brown to the Executive Committee of the Democratic National Committee, Chicago, Ill., November 21, 1991 (for Democratic party receipts figures through November 15, 1991). All figures are based on Federal Election Commission data; 1991 receipts figures are first reported here. The Rep./Dem. receipts ratios were specially calculated for this table.

- the striking expansion of Republican National Committee and allied congressional campaign committee staff and financial resources in the period from the early 1970s to the mid-1980s;
- the significant yet belated and less dramatic growth of Democratic National Committee staff and receipts during the early to mid-1980s;
- the growth of both parties' congressional campaign committees as significant partners with the two national party committees in terms of staff resources and fund-raising;[12]
- the failure of the Democratic congressional campaign committees—despite their linkage to persistent majorities in both chambers—to offset significantly Republican partisan staff and financial advantages; and
- the overall development in both national parties of new levels of staffing and financial receipts (hard money alone or in combination with soft money), thereby allowing the national organizations of both parties to exercise far greater degrees of influence over and involvement in electoral politics and party organizational processes.

In short, the national parties, including the national committees, now command the resources to ensure that their activities are marked by more than "politics without power." Although the national parties and the national committees do not—and never will, given our federal and separation-of-powers system—control the state parties or dominate independently elected officeholders, they have gathered the means to ensure their political relevance in elections and their importance to officeholders, candidates, and state parties. Various scholars and party analysts have described this new role for the contemporary national party: as the "service vendor party,"[13] as the "broker party,"[14] and as the "candidate service center."[15] Whatever the term, what is being described is an involvement of national party organizations in electoral campaigns of an unprecedented nature.

This support role for the national parties takes many forms, ranging from direct candidate financial assistance to such "in-kind" campaign assistance as polling, campaign management, and other technical services. In the Democratic party, this conception of party organizational assistance and cooperation with candidates and their campaigns has been formalized in recent years in terms of what has come to be called the "Coordinated Campaign"—the hallmark of DNC Chairman Ronald H. Brown, who became head of the Democratic National Committee in early 1989, and DNC Political Director Paul Tully. The Coordinated Campaign involves the strong encouragement by the DNC for the creation of independent campaign structures within state Democratic parties financed in large part by individual Democratic party nominees and supported by other Democratic power centers, including Democratic elected officials not on the ballot and constituency groups such as organized labor. The Coordinated Campaign in each state performs key campaign organizational tasks such as voter registration, voter identification, absentee ballot and get-out-the-vote drives, and, in some cases, such additional tasks as polling, scheduling, targeting, press relations, and purchasing paid media. In the 1990 campaign alone, the DNC recognized and supported more than thirty-six such statewide Coordinated Campaign programs, and efforts are under way to create 1992 Coordinated Campaign structures in virtually every state.[16]

In presidential election years, such as 1992, these state-by-state Coordinated Campaigns will work closely with the presidential campaign, on both the national and state levels, in setting overall strategies as well as conducting polling, focus groups, and other voter-research activities. One late 1991 account described the 1992 presidential electoral strategy being developed by the DNC political staff as a complement to the above enumerated campaign support services: "Target key coastal, midwestern and southern border states, revive efforts to mobilize black voters who were generally neglected in 1988, and concentrate extraordinary resources in California, which, with 54 electoral votes, is assured of a pivotal role in any close presidential contest."[17]

Although such electoral strategies are obviously always subject to subsequent review or even rejection by the presidential nominee when determined or evident, this type of forward planning of electoral priorities is further evidence, along with the fervently sought and emphasized linkage on the state level between state party Coordinated Campaigns and the presidential campaign, of the new involvement and significance of the Democratic National Committee in electoral activities. The new campaign-centered role of the DNC, then, entails services for candidates, together with vigorous efforts at the coordination of multicandidate activities. The purpose underlying that role is to ensure that the total electoral effort is at least as great as—or greater than—the sum of its parts.

THE DEMOCRATIC NATIONAL COMMITTEE TODAY

Thus far, we have been examining the gradual institutionalization of the national Democratic party—especially that of the Democratic National Committee—in terms of numerous indicators and programs. Next we will step a bit closer to the DNC itself as a national party organization to

TABLE 3.5 Size and Composition of Democratic and Republican National Committees in Late 1991

Democratic National Committee	Number of Members
Chair and next highest ranking party officer of opposite sex from the Chair from each state and from D.C., American Samoa, Democrats Abroad, Guam, Puerto Rico, and Virgin Islands	112
Members additionally apportioned to states and territories on the same basis as delegates to national convention (2 to 17 per state or territory)	212
Members-At-Large elected by the DNC upon recommendation of the Chair	50
Representatives of various Democratic constituency organizations such as Democratic Governors Association, Democratic State Legislative Leaders Association, and National Federation of Democratic Women	30
National Committee Officers not otherwise DNC members (potentially up to 9)	6
Total DNC members (as of mid-November 1991)	410

Republican National Committee	Number of Members
Chair, National Committeeman, and National Committeewoman (3 total) from each state and from D.C., American Samoa, Guam, Puerto Rico, and Virgin Islands	165
Total RNC members (as of mid-November 1991)	165

Sources: Calculated from the Membership List of the Democratic National Committee, November 15, 1991, and from information supplied by the Republican National Committee in mid-November 1991.

consider what its characteristics are from the standpoint of a National Committee member. In mid-1989, I was elected by the Wisconsin Democratic State Convention—in a surprising upset—to represent Wisconsin as a member of this key national party organization. The following paragraphs provide some reflections and observations, then, of a political scientist and political activist about the state of the DNC as of early 1992.

Clearly the Democratic National Committee—a large body currently totaling 410 members (see Table 3.5)—is ill-suited to function effectively as the supreme governing body of the national Democratic party. It is just too large and unwieldy a gathering. When DNC meetings are held, the hall is filled with 400 or so official members, 50 to 100 party officials and staff, 100 or more journalists, and dozens upon dozens of honored guests (as well as some less honored political hangers-on). The scene, in fact, looks more like a good-sized annual state party convention or a mini-national convention than the convening of a working national party governing organization.

In addition, the DNC is still predominantly made up of state political activists—party chairs, vice-chairs, and elected members, together with assorted governors, members of congress, mayors, county officials, and the like—who were selected almost entirely on the basis of their personal stature within their state rather than because of their particular breadth of viewpoint concerning national party issues. Still inherent in the contemporary DNC, then, is a built-in localism—or even parochialism—of viewpoint.

To some degree, these two limitations of the DNC have been addressed by means of institutional reform. The DNC continues to be a huge entity, but a number of standing committees and specialized groups of the National Committee also now operate as meaningful and manageable policymaking bodies. The DNC Executive Committee, the State Chairs Association, the three powerful DNC standing committees on Credentials, Resolutions, and Rules and Bylaws, numerous less official caucuses (Labor, Hispanic, Women, Blacks), together with highly informal political "networks," provide the locale for the personal advancement, policy evaluation, and effective decisionmaking so difficult in the DNC as a whole.

A member of one of the important subunits within the DNC is potentially able to play a significant role in DNC affairs. Those DNC members not holding such a position, however, can easily feel left out of DNC decision-making. Resulting from the discontent of DNC rank-and-file members, who had come to perceive themselves essentially as National Committee cannon-fodder, was the formation, in September 1991, of a new caucus of DNC members determined to work within the DNC to ensure active participation in National Committee affairs of those members *not* holding DNC commit-tee or other internal leadership roles. The creation of this semi-insurgent group of DNC members was greeted with a notable lack of enthusiasm by party leaders, and the fate of the new Association of DNC Men and Women rank-and-file group was, as of early 1992, unclear.[18]

The state focus of most DNC members has also been addressed by several means, including presentations to National Committee members of detailed assessments of national issues, political trends, and in-depth polling results. And in recent years some fifty "additional members," selected by the DNC upon the recommendation of its leaders, have been added to the National Committee. These "At-Large" DNC members, who include a number of prominent national Democrats, usefully supplement the predominant vigorous articulation of state viewpoints.

What does the Democratic National Committee do, as the governing body of a national political party? Among its duties are to elect national party officers, to write and approve detailed plans for each national party convention, to govern the national party during the four years between national party conventions, to support Democratic candidates at all levels, and to express party concerns on national issues of the day. The DNC has recently been deeply engaged in each of these activities.

Early in 1989, the DNC decided on the leader of the national Democratic party by electing Ronald H. Brown as DNC chairman—the first African American ever to head a major national political party. At its September 1989 meeting, another election of party leadership occurred, and after a heated campaign involving countless letters, telegrams, and imploring phone calls from candidates and their celebrity supporters, Kathleen M. Vick of Louisiana was elected as party secretary.

At a subsequent meeting late in 1990, the Democratic National Committee completed work in a second area: setting the processes and rules in place for the 1992 National Convention. By a unanimous vote (always a notable level of consensus for Democrats), the DNC adopted its official *Call for the 1992 Convention* and its detailed specifications concerning the method of delegate apportionment among and selection within the various states—as well as the rules and procedures that will govern the process. It was a remarkable achievement to be able to wrap up—early on and in unanimity—what has been so often in the past a highly contentious and polarized process, and to do it well before presidential candidates had the opportunity to manipulate the rules in pursuit of some perceived political advantage.

In the past several years, the DNC has also acted as the official governing body of the national Democratic party. By action of the National Committee in September 1989, for example, the National Democratic Charter (the party constitution first adopted in 1974, as previously discussed) was amended to provide that the terms of national party officers would run *not* from national convention to national convention—a practice that gave excessive opportunity for presidential nominees to replace party-building national party leaders with personal loyalists—but, instead, from national election to national election. Party leaders will seek election or reelection in the future in light of what has gone on in the course of the *entire* presidential campaign, not just its nomination phase.[19]

The DNC also modified the National Democratic Charter in September 1989 to provide that actions of national conventions that affect the governance of the party will be subject to ratification by the DNC itself *prior* to going into effect—a useful check on actions adopted in chaotic convention sessions, sometimes in the political heat of the moment. Finally, the National Committee voted late in 1989 to make permanent the presence of a significant group of uncommitted Super Delegates at national conventions—some 771 individuals selected because of their public office or party post rather than their candidate support—thus providing a degree of "peer-review" of presidential candidates. (This development will be discussed further in the next section.) The latter innovation was particularly easy for the DNC to accept, for most of the newly enfranchised Super Delegates were National Committee members themselves!

Appropriately enough, a growing focus of DNC activities has had to do with the involvement of the Democratic National Committee with campaigns in the various states—congressional, gubernatorial, and even state legislative campaigns. The primary vehicle of this involvement has been the statewide "Coordinated Campaigns"—discussed earlier in this chapter. Noteworthy in this development is the fact that the National Committee is increasingly devoting its energies and resources to first purposes—the contesting of elections.

Another important activity of the Democratic National Committee has been fund-raising, key because financial resources are precisely what allow a party organization to play a meaningful role in elections. Earlier in this chapter (see Tables 3.3 and 3.4) we traced the gradual expansion of DNC fund-raising activities over the past fifteen years; most significantly these activities have included the raising of significant dollar amounts in nonpresidential years.

In calendar year 1989, for example, the DNC by itself raised $6.8 million (see Table 3.3) and, in addition to that officially reported total, raised $2.7 million of "unregulated funds," or "soft money," for a year-end total of $9.5 million. This figure compares favorably—but just barely so—with comparable "off-year" DNC fund-raising totals (hard and soft money combined) of $9.2 million in 1987 and $8.4 million in 1985. As of November 15, 1991, the comparable combined year-to-date hard and soft money receipts for the DNC was $10.2 million—another increase over the off-year totals for 1989, 1987, and 1985. In short, the DNC is proving its ability to expand its fund-raising abilities, gradually yet steadily—even in nonelection years.[20]

Where the DNC financial success is far less impressive, however, is in contrast with the enormous sums raised by the Republican National Committee. Federal Election Commission data for 1989 show that the DNC's hard and soft money combined figure of $9.5 million was eclipsed by the RNC's fund-raising total of hard money *alone* of $30.6 million! Adding the 1989 hard money campaign money raised by the two "Hill" campaign committees—the Democratic Senatorial Campaign Committee and the Democratic Congressional (House) Campaign Committee—to the hard money receipts of the DNC, one finds that the three national Democratic partisan organizations raised a grand total of nearly $19 million in 1989. This is an impressive achievement—until one looks again at the comparable total money raised in 1989 by the RNC and the two Republican Hill committees: $80 million! Similarly, the receipts data covering the first six months of 1991 show a continuing sharp Republican advantage: 5.3 to 1 in the case of the RNC/DNC hard money-only receipts; 4.5 to 1 for national committee fund-raising totals combining hard and soft money; and, for total funds raised by the national committees *and* the congressional campaign committees, a Republican advantage of 4.3 (hard money only) and 4.0 times (combined hard and soft money receipts). In short, the DNC and its allied Democratic Hill campaign committees have made noteworthy progress in their fund-raising activities but, as of the early 1990s, still lag far behind their Republican counterparts.

Finally, concerning issue articulation, note should be taken of the ample opportunity the DNC provides for the expression of member concerns on major national policy questions, often after vigorous debate. Bella Abzug, a long-time DNC member, and Paul Wellstone, also a DNC member until his 1990 election to the U.S. Senate, could always be counted on to express their viewpoints, as could many more centralist members of the National Committee. At times (but unfortunately not always), the DNC can indeed be an exciting forum for the exploration of issues and controversies—on matters as disparate as social security reform and the Gulf War.

As earlier noted, two prominent political scientists once disparagingly described the national party committees as "politics without power." The Democratic National Committee is inherently and appropriately involved in politics—for politics is, above all, the purpose for which the national party organization is organized. But to "politics" has now increasingly been added some measure of meaningful power. The Democratic National

Committee *is* the national governing head of the national Democratic party, and in the 1990s it is finally beginning to live up to that responsibility and opportunity. As Paul S. Herrnson put it, "The United States may be embarking on a new era of party politics, one characterized by strong and highly active national parties."[21]

A SUPER OPPORTUNITY FOR
THE NATIONAL DEMOCRATIC PARTY

One other development affecting the national Democratic party—especially its individual members—remains to be mentioned. The dynamics of the presidential nominating process of 1992 may accord national Democratic party leaders, as well as individual members of the Democratic National Committee, a central opportunity and responsibility in determining their party's presidential nominee. Underlying this analysis is the assumption that the 1992 Democratic nominating process is unlikely to produce a swift and decisive choice. If this should be the case, then a large group of so-called Super Delegates—Democratic senators, members of Congress, governors, other elected officials, but most important, all 410 individual members of the Democratic National Committee—could play a role of unusual significance in deciding the Democratic presidential candidate of 1992.

But will the 1992 nominating process be slow to resolve? It is undoubtedly hazardous to be predicting in early 1992 the outcome of volatile political events occurring later in the election year; but with the disclaimer that all that follows may be made false by subsequent events, I shall now outline a scenario in which the nomination decision is deadlocked for a considerable time, and the uncommitted Super Delegates of 1992 end up playing an instrumental role in its resolution.

Several factors explain why the Democratic nomination in 1992 may be undetermined even very late in the process: (1) The field of Democratic candidates is largely unknown and devoid of national campaign experience and exposure; (2) the nomination contest of 1992 was a late-starting one, allowing less time for a dynamic of inevitability to build; (3) a new strict proportionality rule in awarding delegates will make it harder for candidates to win large blocs of delegates; and (4) as many as 18 percent of all the national convention delegates—the unpledged Super Delegates—will not be decided upon or bound by the primary results, thus making it more difficult for one candidate to accumulate close to a majority of the delegates.[22]

The first of these factors arises from the nature of the contenders for the 1992 Democratic nomination. Among the Democratic candidates as of early 1992—Senators Tom Harkin and Bob Kerrey, Governor Bill Clinton, former Governor Jerry Brown, and former Senator Paul Tsongas—none but Brown has ever run for national office or, for that matter, has run anywhere outside his own state. (Former California Governor Brown enjoyed a short but impressive campaign for the presidency sixteen years earlier, in 1976, and mounted a considerably less noteworthy effort in 1980.) The group of five—capable as they may be in varying degrees individually—were largely unknown initially to the general public in early 1992. Further, unlike former Vice-Presidents Fritz Mondale in 1984 and Hubert Humphrey in 1968, none are towering figures in their party, able to draw upon the long-time personal loyalties of party leaders. Any of this group of contenders, of course, could strike political fire during the primaries of 1992, but none can build that fire upon a solid base of national exposure and extensive ties to national political leaders.

Compounding the difficulties any of the Democratic contenders will face in surging to an apparent nomination in 1992 is the late start of the field. By September 1991, there were but two announced candidates for the 1992 Democratic presidential nomination, former Senator Tsongas and Senator Harkin, and the set of contenders did not become complete until late October—only about fourteen weeks prior to the first delegate contests in Iowa and New Hampshire. The abbreviated pre-primary period of 1992, lauded by many as saving America from elongated presidential nomination campaigns extending for a year or more *prior* to the first primary or caucus contests, makes it more difficult for any candidate to have the time to "break out of the pack" and surge in delegate total toward the nomination.

The third factor creating the possibility of a slow-to-resolve Democratic nomination in 1992 results from a subtle, yet significant, rules change in 1992 concerning the division of delegates resulting from a given primary or caucus. In 1984 and 1988, proportionality was the general rule, but major exceptions in so-called "loophole primaries" and "bonus delegate" practices allowed the winner in many primaries to garner a much larger share of delegates than his share of the actual vote. This magnification of candidate strength was a significant factor in the ability of former Vice-President Fritz Mondale in 1984 to turn back the insurgent candidacy of Senator Gary Hart; it was also important in the eventual nomination success of Governor Michael Dukakis in 1988 over Jesse Jackson and others. In short, nonproportionality allowed leading candidates in both years to move even closer to the "inevitability point" when, because of their increasing delegate total, their nomination seemed sufficiently likely to swing remaining uncommitted delegates to them.

In 1992, however, the rule across-the-board is that delegates in each state are to be allotted to each candidate—who receives at least 15 percent of the vote—in strict proportion to the vote that candidate wins in that state's primary or caucus. There are *no* bonus delegates and *no* loophole primaries that would otherwise add extra delegates to a front-runner. As a result of this rules change, together with the limited national stature of the candidate field and the compressed pre-primary campaign, any candidate will find it unusually difficult to accumulate a delegate total coming anywhere close to a majority. A more likely pattern is that of two, three, or four serious candidates, each slogging his way through countless primaries and caucuses, each "winning" or "partially winning" some and losing others, and each picking up only portions of blocs of delegates and nowhere winning an overwhelming majority. The proportional division of delegates, not the accumulation of majorities, will be the pattern in 1992.

One final development in 1992 makes it even less likely that any candidate will easily and swiftly win a majority of national convention delegates. In 1992, an unprecedentedly large number of delegates will be determined automatically, independent of any primary or caucus outcome. The 1992 Super Delegates, totaling 772 of the approximately 4,288 national convention delegates, will constitute 18 percent of all those participating in the nomination. This group of uncommitted delegates in 1992 is about 120 delegates greater than in 1988, and about 200 more than in 1984. Made up in part of U.S. senators, members of Congress, governors, and other party leaders, more than half of the unpledged Super Delegates—410 in all—will be the members of the Democratic National Committee.

The practical effect of removing 18 percent of all the delegates from primary or caucus determination is to diminish further the likelihood that a candidate, through strong primary showings, will surge to an apparent nomination based upon the accumulation of pledged delegates. The field of non-nationally prominent candidates, the late-starting contest, and strict proportionality make a quick nomination unlikely; in addition, a candidate attempting to win committed delegates sufficient for the nomination—or a total seen as sufficiently close to it—will have to win not just a majority of electorally determined delegates but actually slightly over 60 percent of them!

Of course, some of the unpledged Super Delegates may well, for various reasons, favor a leading candidate and even make this preference known, thus lowering the number of primary or caucus-pledged delegates necessary for an apparent nomination. Nevertheless, there are conditions present in 1992, with 18 percent of the delegates outside the primary or caucus process, that suggest the nomination process will be long unresolved—through the early primaries, through the middle collection of contests, through the final primaries, through the pre-convention stage following the primaries, and even until the convention itself. It is not difficult to envision a situation in which the Democratic nomination of 1992 will be undecided until the National Convention meets in New York City, starting on July 13, 1992, and there be determined only by means of more than one roll-call vote. (If this should be the case, it would constitute the first multiple roll-call nomination of a presidential candidate in either party since 1952—a span of forty years!)

The key to the outcome of such an unprecedented presidential nomination situation would lie with the 772 Super Delegates, who are substantially uncommitted and largely devoted to the interests of party and candidate in their particular state or locale. This "peer-review" of presidential candidates would be profoundly influenced by assessments of the "winability" of the various presidential contenders and, especially, by the impact of particular presidential nominees on the Super Delegate's own local area of concern. This evaluation, further, would occur relatively late in the nomination process, after the candidates had been tested in a wide range of primary and caucus contests. Some candidates, even with significant delegate totals, might be seen by the Super Delegates as losers and, even more important, as losers whose nomination would have profound consequences on local candidates and party. Another candidate might be seen as enjoying steadily growing political strength and wide appeal, and be judged as a potential nominee who would bode well for candidate and party fortunes in a particular state or locale. In short, the calculations of this hard-eyed group of political professionals would not likely be ideological, and certainly not whimsical; rather, they would be extraordinarily calculated in terms of the political and candidate goals closest to themselves. Paramount among Super Delegate concerns would be both a potential nominee's ability to win the presidency and his political attractiveness to and consequences in a given area.

Of course, it is possible that the nomination process of 1992 will work out far differently from the scenario outlined here. Perhaps a candidate will surge to an easy nomination, building on initial successes in Iowa, New Hampshire, or "Super-Tuesday" contests, leaving the Super Delegates with at most a minimal confirming role. On the other hand, there is considerable evidence, as presented here, that the Super Delegates *could* be the deciding element in the 1992 Democratic nomination, and thus mark a further revival of the role of the national Democratic party, its leaders, and also its rank-and-file National Committee members in a crucial national political decision.

CONCLUSION

This chapter has advanced the argument that the national Democratic party can lead. It is undergoing a long-term process of revitalization and institutionalization, including the incorporation of some of the ideas of the Democratic Charter Movement reformers of the early 1970s. In addition, the national Democratic party is becoming increasingly electorally relevant and sufficiently mobilized to affect those critical democratic decisions, and national party personnel—including DNC rank-and-file members themselves—may possibly play a central and perhaps determining role in the presidential nominating politics of 1992. What, however, are the implications of this renewal of national party to progressives and others concerned with the programmatic purposes of party activity?

It has been customary in the past to view party organizations and party leaders as the enemies of progressive ideals. Certainly in the insurgent years of the 1960s and early 1970s, it often seemed that progressives were recurrently on the outside of political parties, seeking without much success to get party regulars on the inside to do what they were loath to do. Events of the past two decades, however, have transformed this simple picture. In the 1990s, progressives are now well entrenched within Democratic party organizations on the local, state, and national levels. The enemies of progressive ideals are no longer party organizational regulars, for today in many cases progressives are those very organizational leaders. Rather, the enemies of progressive ideals are Democratic party weakness and irrelevance, allowing for candidate-driven, media-adviser-shaped, consensual electoral politics to prevail.

The revival of the national Democratic party provides a crucial opportunity for progressives to harness that great engine of progress to innovative and socially progressive ideals. The national Democratic party *can* lead, the Democrats *must* lead, and progressive principles and values *will* provide the vision for that leadership.

NOTES

1. Cornelius P. Cotter and Bernard C. Hennessy, *Politics Without Power: The National Party Committees* (New York: Atherton Press, 1964).

2. See E. E. Schattschneider, *Party Government* (New York: Reinhart, 1942), p. 133.

3. V. O. Key, Jr., *Politics, Parties, and Pressure Groups*, 5th ed. (New York: Crowell, 1964), p. 334. "The national committee," Key wrote further, "is a gathering of sovereigns (or their emissaries) to negotiate and treat with each other" (p. 330).

4. Cotter and Hennessy, *Politics Without Power*, p. 39. An example of the unique character of state election of national committee members occurred in the early 1970s, when one candidate for national committeewoman in Wisconsin centered her campaign around hundreds of posters of herself wearing a mini-skirt and knee-high white boots; these posters were headlined "Make Wisconsin Happen Again." Despite widespread curiosity as to the proposed happening, this candidate was unsuccessful.

Another national committee candidate in the same state in 1989 (in fact, the author of this chapter) adopted a more restrained and agrarian theme for his campaign: "Elect a Grass-Roots Democrat." Despite a lack of relationship of this theme to any issue of national party affairs, he managed to win. These examples might suggest the primacy of localism over mini-skirts in national committee elections, along with the usual absence of broader national party policy issues.

5. Frank J. Sorauf, *Party Politics in America*, 3rd ed. (Boston: Little, Brown, 1976), p. 132.

6. The unhappy history of the Democratic Advisory Council from 1956 to 1960 is recounted briefly in Key, *Politics, Parties, and Pressure Groups*, pp. 318-319. It is instructive to note that the Democratic Advisory Council was opposed not only by Democratic congressional leaders at its inception in 1956 as a potential policy rival but also by the newly elected Democratic president in 1960 as unnecessary and intruding on presidential policy prerogatives.

Such innovative independent action by national committee chairmen is unusual; more often they serve as subordinates of their party's officeholders. Sometimes such subservience has proved to be useful. Senator Robert J. Dole (R-Kan.) has often ironically expressed relief over the fact that his service as Republican National Committee Chairman from 1971 to 1973—during the Watergate break-in and White House tapes period—consisted primarily of his nodding yes in the Oval Office.

7. Cornelius P. Cotter and John F. Bibby, "Institutional Development of Parties and the Thesis of Party Decline," *Political Science Quarterly* 95 (1980): 2.

8. See David S. Broder, "Rift Ends Charter Session," *Washington Post*, August 19, 1974; and Michael J. Malbin, "Controversy over Charter Reflects Democratic Party Division," *National Journal*, September 21, 1974, pp. 1407-1417. The reconstruction of events in this section of the chapter is based on my observations as a Charter Movement participant as well as Alternate-Delegate to the 1974 National Democratic Party Mini-Convention, which adopted the first-ever Charter of the National Democratic Party. For a useful overview of the Democratic Charter Movement of 1972-1974, its proposals, and their demise in 1974, see William Crotty, *Party Reform* (New York: Longman, 1983), pp. 110-114.

9. David E. Price, *Bringing Back the Parties* (Washington, D.C.: CQ Press, 1984), pp. 40-43; John F. Bibby, "Party Renewal in the National Republican Party," in Gerald M. Pomper, ed., *Party Renewal in America: Theory and Practice* (New York: Praeger Special Studies, 1981); Cotter and Bibby, "Institutional Development of Parties"; and Paul Allen Beck and Frank J. Sorauf, *Party Politics in America*, 7th ed. (New York: HarperCollins, 1992)

10. Paul S. Herrnson, "National Party Organizations and the Postreform Congress," in Roger H. Davidson, ed., *The Postreform Congress* (New York: St. Martin's Press, 1992); and Cotter and Bibby, "Institutional Development of Parties."

11. Paul S. Herrnson, "Reemergent National Party Organizations," in L. Sandy Maisel, ed., *The Parties Respond: Changes in the American Party System* (Boulder: Westview Press, 1990), p. 48.

12. The premier chronicler in recent years of the renascent congressional campaign committees is Paul S. Herrnson. His major work is *Party Campaigning in the 1980s* (Cambridge, Mass.: Harvard University Press, 1988), and his analysis is extended and updated in Herrnson, "Reemergent National Party Organizations" and "National Party Organizations and the Postreform Congress," as well as in Paul S. Herrnson and David Menebee-Libey, "The Dynamics of Party Organizational Development," *MidSouth Political Science Journal* 11 (1990): 3-20.

13. Christopher Arterton, cited in Beck and Sorauf, *Party Politics in America*, p. 103.

14. Herrnson, *Party Campaigning in the 1980s*.

15. Beck and Sorauf, *Party Politics in America*, pp. xiii and 143-146.

16. See Coordinated Campaign Briefings for Democratic Party State Chairs and DNC Members, Chicago, Illinois, November 21-23, 1991. For further discussion of the Democratic Coordinated Campaign, see also Herrnson, "National Party Organizations," pp. 65-67; and for additional detail and definition, see the document entitled "1992 Coordinated Campaign: What Is The Coordinated Campaign?" distributed by the Democratic National Committee in November 1991.

17. Thomas B. Edsall and Dan Balz, "The Democrats Put Together Their Teams," *Washington Post Weekly Edition*, September 30, 1991.

18. Letters to Democratic National Committeepeople from DNC member Sherrie Wolff of Colorado and others, June 25, 1991, and September 10, 1991; letter to DNC Chairman Ron Brown from DNC member Patrick A. Shea of Utah, September 25, 1991; letter to Democratic Committee Women and Men from Sherrie Wolff, Chairperson, Association of DNC Men and Women, October 20, 1991; letters to DNC members Patrick A. Shea, October 10, 1991, and Sherrie Wolff, October 22, 1991, from DNC Chairman Ronald H. Brown.

Following an organizational meeting of the rank-and-file DNC members' association in Los Angeles on September 20, 1991, fifteen DNC members were elected to constitute a steering group for the new association; more were expected to be added subsequently. In addition, Sherrie Wolff was elected chairperson of the new Association of DNC Men and Women.

19. To some degree, this change in the term of office of national Democratic party officers reflects at least partially the aspirations of the Democratic Charter Movement reform activists of 1972-1974 (see discussion earlier in this chapter). The goal in the 1970s, however, was for a possible midterm election of DNC officers, which, it was hoped, would remove that decision completely from presidential election-year politics. The 1989 reform was more limited, but it did set national party officer elections in a post-election period, rather than in its middle.

20. See Richard L. Berke, "Contributions to Democrats Lagging," *New York Times*, February 2, 1990, p. A12, as well as the sources cited in Tables 3.3 and 3.4. In comparing the data discussed in the text with the figures earlier reported in these tables, we must keep in mind that most of the data examined here are totals *combining* hard and soft money receipts. By contrast, Tables 3.3 and 3.4 predominantly report *only* hard money receipts.

21. Herrnson, *Party Campaigning in the 1980s*, p. 130.

22. The fullest analysis of the 1992 nominating process possibilities resulting from these new circumstances, and one which has greatly influenced this discussion, is by a young political scientist with senior experience in delegate-counting activities, Anthony J. Corrado (1991), "Party Rules Reform and Candidate Nomination Strategies: Consequences for the 1990s," paper presented at the Annual Meeting of the American Political Science Association, Washington, D.C. A revised and expanded version of this provocative essay is Anthony J. Corrado and Thomas A. Devine (1991), "Party Rules Reform and Candidate Nomination Strategies: Consequences for the 1990s" (unpublished paper).

4

WILLIAM CROTTY

Who Needs Two
Republican Parties?

A REPUBLICAN LEGACY

The real question may well be: Who needs *one* Republican party? Indeed, as we review the excesses of the last few Republican administrations, we cannot help but ask: Who needs economic exploitation; environmental devastation; a bloated military and a succession of invasions ranging from Afghanistan, Lebanon, Grenada, and Panama to the covert wars in Nicaragua, El Salvador, and Africa; a class-polarized social agenda; insider trading and Wall Street buccaneering; race-baiting politics, from Willie Horton to Clarence Thomas; a $100 billion plus "off-budget" Savings and Loan bailout; budget deficits that double those of all previous administrations combined; a for-profit health care system that fails miserably to meet the nation's needs; a homeless population that has become a source of disgrace in the world's wealthiest country; and a hemorrhaging of the educational and cultural resources of a nation that is not overly generous in these regards to begin with? Who needs policies that make the rich richer and the middle and working classes poorer, policies that leave the poorest of the poor (according to the mythology of Reaganism-Bushism, the source of the problems) outside the system?

All is sacrificed for short-term, quick-fix profit. The future is left to take care of itself. The consequences: a more class-stratified, more polarized society; an economy in decline; constant trade imbalances; a neglect of social problems; a nation's infrastructure badly in need of repair; a tax system both more onerous and substantially more regressive than that of its predecessor; the largest, most expensive budget deficits in history; and an educational system in retreat. For good measure, finally, add two constitutional crises—Richard Nixon's Watergate and the Reagan-Bush administrations' Irangate, products of conservative governments too arrogant to believe that the Constitution should stand in the way of their political ends. The record is a sorry one!

The foregoing assessment may be harsh. Perhaps George Bush, Ronald Reagan, and Richard Nixon will be found to have provided some yet-to-be discovered social benefits that will rescue their place in history. Perhaps the economically privileged do require a constant overrepresentation of their interests, and perhaps fate, or a market economy, has decreed that they should be enriched at the expense of society more generally. Perhaps this is the natural order of things, perhaps the best way to run a society.

Personally, I think not. Nonetheless, several caveats are in order. Clearly, there is a place for a Republican party. It does represent viable interests in the society. The vast majority of its supporters have good reason to voice and vote their concerns, and are unlikely to endorse much of the worst that happened (though they may decry the absence of an effective alternative). The indictment offered is not of them or, notwithstanding the title of this chapter, the Republican party per se. More to the point: It is an indictment of the record of conservative Republican administrations that have provided most of the governance of the country for the last quarter of a century.

These qualifications will not alleviate the anger of the lost souls, politically speaking, who have voted Republican in the last six presidential elections, possibly with results not foreseen or believed to be so stark as those depicted earlier. Nonetheless, the picture presented is depressing, and any corrections introduced represent a bow toward a bit more fairness and balance.

THE NO-OPPOSITION PARTY

In another context, and even more to the point, the Democrats have had a hand in all that has happened. To be clear: I do not suggest they are the sponsors or chief culprits. They are not. But they did consent, directly and indirectly, to much of what has occurred. By holding a basically 2 to 1 majority in the House of Representatives and control of the Senate through most (though in the case of the Senate, not all) of the period in question, they had to acquiesce, actively and through their legislative vote, to each of the major policy options endorsed. Through their refusal to aggressively exploit not only the power of opposition in national elections but also their control of the legislative branch of government; through their failure to maximize their powers over budgetary allocations, legislative fact-finding hearings, and congressional oversight investigations into the bureaucracy; through the rush to co-sponsor Republican initiatives (e.g., the "Tax Reform" Act of 1986, the efforts to reduce the tax on capital gains, support of the Contras in Nicaragua and the government of El Salvador, the funds allocated for military build-ups, the limits placed on social programs)—all in the name of political expediency and the illusion of a balanced budget; and through tepid legislative (and invisible national party) leadership, the Democrats went along with much of what took place, in the process making their own distinctive contribution to all that has resulted.

At a minimum, they chose not to openly oppose much of what was being done. They did not vocally oppose the trends under way, nor did they offer viable policy alternatives or persistent arguments to counter conservative claims. The Democrats (and the media) bought into the idea of a conservative revolution, when the electoral and survey data available indicated no such profound change in public attitudes. The Democrats failed, for whatever reason, to mobilize effective liberal candidacies for national office, and they proved incapable of framing and delivering a liberal message that activated their core constituency groups. In short, the Democrats did not fulfill the role of a viable, legitimate opposition party within the American two-party system. With the interests of their constituent groups effectively unrepresented, is it any wonder that the Nixon-Reagan-Bush message of class privilege on the domestic front and a policy of military build-ups and force in foreign affairs prevailed?

This is the point of this chapter. The Democratic party lost its way. The differences between parties became blurred. The Democrats had no distinctive message and ignored their core constituency. They found themselves unable to compete effectively with the Republicans in presidential elections or even to oppose in strong and unambiguous terms what Nixon, Reagan, and Bush stood for. The party was unable to fashion a message or to find the national-level candidates capable of popularizing it and bringing it home to the American people. Quite the contrary: The Democrats became a shadow Republican party, attempting to mimic Republican appeals and targeting much the same electoral groups. In the process, they left their basic value commitments and traditional constituency behind. And they have suffered for it, along with the country, not incidentally.

Republicans are much better at being Republicans than Democrats are. If voters are presented a choice between two Republican alternatives, why not take the real thing? The Republicans are authentic, and there is a sense of integrity (notwithstanding the cataloguing of ills presented here) in what they say and who they represent. The Democrats would have difficulty making any such claims. Republicans really are for lower taxes and balanced budgets, reduced social programs, government subsidies for business development, less government regulation, a strong defense, and maximized profitmaking. The Democratic party's efforts in presidential elections to capture the ideological tone and to copy the policies and electoral strategies of its opponent have failed. Republicans are better at "Republicanism" than Democrats, and the electorate senses it. A political party unsure of itself and what or whom it represents is not a political party with which to entrust the nation's leadership. The alternative, however, is even more costly.

THE CLIMATE OF OPINION

There are a number of ways to chart the Democrats' efforts to reformulate their appeal and prove themselves more attractive to a different constituency. The Democratic party lost its way attempting to gain electoral success in presidential elections. The strategy was to counter Republican victories by modeling itself—in terms of policy stands, voters targeted, and even funding efforts and a reliance on media strategies—after the Republican party. The effort was not totally nonrational. The Democratic planners were reacting to what they saw as the prevailing mood of the country and to the belief that the times were unsympathetic to their traditional emphases. But the "L" (for liberal) word became a no-no, and their normal constituency appeared unresponsive to their appeals.

The Dominance of Conservatives (the Republicans)

The climax of a conservative resurgence was seen by Democrats in the election of Ronald Reagan as president in 1980. For decades, Reagan had presented a starkly conservative, even rightwing, ideological agenda both within the Republican party itself and, more broadly, to the nation's electorate. He had been a highly visible spokesman for corporate interests generally and for specific sponsors (General Electric, for example), even before running for political office. In his tenure as governor of California and his repeated efforts to win the Republican party's presidential nomination, his message and his commitments could not have been clearer. He positioned himself at the far right within the party and within the electorate, and he made no apologies for his truculent antiwelfare, anticommunist, antitax, antispend, and antigovernment stands. Even while in office and throughout his reelection campaigns, he basically ran against government. He was adamantly opposed to social spending of any type and in favor of laissez-faire economic and governing systems that would have been familiar to voters of the 1920s. There could be no mistaking his position or the ideological credo he represented. In issue terms, Ronald Reagan was the most clearly defined conservative candidate on the American scene.

Yet, in violation of what many believed was the electorate's historical endorsement of centrism and pragmatism in presidential choices, the American people had elected him president. He was reelected by an overwhelming margin, as was his successor and heir, George Bush. The victories, of course, followed first the narrow and then the landslide wins of Richard Nixon in 1968 and 1972. The only Democratic break in this string of successes came in 1976, when Jimmy Carter, a southerner and party outsider and the "most conservative Democratic President for his time since Grover Cleveland,"[1] managed to beat another conservative, Gerald Ford, who as vice-president had taken over upon Nixon's abdication. Carter then went on to lose convincingly to Reagan in 1980.

The message was clear: The country had moved dramatically to the right. Only conservatives could win. The Democrats, even if fitfully and not too successfully, would have to refashion themselves into a more conservative instrument to achieve any hope of electoral success. Right? Wrong. This was the message put out by successful conservative politicians, conservative think-tanks, and conservative commentators, and it was offered as an explanation for the overwhelming success of Reaganism. It was bought by the media, by politicians generally, and, most unfortunately, by the Democratic party leadership. It became the blueprint for political success, and it led to a conservative revolution during the Reagan years that threatened the very foundations of the New Deal state.

A few points: First, an analysis of voter attitudes showed no such sea-change in political positions. Reagan's 1980 election is best explained in light of the indecisiveness and leadership failures of the Carter administration. Neither candidate was particularly popular in 1980; yet Reagan in both 1980 and 1984 was able, through skillful use of the media and public relations, to convince the electorate that he was the more attractive alternative. Seen as a choice between two options, and in light of the weak campaign performances of both Carter and Walter Mondale, the outcomes are more explainable.

In many respects, Carter and Mondale, much like Michael Dukakis who followed them in 1988, proved ideal foils for their opponents. Carter, like Dukakis, chose to emphasize "competence" over issues. His record in office undid him. With Dukakis, the Bush campaign, through a clever and viciously negative campaign (to which Dukakis would not or could not respond), drove home the point that he was anything but the competent manager he presented himself as. Walter Mondale, a true New Deal liberal, chose not to emphasize issues or his traditional Democratic sources of support (such as organized labor, for which he seemed apologetic). In an issueless campaign, during which he was depicted as Carter's former vice-president and a tool of "special interests," attention was focused on Reagan's personality and record in office. In none of these cases did much of a contest result.

Finally, we should note that landslides, once considered marking points in American politics, come cheap in today's political marketplace. It took only about 27 percent of the voting-age population (with a turnout of only slightly over one-half of those eligible) to elect Reagan overwhelmingly and set in motion the drastic policy changes that this conservative landslide supposedly symbolized. The conservative revolution in people's thinking, however, never took place. Reagan was elected (as was his successor) by a relatively small percentage of the electorate in low-turnout elections (more on this later). The success of recent conservative presidential candidates is better found in the dynamics of the individual elections than in profound changes in values or priorities within the nation's electorate.

A Party Divided (the Democrats)

The conservative revival came at a critical juncture in the Democratic party's development. As a consequence of the social unrest, the civil rights revolution, and the reaction to the war in Vietnam, the Democratic party (the party then in power) divided in the 1960s. It was torn between the traditional cold war warriors with a New Deal social outlook (which, for many, gave way in favor of support for the more conservative of candidates) and the challenges posed by younger, more liberal, issue-oriented, and increasingly vocal antiwar activists who would come to dominate the party in the 1970s.

The changeover from the professionalized, elitist, and comfortable leadership of the past to the more open, competitive, and policy-driven system of the contemporary period did not come without a political hemorrhaging. The old yielded slowly, painfully, and rancorously to the thinking and the political concerns of a newer generation. To make matters worse, the newcomers seemed oblivious to the contributions and sensitivities of their predecessors. Many of the old guard would eventually turn to the Republican party of Ronald Reagan as their savior.

Whatever the merits of the respective positions of the competing factions within the Democratic party, it divided the party's basic coalition and has persisted to this date. The failure to bridge the gap, to agree on policy positions or candidates representative of the different interests within the Democratic party, has been a principal cause of the party's inability to win presidential elections.

THE DEMOCRATS MOVE TO THE RIGHT

There are any number of ways to chart the Democrats' efforts to reformulate their appeal in an attempt to counter Republican successes after 1968 and to become more competitive in appealing to much the same electorate. Signposts along the way include the party's platforms, its principal statement of its commitment on issues, and its effort to reward the groups to which it hoped to appeal; the fight over the party's presidential selection process and party reform, a controversy that has continued to divide the party; and the efforts of a group of party leaders in the 1980s to create a competing organization within the party itself, the Democratic Leadership Council, to move the party further right.

The Party Platform

A comparison of the approaches used in party platforms in 1964 with those employed against Reagan and Bush in the 1980s is instructive. In 1964, the Democratic party was ending four years of presidential rule, an uncertain and in many respects explosive period (the Cuban Missile Crisis, the Bay of Pigs, the erection of the Berlin Wall, the beginning of the build-up in Vietnam, the Kennedy assassination). Yet in domestic affairs, the Democrats could claim "42 months of uninterrupted [economic] expansion under Presidents Kennedy and Johnson, [during which] we have achieved the longest and strongest peacetime prosperity in modern history," and "prices [that] have been more stable than in any other industrial democracy."[2] The platform went on to call for a full range of domestic programs: federal investments in hard-pressed economic areas; tax reductions; "a job and a fair wage for doing it" for everyone who wanted to work; a commitment to civil rights; increased housing and home financing; additional funding for health, education, and domestic welfare;

the rebuilding of urban America; the conservation of wilderness areas and natural resources; help for the poverty-stricken; and the expansion of school lunch, Head Start, and Medicare programs. In similar language, the pledges were repeated in the 1968 platform.

The proposals are unabashedly liberal. It was the "Great Society's" contributions to the unfinished agenda of Franklin Roosevelt's "New Deal." The later program had provided the basis for the contemporary Democratic coalition as well as the electoral divisions that distinguished the two major parties. An aggressive Democratic party was prepared to build on this foundation in the 1960s.

By the 1980s, the message had changed but not the coalitional base of the parties. The Democrats had begun in earnest their move toward more centrist positions in reaction to the Republican interpretations of what the elections of 1980 and 1984 signified. In a fundamental way, it appeared that the party had lost its sense of direction. The 1984 party platform had grown to a bulky 45,000 words, and catalogued without thematic cohesion or much sense of purpose was a series of group demands opening the Democrats to the curious charge, as leveled by Reaganites, that it was the party of "special interests." Yet the platform did not call for any major new social spending and was "economically more conservative than Democratic documents of the past 50 years."[3]

By 1988, the Democrats had come full circle. The Republicans drafted a long, conservative platform (also 45,000 words, far more specific than their usual) that the Democrats, for some reason, had difficulty in attacking. Perhaps they did not want to. The Democrats, under the direction of candidate Michael Dukakis, chose to offer a brief statement (one-tenth the size of the party's earlier platform and that of the Republicans). Predictably, the platform was criticized as "lacking in commitment" and as being "vague" and "evasive," charges later directed by Republicans at the Dukakis campaign more generally.[4]

Dukakis chose to place his emphasis on technocratic and managerial abilities ("competence not ideology") rather than on hardcore liberal appeals. The result was that the Republicans and their allies in the conservative movement were able to frame the issues in the campaign: gun control; the death penalty; toughness on crime; and racism (recall the Willie Horton commercial); a strong defense (the Democrats helped here with the news clips showing Dukakis in an oversized helmet riding around in a tank, a visual image the Republicans adopted in their commercials to their own ends); and patriotism, the flag, and the Pledge of Allegiance. These were combined with an attack on the competence issue (examples include pollution in Boston Harbor and the deteriorating state of the Massachusetts economy).

It could be argued that neither side addressed the fundamental issues. The Republicans decided to emphasize the themes of the Reagan revolution and to use a negative campaign to belittle their opponent; the Democrats chose not to respond to the dirty tactics (and charges) of their opponent and found themselves unable to make the economic and foreign policy failures of the Reagan years foremost in the campaign. Consequently, the Dukakis strategists fell back to basically emotionless, centrist calls for efficiency and better political management, issues that Republicans have historically used more effectively. The 1988 Democratic platform was an accurate introduction to a lifeless Democratic campaign.

By the late 1980s, the Democratic party had lost faith in its traditional issues and appeared almost embarrassed by the coalition of the less well-off that normally supported it.

Presidential Selection

The reforms introduced in the Democratic party's presidential selection proceedings after the 1968 election were in response to the divisions caused by the racial strife of the 1960s and by the split over the war in Vietnam and the riots and violence that marked the Democrats' National Convention in Chicago. They were meant to open the process, provide fairness for all who participated, modernize deliberative procedures, and unify the party. Whatever the score on the other objectives, they did anything but unify the party.[5]

The opposition to the reforms was intensive, aggressive, and long-running. It began as soon as the new rules were adopted and lasted through the mid-1980s. To counter criticism of the new selection system and to placate its opponents, concessions were made. One was the creation of "Super Delegates," elected and appointed party officials who did not have to contest their seats at the national conventions or commit themselves (unlike those who contested in the primaries or caucuses) to any one candidate. They would remain uncommitted and, it was hoped, would cast their ballots at national conventions for the centrist, less ideological candidate, the one closer to the traditional center of the Democratic party (I refer here to organized labor, big city mayors, party funders, and officeholders). In short, the Super Delegates would provide a check on the grassroots activists represented through the primaries and push the party, especially in the contested nomination races that had become the norm, toward the centrist alternatives.

This is exactly what happened in 1984 (arguably Walter Mondale could not have won a first-ballot victory without his strong support from the Super Delegates). And in 1988, the Super Delegates solidified behind the frontrunner, Dukakis.

The party's long-run gains from these tactics are debatable. The presidential selection system remains hostage to the party's squabblings. In practice, and with obvious amendments, a grassroots nominating system prevails. Many traditional centers of power in the party, however, refuse to accept it.

A Secessionist Move Within the Party: The Democratic Leadership Council

Symbolically and politically, the most significant move to the right within the Democratic party occurred with the creation of the Democratic Leadership Council (DLC), a vehicle intended to give the conservatives a dominant voice in party politics. The DLC was established in 1985, according to its own account, after the Mondale defeat "by a group of rising Democratic leaders [who] decided it was time for a new kind of politics. They started the DLC to lead the Democratic Party back to the political mainstream and [to] restore America's sense of national purpose."[6] The "political mainstream" would be decided primarily by Sunbelt Democrats and elected officeholders (governors, state legislators, and mayors), although in reality the DLC's two-thirds congressional membership dominated its activities. The council was to be led by Representative Richard A. Gephardt of Missouri and Senators Charles S. Robb of Virginia and Sam Nunn of Georgia. Its political agenda was to be fashioned largely in response to the Reagan victories of 1980 and 1984.

The DLC originated in early 1985 at a retreat with speakers including, among others, a motivational psychologist and consultant to big business (Topps Bubble Gum, Polaroid, and Elizabeth Arden) and Reagan's former communications director. It intended to free the Democratic party from the shadow of organized labor and the other "special interests" of the 1984 campaign and, according to Nunn, to "move the party—both in substance and in perception—back to the mainstream of American political life."[7]

Others would echo the same themes. The DLC's executive director spoke of the group as consisting of "entrepreneurs" of ideas and as representing an effort to free the party from traditional Democratic views. Florida Senator (and later Governor) Lawton Chiles referred to the council as a "caucus for . . . Middle America," and Gephardt saw it "as a way station or bridge back into the party for elected Democrats" (a reference to the changes in power configurations brought on by party reform). The DLC's literature described the group as attempting to fashion "a national party" with "a message that touches everybody, makes sense to everybody, and goes beyond the stale orthodoxies of 'left' and 'right.' A message that resonates with the hopes and dreams of ordinary Americans. That's what the DLC has set out to do."[8] This statement on behalf of the DLC was signed by Bill Clinton, governor of Arkansas and Democratic presidential contender in 1992.

The DLC initially numbered its membership at roughly 40 people. In preparing for the 1992 elections, however, it could claim more than 1,000 Democrats in attendance at its policy convention and as contributors to its statement of principles.

The major concerns of the DLC at the end of the 1980s were a strong defense (modified somewhat after the collapse of the cold war) and an emphasis on fiscal responsibility, economic growth, and opportunity—stands it hoped would appeal to the middle class. In a real sense, the DLC had been seduced by the Republicans and, more pointedly, by Reagan's definition of the major concerns facing the nation. It rejected "quotas," favored free trade, avoided a discussion of abortion, came out against higher taxes (except for the wealthy), proposed a modified form of budget-balancing, emphasized "family values," endorsed choice in schools, and pledged "vigorous" welfare reform.

In all fairness, the DLC was not the Republican party in sheep's clothing. The DLC attacked the "fantasy world" of the 1980s, the glorification of "the pursuit of greed and self-interest," the unwillingness to admit major national problems, and the failure of the "national political leadership to assume responsibility for doing something about them."[9] In line with its style, it failed to mention any names or hold any party or individual responsible for the problems it identified. And, for a centrist/conservative group (conservative, that is, for Democrats), its message was couched in more traditional Democratic terms:

> Of all the major countries in the world, we're the only one to send millions of men and women off to work with the gnawing insecurity that if someone in their family gets sick, they don't know how they'll pay the bills or whether they'll get the care.

Eighteen other nations do a better job than we do at the simple task of bringing babies into the world alive. A dozen do a better job of preparing their children to perform on international math and science tests. At least ten give their workers better reading skills that are so necessary to compete in a world where what you can earn depends largely on what you can learn.

Of all the major industrial nations, we're the only one that has no system for moving kids who don't want to go to college into good jobs with a high wage and a bright future instead of dead-end jobs.

Last year, we became number one in another category. We . . . now lead the world in the percentage of people we put in prison.[10]

Although the DLC's identification of the problems was different from that of the Republicans and its concern for working people was more pronounced (notwithstanding the fact that the group focused its main appeal on the middle class), its solutions—providing an emphasis on universal economic growth and productivity—would not have made Republicans uncomfortable. According to co-founder Robb, it was "time to approach the electorate on a different basis . . . consistent with our values."[11] To accomplish this goal, the DLC would have to change the Democratic party from within.

The DLC both succeeded and failed. Its membership grew to include many of the most influential Democrats in American politics. Among these were 32 Senate Democrats (just under 60 percent of the party's average Senate membership for the period 1985-1992); 140 U.S. representatives or former representatives numbering committee chairs and northerners among them, such as Les Aspin (Wis.), Michael Barnes (Md.), David E. Bonior (Mich.), Tony Coelho (Calif.), Tom Lantos (Calif.), William O. Lipinski (Ill.), Tom McMillen (Md.), Norman Y. Mineta (Calif.), Leon E. Panetta (Calif.), Stephen Solarz (N.Y.), and former speaker Jim Wright (Tex.).

The 25 governors or former governors affiliated with the DLC were dominated by southern and border-state moderates but included the Democratic governors of Pennsylvania, Connecticut, Colorado, and Michigan. Anne Richards of Texas, an outspoken liberal, was also a member. Other DLC members holding state and municipal offices included several, such as Lieutenant Governor Harriet Woods of Missouri, Mayor Diane Feinstein of San Francisco, and Mayor Henry Cisneros of San Antonio, recognizable beyond their immediate localities. The DLC membership also welcomed a number of prominent blacks—Willie Brown, Speaker of the California Assembly; Roland W. Burris, Attorney General of Illinois; Mayor Maynard Jackson of Atlanta; former Atlanta Mayor and United Nations Representative Andrew Young; Mayor Tom Bradley of Los Angeles; and U.S. Representatives William H. Gray III (Pa.), John Lewis

(Ga.), Cardiss Collins (Ill.), Mike Espy (Miss.), and former Representative Barbara Jordan (Tex.). The DLC even welcomed an occasional Kennedy (State Representative Patrick Kennedy of Rhode Island). A number of members used the council for tries at the Democratic presidential nomination—namely, Gephardt, Clinton, Joseph Biden, Jr., Alan Cranston, John D. Rockefeller IV, Bruce Babbitt, Lloyd Bentsen, and Albert Gore, Jr.

Its strength, however, was its weakness. Although its ranks included many of the shakers and movers in Congress and, to a lesser extent, the state parties, many of its members were avowedly liberal. As it grew, and though still dominated by party centrists, it attracted a range of individuals who diluted its initial emphasis and reduced its aim to one of serving as a policy vehicle for officeholders, one of the objectives Gephardt, among others, originally had in mind for it. From the beginning, it fostered a cordial relationship with the national party and its chair, a tactic that implicitly limited whatever disruptive or redirective role to which it might aspire.

Although the DLC does provide a base for presidential candidates, its impact in 1988 appeared minimal (a presumed liberal—Dukakis—won, and its message of economic growth and sound fiscal management did little to sway voters). One of its principal stratagems backfired—namely, a Super Tuesday primary in the South meant to maximize the influence of the more conservative voices in the Democratic party. The candidacies of Albert Gore and Richard Gephardt went down to defeat. Dukakis won, and the political credibility of the most liberal of the contenders, the Reverend Jesse Jackson, improved dramatically. Jackson's 33 to 45 percent of the vote in such states as Alabama, Georgia, Louisiana, Maryland, Mississippi, North Carolina, and Virginia (29 percent overall in the southern and border-state primaries) in a multicandidate field established him as the principal alternative to Dukakis, not the outcome the DLC had anticipated.

Many recruits joined the DLC out of a need for some sense of national party identification and out of a hunger for ideas and issues relevant to a changing political climate. Clearly, they did not find these in either the administratively oriented national party operations of the 1980s or in the issue-weak Democratic campaigns of the party's presidential contenders. Its success (to the extent it has enjoyed success) and its eventual influence in party politics may best be explained in this context. Its attractiveness for officeholders may speak more to the weakness of the national party than to the message it hoped to convey or the constituency it planned to develop. The ultimate lesson of the DLC is that there is a place for ideas in American politics and that those most receptive to them may well be the politicians who face the voters in elections. The Republicans, with their think-tanks and issue-oriented, ideological politics, have recognized this. The Democrats have been slow to respond.

A CLASS-SKEWED ELECTORATE

The Democrats' turn toward the center/right wasn't entirely nonrational. The impression made by the Reagan victories and their acceptance as confirmation of a rightward swing of the electorate have already been commented on. Another, more fundamental development had been under way for at least a generation: The electorate was undergoing a restructuring, becoming smaller and more select, wealthier, better educated, and more professionalized—in short, more middle- to upper-middle-class in orientation and values. In the process, the working class and underclass, always at a disadvantage in terms of turnout, were further disadvantaged in a presidential electorate that continued to contract. The losses occurred disproportionately among those needing representation the most: the less well-off economically, socially, and politically. Those with the most to gain and with the least influence within the system, and for better or worse the mainstays of the Democratic party's constituency, were represented among the voting public at successively lower levels. Conversely, the electorate to whom presidential candidates needed to appeal increasingly came to resemble the traditional base of Republican support. The mathematics are there. Assuming a 50 percent turnout (or slightly more) in an upwardly scaled voting population, the victory of a conservative candidate would require only one-quarter (or a little better) of the voting-age population, or a little more than one-half of those voting, in an electorate receptive to that candidate's appeal. This is exactly what happened.

If a blueprint for a conservative victory existed, it could not have been better executed. Shrink the electorate. Squeeze out the lower end, those most likely to be receptive to Democratic appeals on economic issues. Divide the remainder on racial issues. Then present a broad, if vague, conservative agenda for endorsement by those voting. Win with a distinct minority of the voting-age population. Convince your opponents that your success depended on a conservative to rightwing ideological appeal and that, to succeed, they should copy, as best they could, your appeals to your constituency. Once in office, back policies (now supported by the opposition) that further reward your coalition and further alienate the supporters of your opponents. Begin the cycle anew at the next election.

TABLE 4.1 Social Class and Party Vote by Decade

Indicators	1950s D	1950s R	1960s[a] D	1960s[a] R	1970s[a] D	1970s[a] R	1980s[a] D	1980s[a] R
Education:								
Grade School	51	49	58	37	54	46	53	46
College	33	67	43	54	40	59	39	57
Occupation:								
Professional								
and Business	34	66	43	53	37	63	39	60[b]
Manual	53	47	60	35	51	49	47	51

[a] Excludes third-party votes in 1968 for George Wallace, in 1976 for Eugene McCarthy, and in 1980 for John Anderson.
[b] 1988 election data were not available.

Source: Calculated from survey data reported in *The Gallup Report* (November 1988), Report No. 278, pp. 6-7. Figures have been rounded.

No such blueprint exists. If it did, it would simply be a good campaign strategy. This strategy did place the Democrats in a bind. By becoming more centrist/conservative, they attempted to appeal to an increasingly more upscale and, in terms of the groups likely to vote, more conservative electorate. One approach was to reconstruct the party, as the DLC had envisioned, into a vehicle that could compete more aggressively for conservative votes. The gamble was that such a change could result in a rejection of the party's traditional base.

The strategy did not work. However the Democrats chose to package themselves, their core support remained strongest among lower socioeconomic status (SES) groups (Table 4.1). One thing is clear: When the Democrats lose the working-class vote, they lose the election big—as was the case in both 1972 and 1984. They do not compete effectively with Republicans for the higher SES vote. This is not their strength.

The United States may well have, as is sometimes claimed, the most class-polarized electorate among democratic nations in the world. This is not what Americans like to think about themselves, and it does not fit comfortably into the mythology that surrounds American politics. It may very well fit reality, though—a reality the Democratic party would be well advised to accept.

RESTRUCTURING THE ELECTORATE

First, why be concerned about the American electorate? For one thing, the United States has the lowest voter turnout among major industrial democracies. Compared to other democratic nations, it ranks just above last (surpassing only Switzerland with its multitude of referenda votes) among the twenty, or twenty-four, democratic nations, depending on the listing. No matter how one calculates the figures, whether it is based on the turnout among the voting-age population or on the turnout of registered voters, the United States does quite poorly.[12]

Worse, turnout is in decline. Since the high of 63 percent in the presidential election of 1960, there has been a steady erosion in voter involvement. In the most recent presidential elections, turnout rates averaged just over 50 percent. Turnout is depressed even more in other, less visible contests.

The consequences are significant. First, those most in need of governmental assistance are the ones most likely to be excluded in a shrinking electorate. This is a point of universal agreement: Those at the lowest end of the social and economic spectrum are the ones most likely not to register or to vote (Table 4.2). Minorities, and those with the least income, education, or professional or job skills are the least likely to participate in elections. These groups, in turn, are the most likely to suffer disproportionately from a regressive tax structure, a weak network of social services, the declining quality of public education, poorly regulated public utilities, the absence of job training programs, unaffordable housing, and expensive and restricted medical health care. Those in need are left out. It can be argued, as it has been,[13] that the policy views of those not voting are not significantly different from the policy views of those who are voting and therefore would be unlikely to change substantially the outcomes of elections. The nonvoters are among the least informed, least interested, and least motivated groups in the electorate.

Conversely, it could be argued that participation in elections (much like anything else in life) would most likely create interest and eventually knowledge, and that both would contribute to a more informed vote. A more informed vote, in turn, is more likely to reflect the class interests of the present nonvoters. The class bias affecting the vote is clear. It is also clear that the interests of those who do not vote will not be represented. Nonvoters cannot depend on others to espouse their concerns within a political system based on conflict and competition for power and the

TABLE 4.2 Indicators of Registration and Turnout in Presidential Elections, by Social Class and Year, 1968-1988 (in percent)

	1968	1972	1976	1980	1984	1988
Education:						
Grade School	65	62	54	53	53	48
College	85	85	84	84	84	83
Employment:						
Employed	77	74	69	69	69	67
Unemployed	60	59	52	50	54	50
Not in Labor Force	71	71	65	66	68	67

Source: Adapted from U.S. Bureau of the Census Reports as found in *Current Population Reports*, Series P-23, No. 131.

resulting distribution of awards.[14] And, finally, differences of consequence do tend to appear between voters and nonvoters on issues of economic concern and welfare state policy,[15] precisely the issues that lend support to the argument being made here.

Second, the policy consequences can be great. Consider as an example the fact that a "landslide" can be determined by slightly over one-quarter of the adult population. This is what has occurred in recent elections. Although these figures may not be impressive in themselves, they did result in an attack on the foundations of the welfare state and an attempted return to a politics more familiar to the 1920s than to the 1980s. A small minority of the electorate can direct changes of enormous significance.

Third, and of immediate concern to the Democrats' electoral fortunes, those not voting provide a natural constituency for the Democratic party. There is no guarantee that all, or most, would vote Democratic if they participated in elections. But there is a likelihood that they would be sympathetic to the traditional message of the Democratic party, that they would provide a recruiting ground for Democrats, and that their interests would be best represented by Democrats.

It is also likely that the Democrats would target for mobilization the subgroups in the population most receptive to the party's appeals. The Democrats have done this sporadically. Yet, when they have concentrated their resources and energies on reaching out and incorporating new groups into the voting population, the effects have been telling.[16] It is in the Democratic party's best interests to expand the electorate. Such is not easily done, but the potential gains suggest that sustained efforts along these lines could have a significant payoff.

INCREASING PARTICIPATION
(AND THE DEMOCRATIC VOTE)

There is an argument to the effect that the decline in voting reflects the low quality of political debate, diminished candidate appeal, and the lack of relevance in issue choice presented to the electorate.[17] The political withdrawal that has increasingly characterized elections is seen both as evidence of a contempt for politics more generally and as a reaffirmation of its lack of relevance for tens of millions of Americans.

There may be much truth to these assertions, and in one sense this volume is dedicated to such concerns. It is clear, however, that the biggest institutional barrier to the vote is registration. Among those who register, the overwhelming majority (better than 80 percent) turn out on election day to vote; but the United States has the most onerous registration system in the free world. It has been modernized, codified, and simplified considerably as a result of the civil rights revolution and, beginning in 1965, the successive Voting Rights Acts. Yet even as efforts have been made to systematize the system and to reduce registration complications, turnout has continued to decline.

One argument is that the fall-off in participation would be more severe if change had not been forthcoming. Another is that regardless of the changes that have taken place, the burden (as is not the case in other democratic nations, excluding South Africa), is still placed on the individual to meet registration requirements; that these remain the single biggest institutional obstacle to the vote; that the people who are registered do vote; and that these are the factors in the equation most susceptible to change.

The most promising approach would be to restructure the registration system along the lines of the government-initiated national enrollment program found in Canada, Britain, and many other nations.[18] Even a more modest change, one proposed by the Carter Administration but never fully considered by Congress—namely, election-day registration—could have profound consequences for increasing turnout. Election day registration remains the most practical and most easily supported of the major alternatives available. It could have a pronounced and immediate impact on American politics.

Many other useful plans have been proposed as well.[19] Each of these would help by mobilizing a more representative electorate. Even modest increases in registration and turnout could affect electoral fortunes and, not incidentally, the nature of policy decisions placed before the electorate. Increases of 10 percent or so may well be possible[20] and would substantially change the electoral playing field.

With a revamped and expanded electorate, it would be up to the political parties during the campaign to mobilize their supporters based on the relevancy of their appeals and the attractiveness of their candidates. As one side mobilized its supporters in a relatively open electoral marketplace, the burden would be on the other to counter through the mobilization of its coalition.[21] In a democratic nation, the burden of mobilization rests upon the political parties. For Democrats, there is much to do in these regards.

CONCLUSION

In recent elections, the Democratic party has been "shadowing" the Republican party. That is, it has tried to appeal to voters in presidential campaigns with the same types of issues as those used by Republicans. It has had little success. Strong elements within the party (the Democratic Leadership Council, for example) believe that this is the road to success even though it has led to successive defeats. In large part, this strategy hinges upon a shrinking, increasingly upper-class and pro-Republican electorate. By contrast, this chapter has argued for a broadened, more inclusive electorate, one more likely to be sympathetic to Democratic liberal programs. An electorate restructured through new registration procedures to include the broadest range of social and class interests would constitute a beginning.

Nobody needs two Republican parties. The political system, and certainly the American people, would benefit from an aggressively liberal, forward-looking, and caring Democratic party, one that speaks to the concerns of those least represented in the society.

NOTES

1. Walter Dean Burnham, "The Reagan Heritage," in Gerald M. Pomper, ed., *The Election of 1988: Reports and Interpretations* (Chatham, N.J.: Chatham House Publishers, 1989), p. 21.

2. *Congressional Quarterly Weekly Report,* August 28, 1964, p. 1964.

3. *Congressional Quarterly Weekly Report*, July 21, 1984, p. 1739.

4. *Congressional Quarterly Weekly Report*, October 22, 1988, p. 3041.

5. William Crotty and John S. Jackson III, *Presidential Primaries and Nominations* (Washington, D.C.: CQ Press, 1985).

6. Democratic Leadership Council, *The New American Choice: Opportunity, Responsibility, Community* (Washington, D.C.: Democratic Leadership Council, 1991), inside front cover.

7. *Congressional Quarterly Weekly Report*, March 9, 1985, p. 457.

8. Democratic Leadership Council, *The New American Choice*, p. 3.

9. Ibid., p. 4.

10. Ibid., p. 3.

11. Richard E. Cohen, "Democratic Leadership Council Sees Party Void and Is Ready to Fill It," *National Journal*, 18 (1986), p. 270.

12. Raymond E. Wolfinger, David P. Glass, and Peverill Squire, "Predictors of Electoral Turnout: An International Comparison," *Policy Studies Review*, 9 (1990): 551-574.

13. John R. Petrocik and Daron Shaw, "Nonvoting in America: Attitudes in Context," in William Crotty, ed., *Political Participation and American Democracy* (Westport, Conn.: Greenwood Press, 1991); Raymond E. Wolfinger and Steven J. Rosenstone, *Who Votes?* (New Haven: Yale University Press, 1980).

14. William Crotty, "Political Participation: Mapping the Terrain," in William Crotty, ed., *Political Participation and American Democracy* (Westport, Conn.: Greenwood Press, 1991).

15. Petrocik and Shaw, "Nonvoting in America"; Crotty, "Political Participation."

16. Thomas E. Cavanagh, "When Turnout Matters: Mobilization and Conversion as Determinants of Election Outcomes," in William Crotty, ed., *Political Participation and American Democracy* (Westport, Conn.: Greenwood Press, 1991); Thomas Ferguson and Joel Rogers, *Right Turn: The Decline of the Democrats and the Future of American Politics* (New York: Hill and Wang, 1986).

17. Curtis B. Gans, "Remobilizing the American Electorate," *Policy Studies Review*, 9 (1990): 527-538; E. J. Dionne, Jr., *Why Americans Hate Politics* (New York: Simon and Schuster, 1991).

18. William Crotty, *Political Reform and the American Experiment* (New York: Thomas Y. Crowell, 1977); Crotty, "The Franchise: Registration Changes and Voter Participation," in William Crotty, ed., *Paths to Political Reform* (Lexington, Mass.: Lexington Books/D.C. Heath, 1980).

19. Wolfinger, Glass, and Squire, "Predictions of Electoral Turnout"; Committee for the Study of the American Electorate, "Creating the Opportunity: Voting and the Crisis of Democracy," *Policy Studies Review*, 9 (1990); Francis Fox Piven and Richard A. Cloward, *Why Americans Don't Vote* (New York: Pantheon Books, 1988); Crotty, *Political Reform and the American Experiment*.

20. Wolfinger and Rosenstone, *Who Votes?*

21. E. E. Schattschneider, *The Semi-Sovereign People: A Realist's View of Democracy in America* (New York: Holt, Rinehart and Winston, 1960); Cavanagh, "When Turnout Matters."

5

SAMUEL C. PATTERSON

A Congressional Party Must Stand for Something

In this country, we pay too much attention to the president and too little attention to Congress. The president is highly visible. Talking heads speak on television several times a day in front of the White House, and news reporters dog him incessantly. By and large, the president is portrayed in a positive light; the exceptions, such as Watergate for Richard Nixon or the Iran-Contra affair for Ronald Reagan, have been egregious but rare. Congress gets relatively little attention, mostly negative. "Congress-bashing," like baseball and apple pie, is a truly American pastime.

Of course, the imbalance of attention between president and Congress, though lamentable, is completely understandable. The president is the focus of national, even world, attention. And it is relatively easy for television and newspaper reporters to cover the president, a single individual. Congress is harder to cover. Its 435 representatives and 100 senators are a diverse lot. Congressional policymaking is scattered over scores of committees and subcommittees. In contrast to apparent presidential decisiveness, congressional deliberation often seems cumbersome, contentious, and highly diffuse. Representing a diversity of interests, bearing a membership elected from scattered territories, divided by ideological, political party, and regional conflicts, and piloted by collective rather than unitary leadership, Congress often seems to lack both motor and brakes.

These realities help to account for the difficulties encountered by Congress when it tries to lead the nation. But Congress does have political parties, and it does have leaders. It will not do to be taken in by the oft-proffered assumption that Congress is, somehow, party-less, or to be misled into thinking that the congressional parties do not, or cannot, have forthright, effective leaders. There are, in fact, four quite well-organized political parties in Congress—the House and Senate Democrats, and the House and Senate Republicans. On major matters of public policy, these parties often act in a unified, coherent way. What is more, these congressional parties have well-institutionalized structures of leadership. The congressional Democrats now constitute a firm majority party, and their principal leaders—House Speaker Thomas S. Foley (D-Wash.) and Senate Majority Leader George J. Mitchell (D-Maine)—are highly competent and effective.

The congressional Democratic party takes a distinctive, partisan approach to pressing national problems, and it has a program of action. That program is seldom fully apparent to public view and scarcely adumbrated in any single manifesto; nor does it tend to be assessed, as a whole, in terms of popular or congressional approval. But the congressional Democratic party must stand for something, and it does. The Democratic leaders in the House of Representatives and Senate must lead, and they do. When there is a Republican in the White House, it is doubly important for the congressional Democrats to offer substantial and constructive programs dealing with national problems, and to provide strong, vigorous, aggressive leadership for the Democratic stands.

WHAT ARE THE CONGRESSIONAL PARTIES LIKE?

Fundamentally, the political parties in Congress are sharpened reflections of their counterparts outside. I say they are "reflections" because American political parties are not, and have never been, highly coherent, disciplined fighting organizations that could monopolize political conflict and policy-making as, at least in myth, is sometimes said of party systems in some European countries. In short, we do not have a "responsible party system" in the sense that powerfully unified national parties adumbrate a program of action prior to elections and then systematically put that program into law upon winning. Our political culture, our constitutional system, and our long-standing practice of politics preclude such a rigid system of political responsibility. The congressional parties reflect the nature of our national political parties. They are ideologically relatively diverse, many of their members occupy the political center, interparty compromise and coalitions are frequent, and many issues are considered that do not evoke partisan cleavage.

I refer to "sharpened" reflections because congressional party conflict, such as it is, certainly is sharper, clearer, better articulated than in the extra-congressional party world of the national parties. Members of Congress are more ideological, more partisan, more politicized than their constituents. Accordingly, it is correct to say that Congress is a very partisan institution, and that the cleavages between its party groups are quite salient and keen. Partisan and ideological differences in the country at large are focused on Congress and come to be manifested there.

To lay claim to the importance of political parties in Congress is to contravene the conventional wisdom, which demeans and diminishes the role of parties in our politics. Even when our parties approximate the "responsible party" model, many pundits ignore their performance or deny their role. The conventional commentators relish claims that our parties, including the congressional parties, are not important, that they are weak and ineffective, that "the party's over," or that we reside in a "no-party" system. These claims, so recently underscored in syndicated columns and academic discourse, seem very odd today, after a span of some twenty years during which the scope and intensity of party cleavage have grown, congressional party organization has been strengthened greatly, party leadership has come to dominate the congressional process, and partisan cleavage in decision-making has escalated.

The congressional Democratic parties—in both the House of Representatives and the Senate—have acquired substantial capacity to lead. Because of personal abilities, organizational reforms, and crucial changes in rules, the Speaker of the House has become a formidable leader once again. Of course, the speakership has been in Democratic party hands virtually continuously within living memory. The speakers who have served since the 1970s—Speakers Thomas P. "Tip" O'Neill (D-Mass.), James C. Wright (D-Tex.), and Thomas S. Foley (D-Wash.)—have been in a position to provide genuine direction and leadership to the majority party in the House. The House Democratic Caucus has become a serious venue for consideration of party programs and strategy. The collective party leadership, organized as the Democratic Steering and Policy Committee (chaired by the speaker and including the majority leader, whip, and other party officials), has acquired the potential for real direction of party action in the House. And the party whip system, today including more than fifty whips and embracing many others as a forum for deliberation about Democratic party direction, has enhanced intraparty communication networks and enlarged participation in party affairs.

The Senate Democratic party has grown in strength, as well. Both of its recent leaders—Senators Robert C. Byrd (D-W.Va.) and George J. Mitchell (D-Maine)—have been able and forceful party leaders. The Senate

Democratic Caucus, which meets every Tuesday noon under the auspices of the Policy Committee, has become a singular feature of party life in the Senate. Although the Senate, a body of 100 influential, independent individuals, presents sizable structural and interpersonal challenges to its party leaders, leadership can be effective in that body. In contrast to the House of Representatives, where the majority party leaders enjoy the power to provide decisive party leadership, Senate leaders commonly find themselves required to use deft scheduling and adroit negotiation among fellow partisans in order to compensate for rather weak formal power. Because the institutional capacities for party leadership in the House and Senate are different, successful congressional action in behalf of a party program is sometimes difficult.

The House and Senate Democratic parties differ, but these intraparty differences stem overwhelmingly from more fundamental characteristics of the two houses. One of these is size. The House party has averaged about 263 members (out of 435) since 1961 and has ranged from a low of 243 members in the 91st Congress (1969-1971) to a high of 295 members in the 89th Congress (1965-1967). By contrast, the Senate Democrats have numbered, on average, about 57 members (out of 100) in the last three decades, fluctuating from as few as 46 senators between 1981 and 1985 to as many as 68 members in the 89th Congress. In addition, Senate Democrats are more likely to be lawyers than their House compatriots: When the 102nd Congress convened in 1991, nearly two-thirds of the Senate Democrats were attorneys, compared to less than half of the House Democrats. And almost all the African Americans who have served in the House have been Democrats; today the Congressional Black Caucus includes 25 Democrats and 1 Republican (currently, there are no blacks serving in the Senate). Moreover, women are somewhat disproportionately represented by the congressional Democratic parties: Of the 28 women in the 102nd Congress, 19 are Democrats, and 1 of the 2 women senators, Senator Barbara A. Mukulski (D-Md.), is a Democrat.

Because of its greater size and its historical development, the House is an environment more conducive to aggressive, active majority party leadership than is the Senate. Senate party leaders, by comparison, are more inclined than House leaders to speak for a national constituency, both because they represent states rather than the smaller districts in which most House members are elected and because they more often have presidential ambitions. And a Democratic leadership has controlled the House for most of the post-World War II era (the Republicans held the House majority during the 80th Congress, in 1947-1949, and the 83rd Congress, in 1953-

1955). The House Democrats, it might be argued, possess the advantage of having served as the governing party throughout most of the last half-century, since the New Deal of the 1930s. Senate Democrats were the minority party for six years during the Reagan era of the early 1980s, and their leaders thereby have, perhaps, a more sober view of their hegemony. As a consequence of this historical experience as well as the greater size of the House party, and for institutional and electoral reasons, House Democrats tend toward greater partisanship than their Senate counterparts.

DO THE CONGRESSIONAL DEMOCRATS HAVE A PROGRAM?

In the 1980s, the congressional parties became more programmatic. The Democratic parties in Congress adopted internal reforms in the mid-1970s that helped to strengthen their capacity to be programmatic—reforms that strengthened the powers of the House speaker, invigorated the party caucuses in both House and Senate, and created more effective channels of participation by backbenchers in party program development. There was a time when one could speak of the congressional party caucuses as moribund and ineffective, meeting only rarely and hesitant to formulate party policy positions for fear of alienating some fragment of the membership. But this impression no longer comports with reality. Today, the House and Senate Democratic caucuses are vital and active, they meet regularly, and they have moved a long way toward hammering out comprehensive party programs. Indeed, the Democratic caucuses now provide the central mechanism for the creation of a congressional Democratic party program.

The recent work of the House Democratic Caucus is illustrative. In 1990, the caucus, led by Majority Leader Richard A. Gephardt (D-Mo.), mobilized by Caucus Chairman Steny H. Hoyer (D-Md.) and Vice-Chair Vic Fazio (D-Calif.), and managed by Congressman David E. Price (D-N.C.), who served as task force coordinator, established a series of policy working groups. These included task forces on Crime and Drugs, Defense, the Economy, Education and Employment, Environment and Energy, Foreign Relations, Health, Housing, and Infrastructure. Twenty Democratic members served as chairs or co-chairs of these caucus task forces, and more than 100 House Democrats worked on task force projects. The summary report of the task force efforts—*Investing in America's Future*, published by the Democratic Caucus in August 1990—sets forth the programmatic goals of the House Democrats and presents a wide range of specific policy commitments.[1]

Senate Democrats have forcefully proposed their own policy agenda, growing out of discussions and deliberations in the Tuesday luncheon meetings of the caucus sponsored by the Democratic Policy Committee. The programmatic thrust for Senate Democrats has been articulated publicly on a number of occasions by their leader, Senator Mitchell. Early in the 101st Congress (1989), he laid the Democratic party policy agenda before the Senate, saying that "there is . . . a fresh and powerful consensus emerging for a series of initiatives and a set of priorities that can move our economy and our society into the next decade and toward a new century," and that "our job, as Democrats and members of the Senate, is not to oppose the Administration automatically, but to propose new policies and pursue them cooperatively."[2]

The congressional Democratic party program does exist—in leaders' proclamations on the House and Senate floors, in publications and documents of the party caucuses and policy committees, and in the concrete actions taken by the parties in the course of congressional deliberation on legislation. This program does not often receive prominent attention in the press or on television, and on that account some (the less attentive) might think there was no such program. The conventional assumption has been that Congress is fragmented and inept, that its leaders cannot lead, that it has no program, and that it considers policy issues only in an *ad hoc* and piecemeal manner. Nothing could be further from the truth.

WHAT DO THE CONGRESSIONAL DEMOCRATS STAND FOR?

The policy program of the House Democrats was laid out by the task forces of the caucus and published in *Investing in America's Future*. At its heart, this document elaborates a "nine-point Democratic program for the future." These key elements of the House Democratic party program are as follows:

- Democrats will improve our nation's economic competitiveness by promoting long-term public and private investment in research and development by supporting small businesses and high technology industries, by enacting sound fiscal policies that will reduce the federal budget deficit, by formulating agreements for fair and free trade among nations, by promoting widespread sharing of the benefits of economic growth, and by instituting a progressive tax code under which everyone, including the rich, pays their fair share.

- Democrats will rebuild and strengthen our nation's infrastructure. We will rebuild our nation's crumbling roads, bridges, highways, railroads, and sewer mains, and modernize our air transportation system through investing surplus infrastructure trust funds and by providing incentives for businesses and local governments to invest in infrastructure projects.

- Democrats will increase the number of Americans living in safe, affordable housing by working with state and local governments, nonprofit organizations, and private developers to stimulate construction of low- and moderate-income housing, to assist first-time home buyers using creative public and private financing mechanisms, and to help the elderly remain in their homes.

- Democrats will give the federal government a positive role to play, alongside the states and communities, in providing our children with first-rate education and technical training commensurate with their abilities. We will increase the number of children enrolled in high quality early childhood education programs, expand efforts to eliminate adult illiteracy, improve math and science education, increase access to higher education, and alleviate the present shortage of teachers.

- Democrats will fight to ensure adequate and affordable health care for the American people by phasing in a system of public and private health coverage that provides basic health care first to children and pregnant women, and then to a larger segment of the population.

- Democrats will wage a real war on crime and drugs that guarantees punishment for all criminals and justice for all victims. Our anti-drug program establishes an adequate program of drug prevention and treatment, and calls for enhanced drug interdiction and education. Our criminal justice program includes creative alternatives to traditional incarceration to solve prison overcrowding problems, and reduce the cycle of repeat offenders.

- Democrats will implement a comprehensive, integrated environmental and energy policy that focuses on pollution control, energy preservation, and the development of new, sustainable energy resources.

- Democrats will orient American foreign policy to promote democracy, free market economies, and respect for human rights, and to address the critical problems of global pollution, trade competition, escalating global poverty, and nuclear proliferation.

- Democrats will initiate an effective defense strategy that reduces military spending where threats have been diminished, maintains flexibility through robust defense research and increased utilization of National Guard and Reserve forces, improves the quick-response capability of our armed forces, advances our nation's economic security and competitiveness, and halts waste and inefficiency at the Department of Defense.

These policy goals call for specific proposals and legislation to bring them to fruition. In the House of Representatives, a number of measures have been undertaken by the party leadership and by key committee chairmen to address these goals, which are widely shared among congressional Democrats. The Senate leadership, and Senator Mitchell in particular, spelled out the specific programmatic agenda for the Senate at the beginning of both recent congresses.

The Rich Get Richer . . .

Among a variety of proposals to improve the American economy, the provision of economic justice through fair tax policies is central to the Democratic program. Current federal tax rates greatly advantage wealthy people, and "the rich get richer" while "the poor get poorer." This experience of the last dozen years is abundantly documented in any number of studies. One study showed that the tax burden, calculated in constant dollars for family incomes earned between 1977 and 1992, fell more than 12 percent for people in the top 1 percent of the family income range (earning $676,000 or more), while the tax burden increased for low-income families.[3] The Congressional Budget Office has shown that real incomes in the 1980s rose for the rich but declined among Americans in the lowest income range (see Figure 5.1). Those with incomes in the top 1 percent enjoyed a growth of 75 percent in income—from an average of $313,206 in 1980 to $548,970 in 1990—while the incomes of the poorest fifth of the income distribution fell by 4 percent.

Millions of Americans have been added to the poverty rolls in recent years. In 1991, one estimate was that 13.5 percent of all Americans were poor, defined as living in a family of four earning $13,359 or less.[4] More disturbingly, by 1990 nearly 45 percent of female-headed households with children were living in poverty, and this proportion was even greater for

FIGURE 5.1   Percentage Change in Real Income, 1980–1990

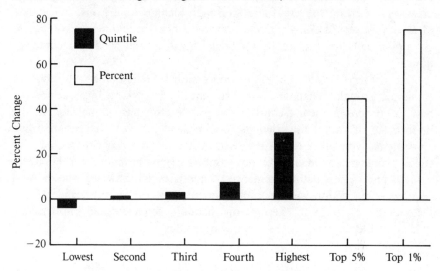

Source: Congressional Budget Office and Joint Economic and Senate Budget Committees, "Another Look at the Republican 'Look at the 1980s': An Analysis" (March 7, 1991), p. 3.

Hispanics and blacks. Of these depressing economic developments, one public welfare expert said, "Welfare rolls have increased for 22 consecutive months and we are at an all-time high in American history."[5] The Tax Reform Act of 1986 (inspired by President Ronald Reagan) did cut taxes, but it egregiously advantaged high-income people and, in short, created a tax system substantially weighted against the middle class.

House and Senate Democratic leaders have proposed tax reform: cutting taxes paid by middle-income Americans and raising the tax liability of the rich. In the Senate, this tax program has been initiated by Senator Lloyd W. Bentsen (D-Tex.), chairman of the Finance Committee. His bill involves a $72.5 billion tax cut, provision of a $300 tax credit for each child, and restoration of Individual Retirement Account (IRA) tax incentives. Senator Bentsen's plan involves offsetting the tax cuts by reducing defense expenditures. In the House of Representatives, the tax reform proposal is that of Representative Dan Rostenkowski (D-Ill.), chairman of the Ways and Means Committee. He proposes to raise the tax rate for high-income individuals and to add a surtax on incomes larger than $1 million. Although taxes would go up for about a million high-income Americans, 80 percent of taxpayers would enjoy a modest tax reduction. In addition, Rostenkowski's plan calls for tax credits for Social Security and Medicare contributions.

Tax reform is not the only congressional Democratic program for economic growth. Other measures are equally important, inasmuch as the new tax proposals do not confront the problem of the national deficit, the importance of stimulating savings, or the need to work out proper trade agreements with other countries. Nor do the tax reforms directly address social problems attendant upon poverty. The growing number of homeless people, and the escalating incidence of public begging in city streets, will require other actions. But economic fairness is the centerpiece of a Democratic program to "restore our nation's economy and improve the quality of life enjoyed by the American people."[6]

Jobs and Housing

The Democratic party has always championed the need for jobs for Americans and for adequate housing. Public policies must foster and stimulate economic growth, represented importantly in growth in employment. Figure 5.2 painfully demonstrates the precipitous drop in job growth during the Bush administration of the 1990s. Beginning in the spring of 1990, the decade thus far has witnessed a severe recession and a decline in the number of jobs; about 300,000 have been lost overall. The protracted economic recession has also meant expiration of unemployment benefits for thousands of workers. By August 1991 unemployment rolls had swelled by 1.7 million workers, and as many as 1.8 million workers had exhausted their regular state unemployment benefits. In order to cope with this problem, the congressional Democrats have sought to extend unemployment insurance to protect the unemployed.

In the summer of 1991, Congress passed legislation extending unemployment benefits for as many as twenty weeks in those states hardest hit by the economic slump. The president permitted the legislation to become law without his signature, but he refused to initiate the emergency provisions of the Budget Act that would have permitted the actual payment of extended benefits. Accordingly, Congress passed a different version of the benefits-extension legislation, but this effort was vetoed by President Bush and Republicans were able to prevent the overriding of the veto in the Senate.

FIGURE 5.2   Average Monthly Growth in Employment, 1953–1991

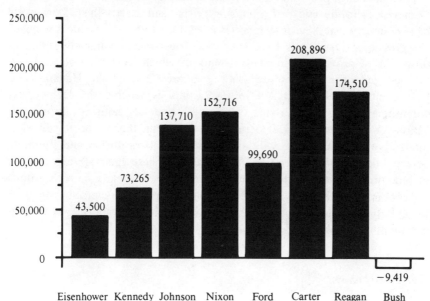

Source: Bureau of Labor Statistics and Democratic Study Group, "The Bush Bust on Job Growth," *Special Report* No. 102–111 (October 1, 1991), p. 1.

Finally, in October, and with the recession continuing, the president reversed his opposition to the extension of jobless benefits. Ultimately, a compromise proposal was hammered out between the Bush White House and congressional Republican leaders on one side, and Democratic leaders—House Speaker Thomas S. Foley (D-Wash.), Ways and Means Chairman Dan Rostenkowski (D-Ill.), Senate Majority Leader George J. Mitchell (D-Maine), and Senate Finance Chairman Lloyd Bentsen (D-Tex.)—on the other. Finally, compromise legislation passed in November extended unemployment benefits to nearly 3 million people, and the president signed it into law. The torturous process, delayed by President Bush's insistence that there was no recession and that extending jobless benefits would "bust the budget," highlighted the need for a change in the system for protecting unemployed workers. As Representative Thomas J. Downey (D-N.Y.) put it, "This is a temporary fix in a program that is completely broken. . . . Until there is a permanent fix in the law, we are going to find ourselves in this situation recession after recession."[7]

The housing program of congressional Democrats recognizes that "America is in the midst of a housing crisis" and asserts that "Democrats believe deeply that American families need decent and affordable housing." Congressional Democrats have sought to "preserve and improve housing programs of proven effectiveness—many of which have been starved and mismanaged over the past decade." Congress passed the Housing and Community Development Act in 1987, thus evidencing the Democrats' commitment to reauthorizing successful federal housing programs. Moreover, congressional Democrats have committed themselves to "develop innovative approaches that will stretch federal dollars further and stimulate new public-private cooperation" in housing. These innovative proposals include programs to assist first-time home buyers, to help nonprofit groups foster community housing opportunities, and to provide "reverse mortgages" for elderly homeowners so that they can use their home mortgages to help pay monthly living expenses.[8]

Our Environment

Beginning in the 1960s, the Democrats in Congress pioneered environmental protection legislation with the passage of the Clean Air Act (1963). And in 1990, congressional Democrats proposed and supported renewal and strengthening of the clean air legislation, which aimed to reduce smog and automobile emissions, provided tougher regulation of toxic chemicals, dealt with the causes of acid rain, created programs to encourage alternative fuels, and directed the Environmental Protection Agency to identify new sources of industrial pollution and control them as much as technically possible. But many of the other environmental advances of the 1970s need to be regained.

Congressional Democrats have pledged not only to work out innovative ways to prevent environmental contamination but also to formulate a comprehensive national energy policy. An effective policy is clearly needed to deal with hazardous waste, to ensure that inland and coastal waterways are free of toxic wastes, and to pursue research on global climate change. Moreover, congressional Democrats are committed to policies designed to explore for and conserve energy, and to develop alternative energy sources as part of "a comprehensive, integrated environmental and energy policy that focuses on pollution prevention, energy conservation, and the development of new, sustainable energy resources."[9]

The Struggle for Racial Justice

Protection of the civil rights of Americans has been a major part of the program of congressional Democrats, especially since the enactment of historic civil rights legislation in the 1960s. In the 1990s, the most serious problem of racial justice has involved discrimination in employment. President George Bush vetoed a civil rights bill in 1990, claiming that it would create hiring "quotas," a charge that Democrats firmly denied. The civil rights legislation passed by the Democratic Congress in 1991 offset the impact of nine decisions by the U.S. Supreme Court that had made it more difficult for workers to initiate and win job-discrimination lawsuits. The new law provides workers greater protection against job bias and harassment, and allows larger money damages and cost reimbursements for those workers who sue their employers successfully. Reluctantly, the Republican White House approved the bill, and President Bush signed it, but not without suggesting that affirmative action guidelines adumbrated by executive branch agencies might be watered down so as to weaken implementation of the new legislation.[10]

The National Health

In their manifesto, House Democrats committed themselves to the national health by asserting that their "long-term goal for health care is to ensure that every American who needs medical care receives it."[11] While in the short run supporting the construction of more health care centers, extending health education programs, and supporting medical cost control measures, "ultimately, Democrats hope to establish a more effective system of national health care delivery that affords all Americans the same guarantee of basic health care that Medicare now affords to the elderly and disabled."[12]

The evidence suggests that health care costs will continue to grow during the 1990s, and that the number of Americans lacking health care insurance (now between 31 and 34 million people) will continue to increase. A variety of proposals to resolve the problems of health care have been proposed, but all of the Democratic proposals agree that "(1) meaningful reform must promote universal health insurance coverage; (2) the health insurance coverage provided must represent an adequate level of benefits; and (3) the health insurance coverage provided must be affordable."[13] The

Senate Democratic Policy Committee worked out a detailed health care policy, which it summarized as follows:

> The [proposed] legislation will assure every American basic health insurance coverage, either through a plan provided by an employer or through a federal-state public insurance program, called AmeriCare, which will replace Medicaid (except for long-term care services). Universal health insurance coverage will be coupled with a comprehensive program to control health care costs and with provisions to reflect the special needs and problems of small business.[14]

Senate Majority Leader Mitchell underscored the need for new national health policy along these lines when he announced the policy agenda of the Senate Democrats at the outset of the 102nd Congress.[15]

Crime and Drugs

The congressional Democrats' policy commitments regarding the intertwined problems of crime and drugs are strongly articulated in the manifesto of the House Democratic Caucus. In *Investing in America's Future*, Democrats commit themselves to strengthening the criminal justice system but recognize that punitive measures alone will not solve the problems of crime and drugs. "Our goals for the 1990s and the twenty-first century include a safe home and community for every family, certain punishment for every criminal, appropriate treatment for every addict, and renewed commitment to laws governing trade, commerce, and the flow of investment capital through the nation's banking system."[16]

In 1991, the 102nd Congress considered new anticrime legislation that, among other things, would have extended the death penalty to more than fifty crimes and restricted the ability of convicted criminals to challenge their death-penalty sentences. The legislation also would have added restrictions to the purchase of handguns. Senate Judiciary Committee Chairman Joseph R. Biden, Jr. (D-Del.) characterized the bill as "the toughest crime bill that has ever come before the Senate." Democrats won a narrow victory in the House on a party-line vote, but Senate Republicans were able to prevent cloture on the bill and preclude Senate action on it. The Bush administration and congressional Republicans particularly objected to the bill because they wanted stiffer restrictions on appeals made by convicted criminals, and they wished to allow evidence seized without a warrant to be used in criminal trials.[17]

Educating a New Generation

Assessments of the quality of American education such as the 1991 *National Education Goals Report* continue to show a substantial need for strengthening the educational system. A considerable incidence of "functional illiteracy" and substantial underachievement in mathematics and science are at the crux of major national education needs. In 1989, House and Senate Democratic leaders met to hammer out consensual goals that would "serve as the Democratic agenda . . . and provide the backbone of our efforts to reinvigorate American education."[18]

Among these Democratic education policy goals are the following: (1) making more comprehensive the program of early childhood development; (2) raising the basic skills levels of all children and reducing skill discrepancies among racial and ethnic minorities; (3) improving the high school graduation rate and reducing adult illiteracy; (4) elevating American students' mathematics, science, and foreign language performance "until they exceed the performance of their counterparts in other industrialized nations";[19] (5) enlarging the access of Americans to higher education "so that all qualified high school graduates have an equal opportunity to enjoy the benefits of a college education or other training by the year 2000";[20] and (6) increasing the number of teachers and upgrading their professional status.

In the 102nd Congress, Democrats undertook two special initiatives in the field of education policy. The first, in reauthorizing funding for the nation's system of higher education, provides direct loans to students and enlarges eligibility for grants and loans to college students. In particular, the Democratic proposal provides scholarships (so-called Pell grants, after Senator Claiborne Pell (D-R.I.), who sponsored the legislation originating these scholarships), thus ensuring assistance to more middle-class families who want to send their children to college. The second—the Comprehensive Neighborhood Schools Revitalization Act—provides enhanced support for local school districts. Both the House and the Senate versions of this legislation furnish block grants to the states for educational improvement and authorize the allocation of state funding, if desired, to both public and private schools (the latter to the extent that parents prefer private education for their children). These issues, fraught with important conflicts and disagreements between Democrats and Republicans in Congress, remain on the congressional agenda.

Foreign and Defense Policy

The rapidly changing international system, and the striking adjustments required in the global role of the United States brought about by these changes, undergird programmatic alternatives. Congressional Democrats have been strong supporters of effective national defense and security policies. But with equal vigor the Democratic congressional agenda calls for speeding up arms-reduction efforts, using the military to counter the international drug trade, enhancing the capacity of international organizations to deal with world environmental problems, providing foreign aid for countries in transition to democracy, and reducing the size of the American military establishment to fit the diminished international threat.

ARE THE DEMOCRATS DEAD?

The congressional Democratic party shows impressive vitality. It has a policy agenda for the nation. Now, that agenda is not rigid, it is not worked out in every detail, and it is not imposed with unflinching discipline on every Democrat. That is not the way our system works. But the agenda is comprehensive, reasonably explicit, clearly alternative to Republican party approaches, and widely accepted by congressional Democrats. In short, the congressional Democrats have a program. As a legislative party, they are not dead.

But Congress is under attack. Many Americans are frustrated with the inability of the nation to resolve irritating and sometimes devastating economic woes. Republicans, including President Bush, use "Congress-bashing" as a strategy to undermine confidence in the Democratic majority. It is time for congressional Democrats to take a strong initiative in behalf of their policy agenda, and in behalf of Congress as an institution. During 1992, they need to pass the full array of bills on their agenda—helping the unemployed, stimulating employment and protecting jobs, stimulating economic growth, relieving the burden of taxes falling on middle-class Americans, establishing a program of national health insurance, enhancing educational performance and opportunities, providing assistance for newly emerging democracies abroad, and reorienting national security policy to comport with the changed world environment.

CONCLUSION

Democratic congressional leaders must assert strong leadership in the weeks and months ahead. They must see to it that their party legislates the Democratic program, and they must demonstrate how sharply their program differs from that of the Republicans. They must establish a record of policy advocacy and achievement that will "show that Democrats can lead."[21] The Democrats in Congress do stand for something. Their policy goals, objectives, and proposals need to be underscored so that they can be seen to stand for something—so that Americans will see, unmistakably, that there is effective, progressive Democratic leadership, that the congressional Democratic party has a coherent and workable program to deal with great national problems, and that this leadership will *lead*.

NOTES

1. Democratic Caucus, U.S. House of Representatives, *Investing in America's Future: A Democratic Issues Handbook* (Washington, D.C.: Democratic Caucus, 1990).

2. *Congressional Record*, April 19, 1989, p. S4226.

3. *Washington Post*, September 13, 1991, p. A23.

4. *San Francisco Chronicle,* September 27, 1991, p. A2.

5. *Washington Post*, September 27, 1991, p. A1.

6. Democratic Caucus, *Investing in America's Future*, p. 28.

7. *Congressional Quarterly Weekly Report*, November 16, 1991, p. 3383.

8. Democratic Caucus, *Investing in America's Future*, pp. 39-49.

9. Ibid., p. 102.

10. *Congressional Quarterly Weekly Report,* November 23, 1991, p. 3463.

11. Democratic Caucus, *Investing in America's Future*, p. 74.

12. Ibid., pp. 73-74.

13. Democratic Study Group, "Alternative Approaches to Health Care Reform," *Special Report*, No. 102-108, July 22, 1991, p. 1.

14. Democratic Policy Committee, "Summary of Health in America: Affordable Health Care for All Americans," *DPC Special Report*, June 5, 1991, p. 1.

15. *Congressional Record*, January 14, 1991, p. S418.

16. Democratic Caucus, *Investing in America's Future*, p. 83.

17. *Congressional Quarterly Weekly Report*, November 30, 1991, pp. 3528-3530.

18. Democratic Caucus, *Investing in America's Future*, p. 62.

19. Ibid., pp. 62-63.

20. Ibid., p. 63.

21. Bruce F. Freed, "'Reverse Truman': A Strategy That Can Win for Democrats," *Roll Call*, November 18, 1991, p. 5.

PART TWO

Getting the Message Across: How? To Whom?

6

JEROME M. MILEUR

Dump Dixie—West Is Best:
The Geography of
a Progressive Democracy

The Democratic party has always been a southern party. It should be one no more. The contradictions within the party that have bedeviled it for a century, contradictions both coalitional and philosophical, would be greatly relieved were the party to look away from Dixie and toward the west. The time for this transition is now, for beyond the logic of party, the realities of American politics—the shifts in political power nationally, and the electoral strengths of the party's presidential nominees—dictate a geographical realignment of the party. Only in this way can Democrats hope to win the White House and govern as a truly national instrument of authentic progressive politics.

A viable progressive politics, one that aspires to greater social justice through more equal economic opportunity, requires a political party that is national in design and organized to harmonize three levels of thought and action: (1) the *philosophical* plane of beliefs qnd values that animate the party; (2) the *programmatic* plane of public policies that are its plan of governance; and (3) the *electoral* plane of the coalition in whose interests it seeks office and promises to govern. Democrats were a model of such a party in their New Deal days, but the last quarter-century has undone that party system and left national Democrats struggling, like Humpty Dumpty, to put the pieces together again.

In this, the South is far more problem than solution for the Democrats. Centered in localism, southern politics have long been alien to national interests. Dominated by race, they have also been at odds with the objectives of national democracy in this century.[1] Beneficiary more than benefactor of its party affiliation, the South is tied more to the Congress than to the presidency. Its politics are at home in an institution given to particularism and horse-trading, not in one of generality and national purpose. The Democrats must end their embrace of the South—or, more specifically, of the Deep South—for Dixie is at the center of the storms that have battered the party, fracturing it as a party of liberalism in national politics and impeding its ability to recover organizationally the progressive impulse that defined and directed its New Deal success. There is no hope of rebuilding the Democratic party as a progressive party of national purpose unless it dumps Dixie and embraces the west.

THE DEMOCRATS' SOUTHERN CROSS

Born as the party of Jefferson, the Democrats have from the outset been a north-south coalition. Built originally on the cornerstones of Virginia and New York, this architecture served the party well before the Civil War, when political liberalism danced to the Jeffersonian tune that government is best that governs least. This coalition was parent to the Virginia Dynasty, which ruled young America through the first quarter of the nineteenth century, and thereafter to Martin Van Buren and Andrew Jackson, who institutionalized it in theory and practice as definitive of both the modern Democratic party and the two-party system. Jeffersonian and Jacksonian Democracy were alike in their devotion to states-rights constitutionalism, laissez-faire economics, restricted government, and a populist politics that was antifederalist in program, localist in spirit, and suspicious of national power. This worked well enough for the Democrats so long as the American nation was in its adolescence constitutionally, institutionally, and culturally; but it has failed as a design for national governance since the American nation came to maturity in the second half of the nineteenth century.

Since the Civil War, the coalition of north and south has been a growing burden on the ambitions of national Democrats, for whom the "positive" state replaced the Jeffersonian maxim as the definition of political liberalism. Reconstruction left a "solid South," a region whose politics were unswervingly Democratic for a half-century, but for which race, not democracy, was the unifying force. Indeed, in the last decades of the nineteenth century, the South embraced a politics of exclusion driven by a populism of race-baiting that was at the same time hostile both to "Yankees" and to *their* federal government. In the first decades of the twentieth century, the region was largely untouched by the reformist and nationalist politics of Progressivism and thus remained an enclave of parochialism, philosophically estranged from the new liberalism and the new presidentialism of American politics.

Electorally speaking, the South was solid for Franklin Roosevelt in all of his runs for the presidency; but it was also an early dropout from the New Deal program, joining with northern Republicans after 1936 in a conservative coalition that ruled Congress for a quarter-century and frustrated the nationalist designs of liberal democracy. After Roosevelt, as Figure 6.1 shows, southern support for the Democrats plummeted—especially in Dixie, that stretch of deep southern states from South Carolina west to Louisiana—and the reason was race. In 1948, Democrats adopted a civil rights plank for their national platform, prompting a number of Deep South delegates to walk out of the party convention and into the arms of Strom Thurmond's third-party Dixiecrat challenge to liberal democracy. Thurmond won over 50 percent of the vote in Dixie, carrying four of the five Deep South states, whereas the Democrat Harry Truman got less than one-third of the region's vote. Nonetheless, the Democrats prevailed nationally, as Truman's Fair Deal candidacy united the Midwest, west, and Midsouth, containing Republicanism to the east and in the plains states and isolating the Dixiecrats. Truman was the first to give the lie to claims that Dixie is critical to democracy.

Through the 1950s and into the 1960s, the Deep South backed Democratic presidential candidates, albeit with vote levels well below those given to FDR. But in 1964, Dixie dumped the Democrats, opting instead for the rightwing Republican Barry Goldwater, who won over 60 percent of the Deep South vote. But despite the defection of Dixie, the Democrat Lyndon Johnson won the White House in a landslide, again showing that liberal democracy can take the presidency without the Deep South. Johnson also carried several dozen new liberal Democrats from the north into Congress, who replaced conservative Republicans and broke the South's stranglehold on national policy. LBJ's Great Society was at once a fulfillment of the liberal agenda left from the New Deal and the last straw for the South. In 1968, Dixie gave George Wallace 51 percent of its popular vote, as he won the electoral vote in four of the five Deep South states—the fifth going to the Republican Richard Nixon. In 1972, the South was solid again, but this time for Nixon.

The decline in support for democracy in the Deep South has its parallel in the Midsouth from Virginia and North Carolina west to Arkansas, but the pattern of defection differs. From 1952 though 1964, the Democratic vote in the Midsouth was more like that of the nation than that of Dixie, fluctuating between six points over and four points under the national ballot.

FIGURE 6.1 Democratic Percentage of the Two-Party Vote in the South, 1932–1988

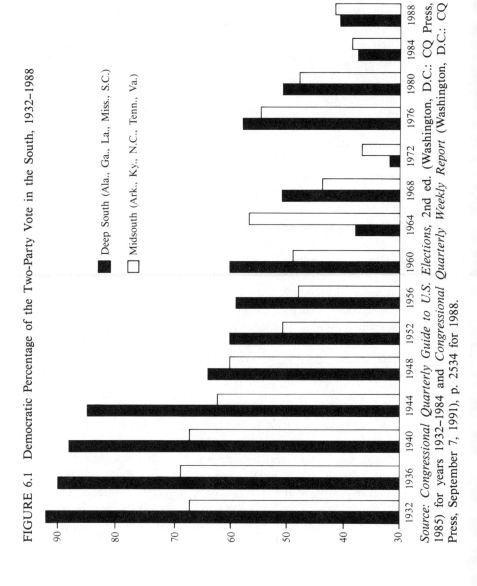

Source: Congressional Quarterly Guide to U.S. Elections, 2nd ed. (Washington, D.C.: CQ Press, 1985) for years 1932–1984 and *Congressional Quarterly Weekly Report* (Washington, D.C.: CQ Press, September 7, 1991), p. 2534 for 1988.

As Figure 6.1 shows, the Midsouth liked Ike more in the 1950s and John Kennedy less in 1960 than did the Deep South, but in 1964 it went all the way with LBJ while Dixie was deserting to Goldwater. In 1968, when the heart of Dixie went to George Wallace, the Midsouth vote split three ways: 36 percent to Nixon, 31 percent to Wallace, and 29 percent to the Democrat Hubert Humphrey. Since 1972, the pattern of the Midsouth vote has been closer to that of the Deep South, although the fluctuations have been more moderate—and in three of these five elections, the Midsouth, for the first time since Reconstruction, gave Democrats a larger share of its two-party vote than did Dixie.

Today, the Deep South may be more restrained in its peculiar passion, but Dixie remains a soil fertile to the seedings of racial politics, as Republican harvests of white votes in the 1970s and 1980s attest. The liberalism of national democracy on civil rights has produced a long-term secular realignment in the South generally and Dixie in particular, as white voters have moved away from their historic Democratic home and made bed with the GOP instead. More than anything, this decline in southern support for democracy may reflect the nationalization of politics in the old confederacy. Nationally, politics are organized by ideology and culture, with majorities shaped by the interplay of class interest and social values. In Dixie, race regularly splits class voting, uniting lower-class whites with upper-class whites in a conservative embrace. But this is not the case in the Midsouth, whose politics are more moderate because the effects of race are not so extreme. It is a terrain more hospitable to national democracy than is Dixie, whose turf resists the tillings of progressivism.

THE NEW AMERICAN NATION

American national politics has been transformed since World War II. The election map has been redrawn as population and thus power has moved from the older states of the east and Midwest to the newer states of the Rocky Mountain and Pacific west, and also from cities to suburbs. There is a new calculus for winning the presidency, defined by the decennial census and measured in electoral votes, as well as both a weakening and a shifting of forces between the nation's two major parties. It is a new math that the Democrats have failed to master.

Table 6.1 reports these changes and shows that, since the 1930s, the old north (northeast, mideast, and Midwest) has lost 57 electoral votes, whereas the far west (mountain, coastal, and ocean) has picked up 54—a net loss of 20 percent for the old east, a net gain of 20 percent for the far west. For

TABLE 6.1 Number and Percentage of Electoral College Votes by Regions and Selected States, 1932-2000

Regions & States	1932-40 N	1932-40 %	1944-48 N	1944-48 %	1952-60 N	1952-60 %	1964-68 N	1964-68 %	1972-80 N	1972-80 %	1984-88 N	1984-88 %	1992-00 N	1992-00 %
Northeast[a]	88	16.6	87	16.4	85	16.0	80	14.9	78	14.5	72	13.4	68	12.6
Mideast[b]	71	13.4	70	13.2	68	12.8	69	12.8	66	12.3	63	11.7	59	11.0
Midsouth[c]	55	10.4	57	10.7	55	10.4	51	9.5	50	9.3	51	9.5	52	9.7
Deep South[d]	50	9.4	50	9.4	49	9.2	47	8.7	46	8.6	46	8.6	46	8.6
Florida	7	1.3	8	1.5	10	1.9	14	2.6	17	3.2	21	3.9	25	4.6
Midwest[e]	137	25.8	133	25.1	131	24.7	129	24.0	126	23.4	119	22.1	112	20.8
Plains[f]	35	6.6	32	6.0	30	5.7	28	5.2	27	5.0	26	4.8	25	4.6
Texas	23	4.3	23	4.3	24	4.5	25	4.6	26	4.8	29	5.4	32	6.0
Mountain west[g]	30	5.7	32	6.0	32	6.0	33	6.1	35	6.5	40	7.4	40	7.4
Coastal west[h]	35	6.6	39	7.3	47	8.9	55	10.2	60	11.2	64	11.9	72	13.4
Ocean west[i]	-	-	-	-	-	-	7	1.3	7	1.3	7	1.3	7	1.3

a New England and New York
b New Jersey, Pennsylvania, Delaware, Maryland, D.C., and West Virginia
c Virginia, Kentucky, North Carolina, Tennessee, and Arkansas
d South Carolina, Georgia, Alabama, Mississippi, and Louisiana
e Ohio, Indiana, Illinois, Missouri, Michigan, Wisconsin, and Minnesota
f North Dakota, South Dakota, Nebraska, Kansas, and Oklahoma
g Montana, Wyoming, Colorado, New Mexico, Idaho, Utah, Nevada, and Arizona
h California, Oregon, and Washington
i Alaska and Hawaii

Sources: For the period 1932-1988, see *Congressional Quarterly Guide to U.S. Elections*, 2nd ed. (Washington, D.C.: Congressional Quarterly, Inc., 1985); for the period 1992-2000, see *Congressional Quarterly Weekly Report*, October 26, 1991.

Democrats, this dramatic shift of power has struck at the heart of the New Deal coalition forged by Franklin Roosevelt in the elections of 1932 and 1936. Centered in the urban and industrial north, the Roosevelt coalition was born when these states cast nearly 56 percent of the electoral vote and their big cities were the keys to victory; and it survived as the nation's political majority for almost four decades. Its demise is measured by the steadily declining electoral importance of the old north, which for the first time cast less than 50 percent of the electoral vote in the 1980s and will cast less than 45 percent in 1992. Yet the old north is still the largest geographic base upon which to build a national majority—and the surest base for a national party of progressive programs.

As the north declines, the far west gains in the new geography of national power. The rise of western power, heralded but not conquered by John Kennedy's 1960 New Frontier campaign, has been led by California, which, as detailed in Table 6.1, has more than doubled its electoral vote from 22 in 1932 to 54 in 1992. The 23 electoral votes added by the Golden State over these six decades is by far the largest number for any state and, indeed, is greater than the *combined* total increase for the next two fastest-growing states, Florida and Texas. But the growth of western power in national politics is not confined to California; it is a regional phenomenon. Eight of the twelve states in the region, other than California, have added electoral votes since FDR first won the White House, and only one has lost a vote. Moreover, the pace of growth in the west has been constant: Half of it came in the three decades before 1960 and half in the three decades since.

It is the west, then, that has remade America's political map. No other section of the country can match its impact. Indeed, except for Florida and Texas, all other parts of the country have *lost* power in national politics since the 1930s. As Table 6.1 shows, the northeast and mideast have lost 32 electoral votes since the 1930s, or 20 percent of their power in presidential elections; the Midwest has lost 25 electoral votes since FDR was inaugurated, or almost 20 percent of its national clout; the plains region has dropped 10 electoral votes, or nearly 30 percent of its punch; and the Midsouth and Deep South have shrunk by 8 votes, or 7 percent of their force. The population growth in Florida and Texas, which together have added 27 electoral votes since the 1930s (resulting in a 5 percent gain in presidential power), has given the impression of the growing importance of the South, but this is largely illusion. Neither Florida nor Texas is truly a southern state; each is more diverse socially and economically than the Midsouth, and neither is dominated by the politics of race that organizes presidential contests in the Deep South.

In the new American nation, the old north alone can no longer elect presidents. This region may still be a solid foundation upon which to construct a new progressive party, but democracy must dig solid footings elsewhere and erect a more expansive edifice if it is to succeed. Moreover, it must adjust its programmatic appeals to include the family rooms of suburbia as well as the living rooms of the Midwest and east; for a viable majority party, as Samuel Lubell argued long ago, must include the alive and growing forces in the electorate.[2] It is imperative that a progressive democracy capture these groups, that it harness their energies and optimism in the service of political change in order to expand opportunity and move the nation in the direction of greater social justice.

The west is unmistakably the alive and growing force in the new American nation, especially the coastal states of California, Oregon, and Washington. The coastal west, moreover, is the epitome of suburbia, steeped in the attendant joys and frustrations. By contrast, the South is not growing as a factor in national politics, especially not the five states of the Deep South. Since the 1930s, Dixie has lost 4 electoral votes, whereas the three states of the ocean west have added 37—a net shift in national power of about 8 percent. Figure 6.2 shows that the Deep South, which had almost half again as much electoral muscle as the coastal west in FDR's first two terms, has today only about 60 percent of the coastal west's brawn. Even if Florida's 25 electoral votes are added to those of Dixie, the coastal west edges them in the Electoral College by 72 to 71. It is thus the old politics of north-south coalition, not the new mathematics of national politics, that argues for the continuing importance of the Deep South to the future of democracy—and not even the old politics mistook Dixie as in any way the foundation for a national progressive party.

LOOK WEST, OR LOOK OUT

The 1988 Democratic presidential campaign of Michael Dukakis has been pilloried by press and party alike; but however muddled in conception or inept in execution, his candidacy produced a national pattern of voting that is a geopolitical model for a new progressive democracy. Figure 6.3 shows the sixteen states that Dukakis either won or came within two and a half percentage points of winning, all of them in one of four regions: the northeast, mideast, Midwest, and coastal west. In addition, he came within five percentage points of winning six other states: three in the mountain west (Colorado, Montana, and New Mexico), one in the plains (South Dakota), and two in the old north (Connecticut and Michigan). Together, these

FIGURE 6.2   Total Electoral College Votes by Region for
Deep South and Coastal West, 1932–1992

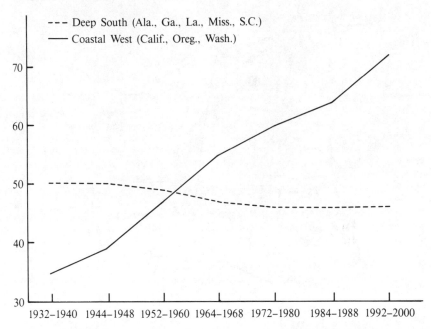

Source: *Congressional Quarterly Guide to U.S. Elections,* 2nd ed. (Washington,
D.C.: CQ Press, 1985) for years 1932–1988 and *Congressional Quarterly Weekly
Report* (Washington, D.C.: CQ Press, October 26, 1991) for 1992–2000.

twenty-two states, including the District of Columbia but *without* a single
southern state, will cast 278 electoral votes in 1992, 8 more than required
to win the Oval Office.

This pattern of support for democracy is not new.[3]   A map of the 1984
presidential election would show almost exactly the same geopolitical
strengths for Walter Mondale, as would maps for George McGovern in 1974
and Hubert Humphrey in 1968.   It is, however, a pattern produced by
liberal Democrats, not moderates.   Maps of the 1976 and 1980 geopolitical
strengths of Jimmy Carter would bear little resemblance to those of Dukakis
et al.   In 1976, of Carter's twelve best states, seven were in the Mid- or
Deep South; in 1980, eight were.   Even more telling is the fact that the four

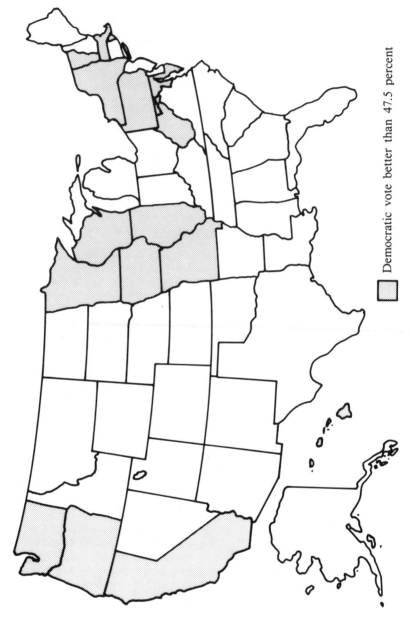

FIGURE 6.3 States with Highest Democratic Share of Two-Party Vote, 1988

Democratic vote better than 47.5 percent

Democratic liberals nominated in the last six presidential elections have, on average, polled 2 to 3 percent *more* of the popular vote in the three states of the coastal west than did Carter in his two presidential runs.

But beyond elections of the last quarter-century, this geopolitical pattern mirrors the historic division between the old Progressive and old Populist states as it emerged in the latter decades of the nineteenth century. Alike in many ways, Progressivism and Populism were different somehow—principally in their attitudes toward the emerging American state and the role of the national government therein. Franklin Roosevelt and the New Deal overcame these differences for a time, increasing the scale and role of the national government dramatically, but in ways that have not always sustained it politically.[4] The Roosevelt coalition broke up in part because the Deep South rejected its nationalism, especially on civil rights, and in part because it never forged a lasting political bond with the philosophically more compatible west. It is this bond that has been emerging in national politics since the 1960s.

The philosophical compatibility of east and west is evident across a wide range of issues. In a study of policy concerns in the north, south, and Pacific west, C. B. Holman found Democrats in the east and west to be similar in their views on social issues, foreign policy, and moral fundamentalism, with their southern counterparts at odds on all of these. He also found northern Democrats to be more like southern Democrats on issues of economic populism, but this similarity was due primarily to the economic liberalism of southern blacks. Holman concludes that there is a "significant degree of tension" between the political ideologies of the South and coastal west, and advises Democrats in search of a national majority to "go west."[5]

A *Times-Mirror* survey of American voters in 1988 affirms Holman's findings, thus underscoring the western opportunity for a progressive democracy. It found the east and west to be much alike in their support for governmental social programs, noting that "the Western region of the U.S. now rivals the East as the region most supportive of an activist governmental role on social issues."[6] This, the *Times-Mirror* adds, represents a "sea-change" in the historic attitude of western voters and divides them sharply from southern voters who were found to be *least* likely to support governmental social initiatives. In general, the *Times-Mirror* found the east, west, and Midwest much more favorable than the South to activist government across the board.

Clearly, the Democrats must go west if they are to build a progressive party able to win the presidency *and* govern the nation. No criticism of the Democrats has been made more often or more convincingly over the last decade than the criticism that the party lacks a national vision, that it has failed to articulate a coherent program of governance grounded in the values that animate the American voter.[7] Burdened by Dixie, democracy has simply been unable to define and integrate the three levels of party—philosophy, program, and coalition—that are essential both to the party's success at the polls and to its ability to link citizens through elections to their government—a linkage that is the measure of responsible democracy. Dumping Dixie with its social and religious conservatism, its hawkish militarism and racial propensities, will reduce programmatic differences among Democrats. Adding the coastal west will at the same time enlarge policy agreement within the party. And by abandoning Dixie for the Pacific west, Democrats will be moving away from a stagnant region of static, if not diminished, power in national affairs toward one of greater and growing national power.

The *practical* reality for Democrats in general, and for progressive democracy in particular, is that a union of east, Midwest, and coastal west, grounded in a common philosophy of politics and joined in support of a common program of governance, is the *only* way to restore democracy as the normal majority in the nation. The logic of public opinion and the new mathematics of national politics add up in these historically progressive states to a coherent party philosophy and program backed by more than enough electoral votes to win the presidency. The old north-south coalition is sustained today not by logic and evidence but by habit—and as Tom Paine taught us two centuries ago, the long habit of not thinking something wrong gives it the appearance of being right. Dixie is wrong for a progressive democracy and should be politely ignored. The coastal west is right for a progressive democracy and should be assiduously courted.

MYTHS AS CONVENTIONAL WISDOM

The unexamined life may be unworthy of man, as Socrates claimed, but it seems par for the course among the party "professionals," elected and otherwise, who direct the destinies of national democracy. Despite their defeat in five of the last six presidential elections, they live with the illusion, fostered by the party's "lock" on Congress, that they are somehow The Government, mistaking the horse-trading localism of the legislative process with responsible leadership of the nation and expecting the American voter to reward their stumbling incrementalism with the keys to the White House. Despite the realities of the new American nation—its new calculus for the presidency and its new divisions in public opinion—they persist in the folly that ideological moderation will restore the old glories of the party's north-south coalitional past, when in truth all it will do is reduce democracy to a pathetic me-tooism. In that case, the Democrats, as in the years between the Civil War and the New Deal, will win the presidency *only* when the Republicans lose it.

The conventional wisdom of too many party professionals admits no possibility of a progressive democracy, for it is wedded to political myths rather than to the present realities of national politics. One myth is that winning the Deep South is critical to the electoral success of democracy. The truth is that the Deep South is less important in presidential politics than it was thirty years ago and that Democrats in Dixie, at least white Democrats, are an endangered species. Owing to white flight, Democratic party identification among southerners dropped by almost one-half between 1950 and 1990, from 70 percent into the mid-thirties, whereas identification with the GOP jumped from 10 to 30 percent. There is no reason to think that this trend will be soon reversed, and there is little chance that black support for democracy can make up for white defections. In short, it is neither in the Electoral College nor in the electorate itself that the numbers add up to significant power for Dixie in national democracy.

The power numbers in American politics today belong, of course, to the west. That said, we are led directly to a second myth embraced by many of the party's "wise men"—namely, that the political philosophy that sells in the South can be marketed successfully on the west coast as well. This tail-wags-dog theory is simply wrong, as surveys of the political beliefs of Americans amply demonstrate. The truth is that, in its support for social liberalism and activist government, as well as in its foreign policy, the coastal west is most like the east and *least* like the South, and is also unlike the South in its views of economic populism and religious fundamentalism. One simply looks in vain for a philosophical affinity between Dixie and the west coast.

The pretend politics that sees the Deep South and coastal west as electoral bedfellows derives in part from a third myth, that only a moderate Democrat can be elected president and that no liberal need apply. This follows from the mistaken but widely held view that American voters have become much more conservative in the 1980s. In fact, there is little, if any, systematic evidence of a major ideological shift from left to right in the electorate.[8] But even if such evidence did exist, democracy would have the leopard's problem of trying to change its spots convincingly. Democrat Stuart Eizenstat makes the point:

[i]n any great democracy there are two parties, one that stresses the marketplace and individuality and the other that stresses the responsibilities of government and community values. . . . We are the party of government in the United States and cannot and should not try to escape it.[9]

The mugging of Michael Dukakis by Democratic pundits and professionals, who construed his 1988 defeat as proof that liberals are persona non grata with American voters, reflected the intensity with which the myth of moderation is embraced. The truth is that Dukakis came very close to winning the presidency, much closer than Democratic moderate Jimmy Carter did in 1980, even though Carter was backed by the muscle of incumbency. The twelve states with 170 electoral votes that Dukakis lost by less than 5 percent of the popular vote could have been won by moving just over a million ballots from the Republican to the Democratic column. By contrast, a switch of 2.5 million popular votes was required to win the 98 electoral votes of the ten Midsouth and Deep South states—and if this had transpired, the Democrats would still have lost the presidency! Moreover, Dukakis did what Carter never could: He won two of the west coast states, the only Democrat since LBJ to do so. Far from being an object of scorn, the Dukakis performance holds the best hope that democracy will win the White House—and the *only* hope of a progressive democracy.

CONCLUSION

Finally, it must be said that the Democratic party has long been far more important to the Deep South than Dixie has been to the party. Dixie's power in national politics derives from the region's history of one-party democracy, which remains strong in congressional and state elections. Today, its power in Washington lies in the pivotal place it occupies between conservative Republicanism in the executive and northern democracy in the legislature. So Dixie is the swing vote on much of what comes down as public policy for America. A Democrat in the White House, unless he is one of their own, threatens the power of the Deep South. Without the political numbers for real national influence, Dixie's power in Washington is preserved mainly by the mythology that passes for wisdom in the council of national democracy. By dumping Dixie and moving west, a national and progressive democracy can emerge—and it will be a winner.

NOTES

1. "The function of the Democratic Party, in this century," John Kenneth Galbraith writes, "has . . . been to embrace solutions [to national problems] even when, as in the case of Wilson's New Freedom, Roosevelt's New Deal, or the Kennedy-Johnson civil-rights legislation, it outraged not only Republicans but the Democratic establishment as well. And if the Democratic Party does not render this function . . . it has no purpose at all." See Galbraith, *Who Needs the Democrats and What It Takes to Be Needed* (New York: Signet Books, 1970), p. 78.

2. Samuel Lubell, *The Future of American Politics* (New York: Harper & Brothers, 1951), ch. 10.

3. In a ranking of overall Democratic party vote from 1968 to 1988, John Martilla, a Democratic party consultant, finds that the top nineteen states are all in the northeast, mideast, Midwest, and far west. See Martilla, "A Daunting Task for Democrats," *Boston Sunday Globe*, March 10, 1991.

4. John Kenneth White and Jerome M. Mileur, eds., *Challenges to Party Government* (Carbondale: Southern Illinois University Press, 1992), especially ch. 5 and Epilogue.

5. C. B. Holman, "Go West, Young Democrat," *Polity* (Winter 1989): 323-339.

6. "West Is Key to GOP Electoral College 'Lock,'" *Times-Mirror* special report (Los Angeles, 1988), p. 20. See also the table on pp. 37-38.

7. See for example, "What's Wrong With The Democrats?" *Harper's Magazine* (January 1990): 45-55.

8. Larry M. Schwab, "The Myth of the Conservative Shift in American Politics," *Western Political Quarterly* (December 1988): 817-823.

9. Stuart H. Eizenstat, "We Have Perverted Liberalism," *Washington Post*, September 12, 1989, p. A21.

7

BETTY GLAD

What to Say and How to Say It?

Can the Democrats win the presidency? There has been only one Democratic president since 1969, a decline in voter identification with the party, and an electoral realignment in the South at the presidential level. Well-educated and affluent individuals, moreover, are both more Republican and more inclined to vote than those less well-off. These factors, when combined with the advantage for the Republicans in the Electoral College, have suggested to several students of the electoral process that the Democrats' problems in winning the presidency are so formidable that they are not likely to be overcome in the near future.

Yet, a Democratic strategy of going for the electoral votes of the largest states—New York, Pennsylvania, California, Illinois, Michigan, Ohio, Texas, plus a handful of medium-sized states in which the Democrats have traditionally been strong (for example, Oregon, Minnesota, Wisconsin, Massachusetts, Hawaii, and the District of Columbia)—has a real chance for success. When viewed as independent events, the odds against winning each of these states may indeed seem formidable. At the presidential level, however, the processes in these states are interdependent, and a trend in one is apt to become a trend in the others. Michael Dukakis, for example, won the electoral votes of New York and could have prevailed in the Electoral College if there had been a shift of 5 percent of the voters in each of the other five big states noted (in addition to minor shifts in nine smaller states). In California, Illinois, and Pennsylvania he lost by a margin of 3 to 4 percent of the vote. In Michigan, Ohio, and Texas the loss was approximately 9 to 10 percent. Moreover, as a 1988 University of Michigan Center for Political Studies survey has suggested, 47 percent of the electorate was composed of strong, weak, or independent-leaning Democrats, as contrasted with 41 percent of the electorate who were strong, weak, or independent-leaning Republicans. To win a majority in these states, Dukakis would have had to run a campaign that minimized the "turnoff" of the Democratic-leaning voters while winning over approximately half of those who were true independents.

To attract the support needed in the future, the Democrats have three major tasks at hand. First, they must continue Democratic National Committee efforts to target possible voters in the battleground states and implement plans to increase the turnout of Democratic-leaning groups at election time. Special efforts must be undertaken along these lines in California and Texas, two states that have gained electoral votes as a consequence of the 1990 census.[1] Second, the party must develop a program for dealing with major problems facing the country and learn how to articulate and present these programs in ways that will attract a broad following. The inability of many party leaders to fashion programs that they believe in has contributed to the loss of party self-confidence in the past several years. This, in turn, has contributed to its inability to articulate messages that have credibility for opinion makers in the country and win attention and positive response from the mass public. Third, the Democrats must choose a candidate who is both politically astute and better able to adapt to the electronic era than its last nominees. I will discuss these latter considerations in this chapter.

CANDIDATE SELF-PRESENTATION

The Democratic nominee must establish himself very early in the campaign as a person who, in addition to being concerned with the needs of ordinary people, is competent and tough. Without that early credibility, he will be in no real position to counter the criticism and problems that will inevitably occur as the race progresses. His image, one hopes, will not have been tarnished by a primary race in which Democratic opponents have undermined his credibility. If so, he must find ways to counter any such harmful negative images.

An instructive example can be found in Mondale's problems along these lines during the 1984 general election. Gary Hart's charges during the Democratic primary campaign that Mondale was a "changeling" politico at the beck and call of "special interests" handicapped him at the beginning of the fall campaign. His decision to appoint Bert Lance to a high campaign position and his subsequent reversal of that decision raised doubts about his decisionmaking skills. These doubts were compounded by his failure to have his national campaign manage skillfully the press coverage of John Zaccaro's financial situation. His old-fashioned campaign oratory, moreover, did not fit the more intimate style that works well on television. Whipping up Democratic crowds may have worked for those on the scene, but television works best with cooler visions. The result was widespread doubt as to Mondale's capabilities that he could never quite dispel. Advertisements tested with focus groups in early September, for example, showed that many voters felt Mondale might be right on the issues but did not see how he was going to accomplish what he had promised. Others saw him as weak and could not believe that he would be a tough arms negotiator or fiscal manager. This perception was confirmed by polling data. As John Reilly, who ran some of the Mondale focus groups noted, "Nothing about Mondale stuck, relating either to his family, or his career, or whatever, because there was no sense of an ideological core, something he stood for."[2]

The candidate must also appeal to the positive emotions of the American people. Mondale, for example, never took the steps that would help people identify with him. His handling of his family life suggests the problem. Unlike Reagan, Mondale had never been divorced and had a close and warm family life. Early in the campaign, however, he decided to shield his family life from public view. The result was that the voters had no real sense of who his wife was or how his relationship to her could be characterized. Indeed, when Joan Mondale toured on behalf of the campaign, her presence was hardly noticed.[3]

Michael Dukakis's technocratic approach in 1988 also gives us some examples of what not to do. He frittered away a strong lead at the beginning of the fall campaign because he failed to understand that politics is about passion and prejudice, and was unable to convey a simple theme. Thus he started the fall campaign with television spots featuring him as a "take charge" person, making many of his points through graphs and bar charts. His response during the debates to the question of how he would feel about the death sentence if his wife was raped furthered the impression that he was a cold man, out of touch with the deeper emotions that contemporary presidential politics brings into play. Generally, his TV spots were unrelated to his statements on the campaign trail, and no consistent theme was maintained throughout the campaign. Even his most memorable campaign slogan—"good jobs at good wages"—was not given sufficient prominence to be connected to him. According to Gallup's surveys for the Los Angeles *Times-Mirror*, the slogan was recognized by 73 percent of the voters, but only 44 percent linked it to Dukakis.[4] Moreover, by not responding earlier to Bush's campaign charges, Dukakis lost control of the campaign agenda. The most salient issues of the campaign were social issues that Bush used to cut into Dukakis's strength among potential Democratic voters. (More will be said on this below.) Overall, his dry and unfocused campaign contributed to the general ennui obvious in that election. A majority of the voters in 1988 (53 percent, according to the *New York Times*, dividing almost equally between Bush and Dukakis voters) thought the campaign dull. The voter turnout was only 50.1 percent, the lowest since 1924.

To avoid these kinds of errors, the nominee needs a good story line, featuring him in intimate settings suited to his own background and place. The story line should portray him as an interesting person and invite popular identification with him and his family. Continuing and positive coverage in the mass media may also be maximized if his story is gradually developed. Carter had a genius along these lines in the 1976 primaries. The good, smart "outsider," he worked with backdrops in his Georgia hometown of Plains—a charming main street where everyone knew everyone else, the Baptist Church, the clear South Georgia skies—thereby feeding the fantasy that, under him, America could return to an earlier day when people knew and loved each other. As Jody Powell has noted, the 1976 election was not just about concrete issues. People were longing for something they "thought they had known once and somehow had lost touch with. I think that pine trees and home towns said something even to people who had never seen a small town, because they suggested something that they wanted."[5]

To maintain credibility, however, the candidate's story line must have some inner consistency. Despite the genius of his 1976 campaign, Carter had some problems with this, having cast his net too widely. In refusing to peg himself clearly along the political spectrum, he enabled his aides to argue to various political groups that he was a conservative or a liberal, according to the bent of the people being approached. The result, however, was the widespread feeling, evident in late April of the primary campaign, that one did not really know who he was or what he stood for. His messages about his religious positions, whether explicit or tacit, presented similar problems. His public discussions of his use of prayer, his missionary work and born again experience, and his hedges as to whether or not he believed in a literal interpretation of the Bible, attracted many evangelical and conservative Christians to his campaign. His scattered quotes from such sophisticated theologians as Niebuhr, Kierkegaard, and Barth convinced the intelligentsia that he was no radical fundamentalist; but when his interview with Robert Scheer in *Playboy* was published during the fall campaign, it became further clear that he was no narrow fundamentalist. His use of colloquial words for cohabitation outside of marriage and his assurance that he had many times committed adultery in his heart, in fact, enraged many fundamentalists and evangelicals who had previously seen him as "one of them." The overall result of this attempt to appeal to such a broad spectrum was uncertainty about what Carter was really like. Gerald Ford capitalized on that uncertainty in his charges during the fall campaign that Carter "wavers, he wanders, he wiggles and he waffles."[6]

Nor should the candidate claim too much for himself. Carter's self-presentation along these lines created problems for him in the election, as well as in his later presidency. In asserting that he had made no political promises to win support, that he had never told a lie, that he loved the people he met on assembly lines, he invited journalists to find chinks in the armor. When it turned out that he played the political game much as others had, he was found guilty of doing something that would not have been perceived as wrong had he not claimed so much for himself. Carter's tendency to raise unrealistically high expectations for what he could do in office also contributed to the generally critical press he received as president.

To avoid the "feeding frenzies" that can sink a campaign, the candidate should be aware of his vulnerabilities and be prepared to deal with them before others can use them to his disadvantage. To preempt questions about possible extramarital affairs, the candidate should take a stand on principle. He should declare that he would never do anything to embarrass the American public, but also that he objects to any candidate being asked such questions as a matter of principle. If his religious or ethnic background is of concern to many voters, he should frame the issue in the best possible way. John Kennedy, for example, responded to the concern of many Protestants about the relevance of his Catholicism to his governance with his address at the Greater Houston Ministerial Association. The separation of church and state was absolute, he noted, and no "Catholic prelate would tell the President (should he be a Catholic) how to act and no Protestant minister would tell his parishioner for whom to vote."

If despite these precautions "feeding frenzies" do occur, they must be dealt with immediately. These episodes can best be handled if one understands that they are little more than minor psychodramas. Most often it is not so much the facts that count as the provision of a psychologically satisfactory ending. This may often require a concession by the candidate to bring a sense of closure to the issue. Carter came to realize this in his 1976 primary campaign. His statements suggesting that he saw "nothing wrong with ethnic purity being maintained" and that he would not "force racial integration of a neighborhood" through public housing programs raised questions about his real attitudes on racial issues. It was only after ten days of play that he put the issue to rest by appearing with several black leaders at a rally in downtown Atlanta. Martin Luther King, Sr., assured a cheering crowd that Carter's slip of the tongue did not reflect his real thinking and that he personally forgave him for it. If the father of Martin Luther King, Jr., was not concerned, then white reporters certainly should not be.[7] Ford suffered from a similar "feeding frenzy" after his statement at the October foreign policy debate that there was "no Soviet domination of Eastern Europe." The issue dominated the media coverage of his campaign for six days until Gerald Ford admitted he had made a mistake.[8]

LEVELS OF ISSUE PRESENTATION

Issue definition and presentation occur at three different levels, and it is important for the candidate and his aides to understand the requirements and purpose of each level. First, the candidate must articulate substantive political objectives for himself and his party, and have some idea of how he can obtain those objectives. Recently, Democrats have fumbled because they have lost faith in their party and its past. One fundamental assumption—that the traditional Democratic commitments to positive government are somehow old hat—has too often gone unchallenged and, accordingly, has gradually become the accepted wisdom. Only if the Democrats can communicate a clear view of the positive role that government can play in our society will they gain the kind of confidence needed to campaign successfully against an incumbent president.

Second, the candidate has to convince both the journalists who interpret what he is doing and potential campaign contributors and party activists who have to decide whether or not they will join in his effort that he has a real chance to win. The candidate's major challenge is to frame his campaign themes in such a way as to attract independents, and possibly a few Republicans, while minimizing internal frictions within the Democratic electoral coalition. The party's commitment to racial integration has been a divisive issue for Democrats since 1948, causing many working-class Catholics and white Southerners to leave the party.[9] Conflict over the Vietnam War, the U.S. relationship with the Soviet Union, and social issues such as school prayer and women's right to choose an abortion have had a similar effect. Several of these issues no longer have the power to divide the traditional Democratic electorate that they once had. If the candidate can show that he understands that fact, and that he knows how to deal with problems that remain, he can gain the credibility that is absolutely essential to creating momentum in a campaign.

Third, the messages going out to the broader electorate must be tailored to fit the characteristics of that audience. The general election is in large part a contest for the swing voters who do not take their cues from party leaders or labels. The number of independent voters since 1980 (assuming no distinction between Democratic and Republican identifiers) has hovered between 30 and 40 percent in each presidential election, and many of these independents make up their minds only in the final weeks of the fall campaign. There is little information to suggest that very many of them compensate for this lack of party identification by identifying with social or economic interest groups.

Many voters do not follow party or interest group cues in voting; they also lack the information levels and historical knowledge needed to formulate independent political judgments. Although some independents are better informed and more likely to vote than traditional Democrats, the "pure" independents lack even issue awareness.[10] National Opinion Research Center (NORC) and University of Michigan polls show that in the 1980s approximately 50 percent of the American public did not know which party controls the House of Representatives, which side the United States was backing in Nicaragua, or that the government of China is Communist. Equally astonishing, a National Election Study of the University of Michigan indicated that in 1986, 23 percent of the people could not identify George Bush. Indeed, the number of voters who can correctly identify a general difference between major party candidates has varied in recent years between 26 and 53 percent. According to a 1980 CBS News poll, only 50 percent of those who voted for Reagan saw him as a conservative. The rest saw him as a moderate or a liberal, or were unable to characterize him.[11] In the 1984 elections, the percentage of voters who knew the candidates' positions and voted accordingly were as follows: Central America (17 percent), defense spending (39 percent), women's rights (27 percent), and jobs and standard of living (27 percent). Only on government spending did the percentage climb higher, and then only to 50 percent.[12]

Most voters take their cues from the mass media. Television, in particular, is the major source of news for approximately 66 percent of all Americans. Yet, the voters are not given the information requisite to making up their own minds on substantive matters. Policy issues, in particular, are not covered adequately on television news shows. Instead, the focus is on the personal characteristics of the candidates and the "horse race" aspects of the campaign.[13] Candidates will also be selectively covered owing to the decision rules followed by the media as to who are winners and who are losers. Sometimes, commentators may stereotype candidates in ways that create serious problems. In 1972, for example, Hubert Humphrey of Minnesota was continually referred to by commentators as a "politician of the past."[14]

The result is that voter opinions tend to reflect what is broadcast on TV. When asked which issues are foremost in their concern, people are inclined to mention those topics that have been most salient in the media. Their judgments as to which candidate is ahead in the race, or has won a debate, often reflects the interpretations provided by news commentators on television.[15] A dramatic proof of this kind of effect was evident in public evaluations of Ford's gaffe on Eastern Europe during the foreign policy debate in 1976. Viewers at first thought that Ford had won the debate. The next day, following an intense discussion in the mass media of his "mistake," they shifted to the view that Carter had won.[16]

This is not to say that even the less well-informed voter presents a *tabula rasa*. The process whereby political attitudes are formed is quite complex, as students of the opinion- formation process now realize. People generally seem to engage in a type of "on-line processing" of political information. Initial judgments are made about candidates and issues on the basis of certain kinds of information. Although most of that information may be dropped from long-term memory, an orientation is formed that influences the way in which new information is received. The new information may confirm the original orientation or cause some adaptation at the margin. The orientation, moreover, is linked to politically relevant attitudes that are already embedded in a complex set of images and feelings.[17] Indeed, as Montague Kern has noted, most students of the process have been "forced to regard attitudes as structures in long-term memory; amalgams of interconnected concepts, feelings, beliefs, and images."[18]

Which attitudes and images will be evoked during the campaign depends, in part, on the themes emphasized by the candidates. Personal economic issues, particularly in hard times, are apt to be the ones to which the voters respond with the greatest alacrity.[19] Yet, foreign policy attitudes have been "primed" by the candidates in some campaigns and worked to their advantage. Social or foreign policy issues may be made salient when a candidate plays on themes that evoke strong feelings—whether positive or negative—that may rebound to his advantage.[20]

Granted, presentations of the issues are apt to fall on deaf ears. This is particularly so when voters have no schema with which to make the given information meaningful. Even on personal finance issues, for example, voters may not blame those in power for what may be objectively bad policies. People are influenced by the things they know best—by unemployment figures, inflation statistics, and interest rates. Expectations about the future require more abstract knowledge than most voters have. It is not surprising, then, that Democratic arguments about the deficit and its ramifications for the future had little impact on voters throughout much of the 1980s. Except during the recession of 1982-1983, most voters considered Reagan and the Republicans to be good at managing the economy.[21]

The goal of the candidate and his campaign manager in these circumstances is to figure out which schemas and deeper feelings can be evoked to the candidate's benefit. These themes must be played up early in the campaign. If the message is to be effective, moreover, it must be simple, clear, and credible. Paid political spots must be used during the final phases of the campaign, for at that point they are the primary source of issue information for many voters. These political advertisements must be internally consistent; they must also accord with the prior history of the party and the candidate's behavior on the campaign trail. If emotions of fear or anxiety are raised in these spots, the candidate must have an alternative to present that relieves those feelings. For an honest candidate and political party, the proffered solutions must also be based on some deeper thinking about how they really work.

THE ARTICULATION OF CANDIDATE AND PARTY GOALS

Communication at each of these three levels presents various problems and requires various kinds of messages. To meet the first objective—definition of candidate and party goals—the party must continue its commitment to the basic values of its core constituency. This commitment includes the promotion of women's rights and the maintenance of equal opportunity for those who have experienced economic deprivation and prejudice. But the issue that can best unite the party and meet the dominant concerns of a majority of the American people in the 1990s is the economy. In approaching the economy, however, the party must not act as if it is a pale carbon copy of the Republican party. Certainly, the consequences of the unregulated economic market of the last decade are cause for alarm. The Reagan-Bush tax and deregulation policies have led to speculative investments and takeovers, rather than to the promotion of real investment through the updating of American factories and infrastructure. At the international level, the Republican commitment to a free trade ideology (which is ignored in practice by major industrial leaders today) has had a detrimental effect on the economy.[22] The United States could hardly lose its primary role in manufacturing and expect to make up for it with high-wage service jobs.

The alternative, however, is not protectionism but an industrial policy that will increase U.S. manufacturing capabilities and provide ways of redressing people hurt by social and economic displacements.[23] Certainly economic productivity cannot be promoted through tax and spending policies that result in corporate takeovers and major inequities in income distribution. In a deep recession or depression, the economy can be stimulated much more effectively through the maintenance of demand (i.e., through unemployment benefits) than through a reduction in capital gains taxes.

Democrats, of course, have to confront the fact that major across-the-board tax increases are politically impossible at this time. To minimize this problem, new major programs that could cost a great deal—such as catastrophic health insurance for all Americans—should be justified in terms that the voters will accept. The best approach is one in which taxes are earmarked for such services. Other popular programs would cost the government relatively little; consider, for instance, the promotion of fair trade at the international level, better regulation of workplace safety, and new tax policies that reward capital development rather than speculation. Several fairness issues, too, cost little. The maintenance of a woman's most basic right to choose an abortion costs the government nothing, as would its support for legislation requiring the larger corporations to provide for short-term nonpaid pregnancy and family assistance leave.

PUTTING TOGETHER A CREDIBLE CAMPAIGN

At the second level of issue articulation, the Democrats have many things going for them. The traditional Democratic coalition held together because people saw that party as the best one to deal with the economy, even though runaway inflation characterized the last months of the Carter presidency and the "successes" of the early Reagan years produced a temporary modification of that view. As early as 1987, voters had come back to seeing the parties as nearly equal in dealing with the economy. By late October 1991, however, 57 percent of the voters polled in the *New York Times*/CBS survey disapproved of Bush's handling of the economy, and his approval rating was 52 percent, a 21 percent decline in little more than a month.[24] If President Bush continues to insist on a trickle-down theory of pump priming and takes only halfway measures to deal with what appears to be at best a long and deep recession, an aggressive Democratic campaign could once again restore the party to its traditional role as the party that protects the economic interests of the common person. The goal should be to show how Republican support of speculative investment, tax cuts for the rich, and a laissez-faire policy toward international trade have contributed to budget and trade deficits and to the faltering economy itself.

An embrace of those programs the Democrats have traditionally valued should cause the party's candidate few serious problems. Indeed, a NORC survey of 1987 indicated that over 60 percent of the voters at that time thought the government was spending too little on protecting the environment, education, and health care. Michael Dukakis discovered the power of these traditional Democratic appeals in the final days of the 1988 campaign. When he resorted to more traditional Democratic proposals for programs that help people, he recovered in the polls. Voters who made up their minds late in the campaign, for example, tipped toward Dukakis by 60 to 40 percent in the last week of the campaign, decreasing Bush's 17 point lead to only 6 points.[25]

The Democratic candidate, however, should call himself a "moderate." From this perspective, he stands to pick up individuals both at the center and at the left of the American political spectrum. As several NORC, Harris, and *Public Opinion* polls have indicated, between 38 and 50 percent of the electorate since 1970 have characterized themselves as "middle of the roaders." Add to this figure the liberal identifiers (whose numbers, according to Harris and NORC polls, have actually increased in recent years, from 17 percent in 1981 to 28 percent in 1987) and you have a substantial majority.

The "liberal" label, moreover, should be handled with care. Liberal identifiers, as we have seen, are still in the minority. Moreover, as a Gallup Poll for the *Times-Mirror* has indicated, 50 percent of those who voted for Bush in 1988 specified Dukakis's liberalism as the most important reason for their decision.[26] Largely as a consequence of Bush campaign statements, "liberalism" had come to mean that one was soft on crime and catered to special interests. Ironically, it was a Democrat who paved the way for this latter misuse of the term. When Gary Hart attacked the liberal Walter Mondale as a representative of special interests in the 1984 primaries, he suggested that all liberal Democrats were somehow not representing a general interest.

To restore the term "liberal" to a positive meaning, candidates, when queried, must define it anew. John Kennedy's approach to the matter could be adapted so that it can be partly redefined. The candidate could note that if liberalism means all the bad things its opponents suggest—a lack of concern about crime, drug use, or efficient use of taxpayers' dollars—then he is not a liberal. But if liberal means, as Kennedy said, "someone who looks ahead, welcomes new ideas, cares about the welfare of the people . . . then I am proud to say that I am a liberal."

Commitments to substantive issues that motivate the core coalition—blacks, Hispanics, Jews, Catholics, persons earning less than $10,000,
and women (a group that collectively voted 50 percent or more for the
Democrats in 1988)— must be maintained. Otherwise, this coalition will not
work for the campaign or vote in substantial numbers.

These commitments can be framed in ways that both minimize opposition
within the coalition and appeal to a broader audience. Most important, the
Democratic party needs to disconnect from the minds of many voters the
linkage between the party and spending programs offering assistance to
blacks and the permanently poor. Working-class Americans do not like to
think that they are paying taxes to help others less industrious than they.
Indeed, since 1972 a majority of blue-collar workers have not voted
Democratic. Moreover, in America even the poor do not like to think of
themselves in those terms. Given these attitudes, the party should stop
speaking of itself as the party of the *poor*. How much better it would be to
redefine the party commitment to welfare programs as a concern for
working people who are temporarily disadvantaged through no fault of their
own. Programs such as unemployment benefits or Aid to Dependent
Children (ADC) should be presented as an effort to help working people
who have suffered as a result of poor luck or a bad turn in the economy.[27]
A commitment to family leave and nursery schools, framed as an endeavor
to enable the heads of one-parent households to get off relief and return to
employment, could attract a wide range of voters.

Social issues can also be framed in ways that minimize division within
the Democratic coalition. Affirmative action programs should be presented
as "efforts to enforce nondiscrimination in employment" and can be based
on economic circumstances and cultural deprivation rather than on race.
The commitment to choice can be presented not as a pro-abortion position
but as a commitment of each woman to make an individual decision in
accord with her own religious views, not someone else's. Democrats might
consider requiring special processes for women under 18. Focus groups
have shown that the support for the right to an abortion is often linked to the
provision that the family should be responsible for what happens to a minor.

If these so-called social issues were to be made more salient, they might
help to gain independent votes. Consider the gender gap, which has existed
since the early 1980s. Women in 1982, for example, voted Democratic 8
percent more than men. Most individuals who would respond negatively to
the pro-choice position of the Democratic party have already left it. As a
1988 *New York Times*/CBS exit poll showed, 67 percent of those who saw
abortion as the most important issue voted for Bush. But there are many
women *and* men who would be persuaded to vote Democratic if the party

were to clearly articulate its commitment to abortion rights. The gender gap has a positive potential for the Democrats in the states with large numbers of electoral votes. (Working women in urban areas tend to vote Democratic when there are important issue differences between candidates on such issues.) The Bush administration's clear and strong commitment to an anti-choice stance, its support of policies to limit information about the abortion choice at publicly funded clinics, and its early attempts to protect anti-abortion activists who harass women at clinics, have provided the Democrats with an issue that could increase their vote by as much as 10 percent in states with large electoral votes. A survey by the *Los Angeles Times*, for example, showed that 69 percent of the public disapproved of the Supreme Court decision allowing states to prohibit doctors and health care workers in publicly funded family planning clinics from telling pregnant women that abortion was an option.[28]

Attempts to articulate how the national deficit might be reduced is a no-win issue and should not be attempted during the campaign. Certainly the Republicans have not acted responsibly in this area, and it would be counterproductive for the Democrats to try to do so in the heat of a campaign. Reductions in arms expenditures, now that the cold war has ended, will free up some funds for economic and social programs. But if the Democrats promise to try to reduce the debt through a reduction in spending, they will violate the essence of the Democratic commitment. And if they promise that they will increase taxes (as Mondale did in 1984), they are likely to meet his fate. (Exit polls in 1984 showed that most of those who voted Republican said that they did so because the Democrats wanted to increase taxes.)[29] The Democrats might handle that issue by promising the electorate a bipartisan presidential commission to deal with the problem. After the election, this commission would be asked to recommend measures of debt reduction that would be temporary and not cut into the nation's most basic programs.

FRAMING THE MESSAGE FOR THE MASS AUDIENCE

At the third level of issue articulation, the candidate must gain mastery over the mass media. Perhaps the most important thing for him to do is to control the agenda so that his issues *are* the salient issues. Dukakis's mistake in the 1988 election was that he let Bush turn his liberalism, the pledge of allegiance, and the prison furlough program into the major themes of the campaign. As a consequence, the Republicans were able to drive a wedge into several ideological clusters that might otherwise have voted for Dukakis. In May, as a Gallup study for the *Times-Mirror* showed, Dukakis had 8 of 10 "New Dealers."[30] By November he had only 6 in 10. The "God and Country" Democrats defected early and stayed away, with only 6 in 10 voting for him. And the "disaffected" about equally divided between Dukakis and Bush in May, but gave Dukakis only 32 percent of their vote in November.[31]

Democratic stances, moreover, must be framed in ways that reinforce the politically attentive voters in the mass audience and sway the relatively disinterested and uninformed. The messages behind these stances must be simple, short, and repetitive. Interpretations should be provided, but with a focus on only very few themes. (Complex messages, as various focus group studies have shown, only confuse most voters.) Visual and concrete examples can be used to dramatize the messages and make them more memorable. And the behavior of the candidate on the campaign trail, as well as his past record, should reinforce these messages as presented by the media. To be credible, such presentations should not conflict with information already known about the candidate and his party.[32]

Reagan's presidential performance was instructive along these lines. His greatest asset was the feeling of pride and confidence he fostered in Americans through his reaffirmation of American values and patriotism. But he also made his negative issues understandable and graphic. Rather than presenting complex arguments about what government cannot do, he rallied voters behind him with the phrase "Get the government off our backs." And to dramatize misuse of welfare programs, he talked of "welfare queens" who drove up in their Cadillacs to get their checks.

To counter these Republican images, Democrats must evoke powerful images that are connected to their values. People generally perceive the Democratic party as more concerned with the common people, so the Democratic candidate should play to that strength. Spot advertisements, given that they serve as a major source of political information for undecided voters, may be used to make these traditional party commitments more vivid.[33] Thus, a series of spots might run like this: "Remember when the government belonged to you? Protected the worker at the workplace?" The camera then pans to locked doors at the poultry fire in Hamlet, S.C. Pan to another portrait, showing how white blue-collar workers have suffered from lower safety standards. Conclude with a voice-over: "During the Reagan-Bush decade, federal investigations of workplace safety were drastically cut. A Democratic president would make sure that companies don't lock the doors on people." Another possibility: Start by playing on a similar theme: "Remember when the government cared?" Then pan to

GM plants with closed signs on the gates. Conclude with voice-over: "The Republicans *don't* care that the jobs of skilled workers are being exported abroad. They call it laissez-faire. But they don't require that other countries open their doors to goods produced by Americans. The Democrats wouldn't let that happen. They will insist on fair trade." Yet another possibility: "Remember when the government was yours? When it helped children who did not have an equal chance at learning in school?" Pan to a preschool Head Start classroom filled with young black and white children. "Now they will have to clean up the mess left by the Reagan-Bush Savings and Loan bailout." Pan to people left stranded outside a closed Savings and Loan bank. Conclude with figures of what the bailout will cost, compared to a good Head Start program.

The same general theme could also be used to differentiate between Republican and Democratic policies for reviving the economy. Start with a voice-over: "Remember when the government belonged to you?" Show a fat rich man, with Uncle Sam pouring coins into his bulging pockets, a few of which drop to the ground. "Herbert Hoover thought you could jumpstart the economy by putting more money in the hands of the rich. So does George Bush. He wants to cut taxes on the investment incomes of the rich. Democrats don't believe in this trickle-down theory. They know that you get the economy going by putting money in the hands of the working men and women, and by assisting the unemployed. Vote for the Democratic candidate for president."

A positive side effect of such advertisements is that they enable party leaders to directly counter the cliché that Democratic traditional programs are old hat. The assumption that Democratic goals and programs have somehow been discredited—an assumption too often embraced by political commentators as if it were an established truth—has placed an undue burden on Democrats. Unlike the Republicans, they must come up with something completely new if they are to be taken seriously.

Divisive appeals to certain emotions from the Republican camp should be anticipated and dealt with immediately. Such emotions have certainly been catered to in the past, in ways that worked against the Democrats, and they are very apt to be used again. For instance, Americans tend to be more religious and to take more pride in their country than the people of most other major industrial powers. As several NORC studies have shown, they are also very concerned about crime and drugs and disinclined to spend more money on urban development. Moreover, racial prejudice and the belief that the rights of homosexuals and atheists should not be protected are disproportionately strong among poorly educated white voters who have traditionally voted Democratic.

The Bush campaign played on all these issues in 1988 by airing Willie Horton references and advertisements featuring footage of Bush's visits to flag factories, and appeals to permit prayer in public places. Meanwhile, the charge that Dukakis was a "card-carrying" member of the ACLU reinforced suggestions that he was inclined to go along with those people who might want to burn flags or ban prayer from the schools.

Consider how these negative campaign issues, if used again, might be turned to Democratic advantage with a little imagination. A television spot might feature a magician (who looks like George Bush) waving a flag over unemployment statistics. Then, it could shift to a scene showing real people who are unemployed (through no fault of their own). One person can be overheard to say that the Republicans are using the flag to make the real issues go away—that they simply want the same old thing, to give more tax benefits to the rich. Conclude with a voice-over: "Vote for the Democrats. They want to help the unemployed. The Republicans wish they would just disappear." Variants on this theme could show the Republicans trying various types of vanishing acts or shell games.

In short, certain underlying feelings may themselves be tapped by the Democratic party. Pride in America and a desire to fight crime and drugs are not Republican monopolies. The Democrats must make a concerted effort to emphasize these values.

Negative campaign appeals, it should be noted, can change individual conceptions of a candidate's image and issues stances, and are likely to be widely used in the future. Usually, TV spots appeal to emotions such as anger or fear. They work, in part, because many people believe what they see on television, thinking that advertisements may exaggerate but do not lie. Successful advertisements avoid the backlash effect by using individuals other than the candidate in the content of the message; seldom, if ever, do they include the candidate or his family except in a freeze-frame at the end.[34] In 1980 Carter made the mistake of taking on Reagan personally. The media responded by ignoring Carter's substantive message, focusing instead on Carter's "meanness."

The Democrats must ensure, however, that their negative messages do not raise anxiety without providing a resolution at the end. An ad that Mondale tested in 1984 showed a man and a boy holding the bar of an ascending car on a roller coaster. An announcer suggested that Republican economic policies would soon cause a decline. As the car reached the top, the voice became anxious, and the boy took a deep breath. A freeze-frame followed with a voice-over: "If you're thinking of voting Republican in 1984, think about what will happen in 1985." The spot was entertaining, and it induced apprehension in its viewers. But when probed further, viewers rejected the suggestion that the impending decline was the fault of the Reagan administration.[35]

Democrats should be prepared for another possibility, as well. At some point, while they are running high in the polls and receiving favorable media coverage, rightwing attacks on the "liberal" media are likely to occur. Agnew launched one such assault back in 1969, when he attacked the "Eastern establishment" news media as having a "liberal-left bias." New-right critics have continued the assault ever since. The Democrats should have compiled statistics on the amount and kind of television coverage needed to counter these critics, followed by advertisements along the "you can't fool the people" line. Here's one possibility. Start with a voice-over: "The Republicans are afraid." Then show a scroll coming before an irate king (who, again, looks like George Bush). On the scroll are listed the latest unemployment figures, or numbers representing the cost per voter of the Savings and Loan bailout, or the actual loss of individual real income for the middle class during the past decade. Conclude with another voice-over: "You can't kill the facts by killing the messenger. People know that the Republicans are not talking sense when they give us their old trickle-down theories and tax policies that benefit the rich. Vote Democratic."

CONCLUSION

The Democrats *can* win the presidency. A potential Democratic majority exists in most of the states with big electoral votes, as well as in many smaller far western, Midwestern, northeastern, and middle Atlantic states. Moreover, most Americans are politically positioned such that a majority can be formed around the progressive stances traditionally embraced by the Democratic party.

The party nominee must, however, play to Democratic strengths. A Democratic candidate can run a credible campaign on a platform promoting both a government better able to meet the needs of most people and equal opportunity for all its citizens. Moreover, by holding to positions in which he really believes, he can shore up the self-confidence that will enable him to navigate successfully around the shoals of the campaign. Finally, if he emphasizes traditional Republican issues such as a tough foreign policy, efficiency in government, spending cuts, and lower taxes, he can make them the central issues of the campaign—and the voters will go for the party that has greater credibility on those issues.

The race will be a difficult one, however, and the Democratic candidate must show during the campaign that he can make tough, politically sophisticated decisions. Negatives must be handled quickly and efficiently, and issues must be enunciated in ways that will hold together the traditional Democratic coalition and appeal to a broader audience. Above all, the Democratic candidate must recognize the key importance of the electronic media to contemporary campaigning and be willing and able to use them effectively. The suggestion has been made here that he develop appealing, simple, and clear media presentations emphasizing what a caring government can do. He might deal with potential negatives on the spending front by emphasizing programs that cost relatively little or can be paid for out of taxes that are earmarked for those programs. And he can handle social issues through sensitive framing of controversial concerns such as a woman's right to choice. Indeed, with care, the Democratic candidate will be able to retain his core constituency, attract Democratic-leaning independents along with some voters who pay relatively little attention to politics, and win the presidency. Once in power, he can demonstrate to the people of America that government need not be an enemy—that government can be a constructive force for dealing with society's problems and the needs of the nation.

NOTES

1. California, with a gain of 7 electoral votes after the 1990 census, has 54 votes as of 1992. Texas has 32 electoral votes, just behind New York with its 33 votes. These states, along with Pennsylvania, Ohio, Illinois, and Michigan, provide 203 of the 270 electoral votes needed for a presidential victory, thus requiring a winning candidate to pick up only 67 more votes. For a Democrat, these 67 electoral votes could come from the smaller states that went Democratic in 1988: Massachusetts, Wisconsin, Minnesota, Iowa, Hawaii, Oregon, Washington, and the District of Columbia.

2. Montague Kern, *30-Second Politics: Political Advertising in the Eighties* (New York: Praeger, 1989), pp. 120-121.

3. Ibid., p. 129.

4. Gallup Organization, *The People, the Press, and Politics: October Pre-Election Typology Survey* (Los Angeles: *Times-Mirror*, October 1988), p. 26.

5. Betty Glad, *Jimmy Carter: In Search of the Great White House* (New York: W. W. Norton, 1980), pp. 321-322.

6. Ibid., pp. 310-311, 379, 383-384, 391-392.

7. Ibid., pp. 327-328.

8. Betty Glad, "Election of 1976," in Arthur M. Schlesinger and Fred Israel, eds., *History of American Presidential Election: 1789-1984: Supplemental Volume 1972-1984* (New York: Chelsea House Publishers, 1986), p. 102.

9. There is some contrary evidence indicating that as Catholics rose in socioeconomic status between 1952 and 1972 and moved to the suburbs, their identification with the Democratic party did not decrease. See Herbert B. Asher, *Presidential Elections and American Politics: Voters, Candidates, and Campaigns Since 1952*, 5th ed. (Pacific Grove, Calif.: Brooks/Cole Publishing Company, 1992), p. 334.

10. Asher, *Presidential Elections and American Politics*, pp. 64-65, 77-78, 115-116.

11. Ibid., p. 180.

12. Ibid., p. 234.

13. Ibid., pp. 191, 255.

14. Doris A. Graber, "The Transformation of Leader Images: Turning Good Guys into Bad Guys," paper presented at the Midwest Political Science Association Meeting, Chicago, 1990.

15. William C. Adams, "Media Coverage of Campaign '84: A Preliminary Report," *Public Opinion*, April-May (1984): 9-13.

16. Glad, *Jimmy Carter*, p. 391.

17. Doris A. Graber, *Mass Media and American Politics*, 3rd ed. (Washington, D.C.: CQ Press, 1989); John Zaller and Vincent Price, "In One Ear and Out the Other: Learning and Forgetting the News," paper prepared for the Annual Meeting of the Midwest Political Science Association, Chicago, Illinois, 1990; Milton Lodge and Patrick Stroh, "Inside the Mental Voting Booth: An Impression-Driven Model of Candidate Evaluation," Department of Political Science, State University of New York at Stony Brook, 1990.

18. Kern, *30-Second Politics*, p. 14.

19. William Mishler and Roy Fitzgerald. "Interpreting U.S. Presidential Elections: A Continuous Time Series Analysis, 1960-1988," paper prepared for the Annual Meeting of the Canadian Political Science Association, Laval University, 1989.

20. John H. Aldrich, John L. Sullivan, and Eugene Borgida, "Foreign Affairs and Issue Voting: Do Presidential Candidates 'Waltz Before a Blind Audience?'," *American Political Science Review* 83 (1989): 123-141; Asher, *Presidential Elections and American Politics*, pp. 130-207.

21. Asher, *Presidential Elections and American Politics*, p. 186; Mishler and Fitzgerald, "Interpreting U.S. Presidential Elections."

22. Robert Kutner, *The End of Laissez-Faire: National Purpose and the Global Economy After the Cold War* (New York: Knopf, 1991).

23. Stephen S. Cohen and John Zysman, *Manufacturing Matters: The Myth of the Post-Industrial Economy* (New York: Basic Books, 1987).

24. Richard L. Berke, "America Grows Gloomier on Economy, Poll Shows," *New York Times*, October 22, 1991, p. A8.

25. Gallup Organization, *The People, the Press, and Politics: Post-Election Typology Survey* (Los Angeles: *Times-Mirror*, November 1988), p. 3.

26. Gallup Organization, *The People, the Press, and Politics: Post-Election*

Typology Survey, p. 31.

27. As NORC's General Social Science Survey of 1986-1987 suggested, a majority of Americans favor increased assistance to the poor though only 20 to 30 percent would support any increase for welfare.

28. Everett Carl Ladd, "One Year to the '92 Elections and Counting," *The Ladd Report*, 4th ed., vol 1, p. 25; Asher, *Presidential Elections and American Politics*, pp. 180-184.

29. Kern, *30-Second Politics*, p. 56.

30. Gallup Organization, *The People, the Press, and Politics: Post-Election Typology Survey*, pp. 12-13.

31. Ibid. These ideological clusters, as used by the *Times-Mirror*, are somewhat self-explanatory. The "God and Country" Democrats are older, religious, socially conservative, and anti-Communist but pro-social spending. The "New Dealers" are also older, middle-income, protectionist, pro-union, and pro-governmental programs. The "disaffected" are "alienated, pessimistic, and financially pressured." This group leans toward the GOP camp, but has had historic ties to the Democratic party. Disaffecteds are supportive of the military but skeptical of both big government and big business.

32. Kern, *30-Second Politics*, pp. 118-119, 131-133.

33. Ibid., pp. 57, 211.

34. Ibid., pp. 32-33, 93-112, 202-209.

35. Ibid., pp. 122-123.

8

LOIS LOVELACE DUKE

Television, the 1992 Democratic Presidential Hopeful, and Electoral Success

Television has increased our ability to communicate instantly and more comprehensively. Because we see pictures and hear voices simultaneously and so can identify immediately with the scene portrayed on the screen, television is more credible than other means of communication. We tend to believe what we can see and hear as opposed to having to rely on "pictures in our heads." And because this medium of communication is so powerful within our society, television has changed our culture, our lifestyle, and our political system.

Americans get most of their information about politics by means of television; thus, what was once viewed as primarily a technological means of conveying information has now become an instrument of real political power.[1] Television determines electoral success, or failure, in political races at all governmental levels. Today's politician cannot escape television—or hide from its pervasive scope. To be elected, the candidate must know how to use the medium; communication skills are necessary for political success. Unfortunately, however, many Democratic presidential candidates seem to fail to recognize this fact of contemporary American politics.

This chapter explores the importance and influence of television in presidential races, examines how Democratic candidates have failed to use television effectively in recent campaigns, and sets forth television strategies for future Democratic presidential hopefuls. We begin by taking a look at the medium of television as a tool for candidates in political races.

INFLUENCE OF TELEVISION IN PRESIDENTIAL RACES

Television has drastically altered political campaigning in this country. Candidates once relied on political parties for monetary support, campaign organization, communication with the electorate, and encouragement of voters to turn out on election day. Before the days of TV, candidates campaigned door-to-door, spoke at "stump meetings," and ran campaigns in which candidates had more control over the media. During these times, the candidates relied heavily on the print media for newspaper ads and editorial endorsements; candidates also used radio, endorsements from opinion leaders, billboards, and yard signs to get their names and themes before the public. Television changed all of this.

As David Broder points out, the differences between television and print news are basic.[2] Television is a picture medium; its strength lies in images. Words and language, the currency of print journalism and of the informal communication that fills our days, take second place. And television, like radio, is a nearly instant source. When something important happens, television is on the air, often on the scene. That has two effects. It reduces the chance to check and edit information before it goes on the air, thus increasing the risk of error or misinterpretation. It also creates a communications loop that makes the TV coverage part of the very story it is covering.[3]

Marshall McLuhan and Quentin Fiore have argued that, in one sense, societies have always been shaped more by the nature of the media by which individuals communicate than by the content of the communication.[4] For example, the alphabet is a technology absorbed by the very young child in a completely unconscious manner—almost by osmosis. Words and the meaning of words predispose the child to think and act automatically in certain ways.[5]

Given such instant communication filled with drama and imagery,[6] it is little wonder that electronic technology has pervaded our society to the point where television news has become a very personal form of journalism. The television newscast is a direct person-to-person transaction between the journalist or the candidate and the viewer. As a result, television has personalized U.S. presidential elections. It follows that voters are more prone to make snap judgments instead of long-term evaluations, which once were formed with the aid of the political parties and in-depth reports from the print media. In short, the media, and specifically television, have taken over one of the main functions of political parties in this country.[7] The consequence of our new form of politics, as McLuhan and Fiore argue, is that "the living room has become the voting booth."[8]

Television also sets the political agenda in elections by determining what messages will be featured in the evening news and which issues will be downplayed or ignored. For example, the effects of the media on agenda-setting have been studied systematically in a series of experimental and quasi-experimental studies conducted by an interdisciplinary research team at the Center for Urban Affairs and Policy Research at Northwestern University. The first of the studies used an experimental design to test the effect of a televised investigative report concerning home health care.[9] Among members of the general public there was a clear agenda-setting effect. That is, those who viewed the program became more interested in home health care and more likely to see the need for governmental help. Additionally, government policymakers who saw or heard about the program were significantly more likely to change their views about the seriousness of fraud and abuse in home health care. On the other hand, interest group leaders were not significantly affected. Given that both the public and policy leaders were significantly more interested in the problem after viewing or reviewing the media report, it apparently improved the position of home health care on the public agenda.

The second study in this series used a quasi-experimental design to examine the agenda-setting effects of a Chicago *Sun-Times* investigative report on government improprieties in the reporting and handling of rape cases in the Chicago area.[10] The agenda-setting effects of the newspaper series were more limited than those found for the televised report on home health care. This result was attributed in part to the already high level of awareness and concern about crime among all groups.

The third study used a pre-test, post-test experimental design to study the effects of a five-part televised investigative series on police brutality in Chicago.[11] As Jerry L. Yeric and John R. Todd point out, two major conclusions are suggested by this series of studies: (1) Television may have a more significant effect on public opinion than newspapers, at least when the subject is dramatic and the event is short term,[12] (2) It appears that the less information the public has prior to a media report, the more likely it is to be affected by it.

Unfortunately, despite these findings, too many of our recent Democratic presidential candidates appear to continue to run their campaigns as though they are still in pre-television days. They have not kept up with the Republican candidates in developing television expertise—and as a consequence national election-day results have been most gloomy for the Democratic party.

Why have Republican presidential candidates been more successful than the Democrats in this respect? Perhaps a look at the first successful Republican presidential candidate to use TV effectively in a campaign will give us some insight. Let us now turn to Eisenhower and his campaign tactics in 1952.

The Influential Use of TV in a Presidential Race

Even though Eisenhower was not a seasoned television performer, he used the medium effectively in his bid for election in 1952. As Mary Stuckey and Arthur Larson point out, Eisenhower projected an impression of honesty, sincerity, and reliability when he appeared on TV.[13] As a result, even though his delivery was not "Madison Avenue slick," he was beloved and believed. Some scholars even feel that the lack of polish in his delivery served to add to his wholesome image.

Eisenhower's 1952 political campaign also gave rise to the innovation of televised spot announcements. The Republicans came up with the gimmick of filming people asking questions, followed by Eisenhower's prerecorded answers:

> "Mr. Eisenhower, what about the high cost of living?"
> Eisenhower: "My wife, Mamie, worries about the same thing. I tell her it is our job to change that on November 4th."
> "Mr. Eisenhower, I need a new car, but I can't afford it at today's high prices."
> Eisenhower: "Yes, a low-priced car today includes $624 in hidden taxes. Let's start saving the billions now wasted in Washington and get those taxes down."

As J. Leonard Reinsch suggests, those Republican spots offered no specific solutions—only the inplication that Eisenhower had the solution to all problems, whether it was the high cost of living or high taxes.[14]

Eisenhower was also the first presidential candidate to hire a consultant to help him in his political campaign. Rosser Reeves, a creative specialist for an advertising agency in New York, is credited with combining the hard-sell tactics of product advertising with a similar approach to political campaign spots for TV. Eisenhower's successful television ads were a first in political campaign strategy. Reeves wrote the commercials, oversaw the production, and compared the tactics he used to those involved in selling soap to the American public.[15]

Reeves's previous nonpolitical successes included the marketing of a hard-sell commercial for Anacin, a long-time headache remedy, and M&M candy. Reeves, in an interview with Bill Moyers, reflected on the incredible ability of television advertising to penetrate people's minds and thus to disseminate information. An important finding, he noted, was that the Anacin commercial was the most unpopular commercial on television at that time, and yet sales set new records and the product moved quickly off the shelves. Reeves observed that there was no correlation between a commercial's popularity and product sales. Although these effects were difficult to explain, Reeves felt that advertising was but an instrument to disseminate information and to get people to remember the product. Television advertising, he suggested, had a similar potential in presidential politics.[16]

Even though one may conclude that these early TV spots lacked the sophistication of today's TV standards, contemporary Democratic presidential candidates have the same opportunities to use television as creatively and effectively as Eisenhower and Reeves had done. They merely have to devise their own personal manner of communicating a specific message while controlling the medium, much as Eisenhower did. It isn't the technology of television that has changed drastically—only the skill in using it to one's advantage. Television, initially perceived as an entertainment medium, is now respected for its news communication potential. Democratic candidates must recognize and utilize with skill this great resource.

As Mary E. Stuckey points out, Eisenhower had the ability to make grand gestures in the "cool" manner McLuhan tells us is the key to success on television. Eisenhower's usual pattern was to define a problem in dramatic terms: "The military threat is but one menace to our freedom and security. We must not only deter aggression; we must also frustrate the effort of Communists to gain their goals by subversion."[17] According to documented accounts, Eisenhower went on to define precisely the nature of the enemy: "Here, then, is joined no argument between slightly differing philosophies. This conflict strikes directly at the faith of our fathers and the lives of our sons. Freedom is pitted against slavery; lightness against the dark."[18] Eisenhower used tough language and appealed to the values of the average American voter. Yet his words were simple, understandable, forceful, and graphic; they lent credibility to the speaker as a leader.

Reagan as the "Great Communicator"

Any discussion of political communication through the medium of television should point up the great success of Ronald Reagan, who enjoyed tremendous popularity despite obvious gaffes and a poor grasp of the details of issues. In fact, Gerald Pomper and his colleagues summarize the 1984 presidential election as a process whereby Americans voted for a likable person who used stirring rhetoric and broadly defended religion and the family.[19]

On the other hand, Robert E. Denton would argue that one conceivably might not even think of Ronald Reagan in connection with the label "Great Communicator." Denton alleges that our country has always had great communicators and that it is impossible to find a Reagan speech that compares with Jefferson's inaugural address, which described vividly the values, goals, and purposes of government; or Lincoln's first inaugural address, which forcefully promoted unity, or his second inaugural address, which movingly promised forgiveness; or Franklin Roosevelt's first inaugural address, which offered comfort and hope to his Depression era audience; or Kennedy's inaugural address, which stirred the minds and imaginations of the American people.[20]

Denton further argues that it is impossible to find a Reagan speech that is as eloquent as Lincoln's address at Gettysburg; as informed as Wilson's address in support of the League of Nations; as confident as Franklin Roosevelt's declaration-of-war message; as impassioned as Kennedy's Berlin Wall address; or as committed as Johnson's declaration of war on poverty. In fact, he concludes, it is simply impossible to find a Reagan speech that will be studied as a piece of literature or as an exemplary example of human persuasion.[21]

However, future Americans will undoubtedly be shown clips of Reagan asserting himself in an early 1980 presidential debate, congratulating U.S. Olympians, standing on the shores of Normandy and before troops in Korea, saluting the Tomb of the Unknown Soldier, comforting the widow of a slain American soldier, and presiding at the Statue of Liberty celebration. Why is this so? Even though Reagan may not stack up with our great leaders and politicians of the past, he clearly mastered the communications technology of his era—namely, television.[22]

Denton goes on to explain that effective presidents have always been skilled in their use of the communications media of their time. Andrew Jackson utilized a friendly newspaper, the *Washington Globe*, to express his policies. Theodore Roosevelt, a master of public relations, understood the impact of delivering powerful messages reprinted in daily newspapers with dramatic photographs. He seldom refused a photo opportunity. Woodrow Wilson, though he lacked personal charisma, initiated regular press conferences and even commissioned motion pictures to capture newsworthy events. Franklin Roosevelt mastered the media of radio and motion pictures. And Ronald Reagan is proclaimed the "Great Communicator"—because of his mastery of the television medium.[23]

When studying Ronald Reagan's 1984 presidential election strategy, we find that polls continually showed that voters favored Reagan because of his persona and charisma, even though they disagreed with his issue positions. The conclusion to be drawn is that presidents who win are those who perform effectively on television. What are the implications for future Democratic presidential candidates and their use of television? Why have Democratic candidates in general not warmed up to the medium of television as the Republicans have done? Perhaps an analysis of Dukakis's handling of TV in 1988 will give us some insight into this issue.

Dukakis's Failure to Master Television

Much has been written dissecting the negative 1988 Bush/Dukakis presidential campaign. For example, Bush conflated all his themes in one speech: "I can't help but feel his fervent opposition to the Pledge is symbolic of an entire attitude best summed up in four little letters: ACLU. I think it's time [Dukakis] let the Pledge of Allegiance out on furlough. . . . It's one thing to give peace a chance, but we cannot afford a president who would take a chance with peace. I don't understand why my opponent seems to oppose the development of every new weapons system since the slingshot."[24] Dukakis was thus attacked; but instead of counterattacking, he retreated. He told his advisers that the lies and distortions about him would fall harmlessly to the ground—that no one would give them credence. Yet his aloofness made him come across on television as being passive and cold. As Sidney Blumenthal points out, "Who he wasn't was who he was."[25]

Dukakis never recovered. With respect to television strategy, he made virtually all the mistakes that could be made. One cannot help but wonder what would have happened had he responded to Bush and his negativity early in the campaign. Could he have defused some of Bush's negative strategy? For example, it seems that almost any response or retort would have played better than Dukakis's decision to ignore the charges. Consider, for example, what might have transpired if he'd responded, "You are right—I am a liberal and damned proud of it. FDR and Kennedy were liberals and leaders, not wimps; and they certainly weren't born with a silver foot in their mouths."

Unfortunately, Dukakis failed to master the primary means of communication at his disposal. He did not come across on television as a caring leader. He ignored the advice of his political strategists and consultants. As a consequence, he seemed almost fearful of the very medium that had the power to turn the election his way. He seemed to believe that the television camera would pick up his positive attributes—such as his competence and so forth. Instead, the Bush strategists continued to bombard him with charges that never let up. And much as Rosser Reeves had observed, people bought the product even though they disliked the advertisements. They "bought" George Bush even though they deplored the negativity of the 1988 presidential race. In effect, Bush and his strategists set the agenda for the negative campaign, whereas Dukakis merely tried to retreat from most of the attacks. What can Democratic presidential candidates learn from the Dukakis/Bush race? As alarming as negative campaign tactics may be, voters will likely continue to see such attacks in even greater numbers in the future. What, then, are the consequences for Democrats and the presidency?

WHAT CONTEMPORARY DEMOCRATIC CANDIDATES MUST DO TO WIN

Several problems are associated with the Democratic contenders' lack of success as electronic media candidates. As one seasoned political consultant has noted, "In recent campaigns, it's not a matter of the Democratic candidates being unattractive or unpalatable. It's more a matter of the Democratic candidates being unable to counter the negating done by the Republicans. After all, Dukakis was not that bad on television—the Republicans just made him appear to be."[26]

The television medium creates a tough world for a presidential candidate. Faced with rapid transmission of concurrent audio and visual projections, a candidate is forced into a paradox of difficulty. Not only must he come across as relaxed and unafraid of the medium, but he must also exhibit strength and leadership, be credible while using simple words stated briefly and succinctly, be dramatic in his delivery of these statements, come across as honest and sincere in order to be believed, and appear to be cooperating with the press while maintaining control of interviews and questions. In short, the candidate must be credible, composed, and in control before the cameras.

Strategies for Conveying Credibility

Democratic presidential candidates must constantly be aware of the effects of their messages as they face the television cameras. They must assess their television performances and their credibility much as a minister prepares for and faces his or her congregation. The Democratic candidate has to be enthusiastic about his message and must present it with the zeal of a preacher. In this connection, the Democratic party has had too many ho-hum, put-you-to-sleep candidates.

To counteract this trend, Democratic presidential hopefuls must come across on television as both credible and sincere. As they become more skillful in this respect, they can begin to relax. Indeed, apprehension may well have been the reason underlying the stilted and defensive television performances displayed by past Democratic presidential candidates. Reagan, by contrast, was relaxed in front of the TV cameras, largely owing to his many years of acting experience. And his confidence only bolstered his credibility. He actually seemed to be enjoying himself as he communicated his messages to the viewers in their living rooms. Following upon this example, a Democratic presidential hopeful can enhance his credibility by using not only verbal but also nonverbal communication techniques, such as hand movements to emphasize a point.

Another technique he might use is to focus on a central theme that can be communicated repeatedly in twenty-five words or less. (Dukakis would have benefited from this technique, as he never really had a specific theme or slogan for his 1988 campaign. During one week of his campaign he emphasized one problem or area of concern, then shifted focus to another topic for the next week.) Should the theme be the economy, subsequent messages by the Democratic presidential candidate might instead include the following: "Yesterday, I was appalled at the high prices of electric bills in this country." "Yesterday, I was worried about the high unemployment rate in this country." "Yesterday, I saw my next-door neighbor get laid off from his job." "Yesterday, I gathered my thoughts. Today, I begin action. Tomorrow, a change will take place." Although the candidate might vary his simple message, his theme should remain constant so that potential voters can identify him with consistency in his campaign rhetoric. Such consistency will enhance the Democratic presidential candidate's credibility.

The Democrats will have the ultimate political opportunity in 1992 given the numerous viable, pertinent issues accessible to attack. Recall that both Eisenhower and Kennedy replaced sitting presidents of the opposing party. Faced with the opportunity to provide alternatives to the prior administrations, they did so in vivid fashion. As Stuckey points out, change is more dramatic than stability.[27] Certainly the rhetoric of both men bears this out: Eisenhower had his Great Crusade, and Kennedy, his New Frontier. Their talk of change created a dynamic that offered both further opportunity and challenge.

How can the 1992 Democratic presidential candidate become more skillful in utilizing television as a medium of communicating credibility? In most instances, paid political consultants who are trained in this field can help candidates develop expertise. Indeed, the mastery of the art of television performance can be developed much like any other skill such as playing tennis or golf. And just as one would not attempt a tennis match in the U.S. Open without prior tennis training and practice, so one should not take on a presidential race without extensive training and practice in appearing comfortable and at ease before the television camera. Thus, in addition to being credible, the 1992 Democratic presidential candidate must be composed.

Techniques of Composure

Television consultants can point out simple, yet effective, strategies for appearing at ease on TV. One tactic a candidate might use is to think of a television interview as involving two sources other than the candidate: the interviewer and the camera. That is, the candidate should begin by responding to the interviewer's questions, but then turn to the camera to make a specific point or emphasize a specific weakness in one's opponent. This strategy can be quite effective inasmuch as it gives viewers the impression that the candidate is speaking personally to them.[28] Kennedy used this technique skillfully in the 1960 presidential debates. Whereas Nixon scowled at Kennedy while responding to questions, Kennedy began by responding and looking at Nixon and the interviewer, and then turned to the camera as he addressed the nation. Although later studies of individuals who heard the debates on radio felt that Nixon had won, those who watched the televised debates clearly saw Kennedy as the winner.

Television consultants can also help presidential candidates gain confidence in dealing with negative questions, which are sure to come. Consider, for example, the following negative inquiries posed to Bill Clinton in a television interview on October 4, 1991:

- How about your lack of foreign policy experience?
- How do you account for the fact that if elected president you will be unable to complete your term as governor of Arkansas despite your promise to Arkansas voters to fulfill it?
- You have stated that you will not respond to personal "Have you ever" questions. Do you have the right to do this?

- You are a Democrat, but isn't the Democratic Congress more of a problem in this country than the president?
- You stated four years ago that you would not run for president because of personal and family problems. Why are you running now?[29]

One simple technique for defusing negative questions of this sort is to turn them into television opportunities for communicating *one's own positive message*. For example, Clinton might have responded to the fifth question by saying, "Circumstances change in all of our lives overnight—let alone over a period of years. I am running today because our country is in a Republican mess." In other words, the question should be turned around so that the Republican candidate is attacked.[30]

Of course, a novice should not attempt this on his own. Behind-the-scenes training is necessary to instill confidence in the candidate, and it must be accomplished over a period of months, perhaps even years. Indeed, the candidate must be briefed and prepared much as contemporary presidents are coached and rehearsed by their advisers before press conferences. Presidents are generally briefed in advance on most of the questions they will likely be asked; in a similar manner, political consultants can assist candidates by interacting with the news media beforehand.

Strategies of Control

Democratic presidential candidates should also be coached to provide responses to television interviewers that are suitable for the medium. In particular, as Kenneth Reich contends, presidents and candidates should answer questions in such a way that "every remark is going to be 30 seconds long," so as to "fit" the TV format.[31] Indeed, those candidates who are cognizant of the needs of the medium in terms of editing and time constraints are much more likely to have their statements aired. Again, political consultants are experts in giving the advice needed in these circumstances.

Today's presidential candidates must control and manage the news in much the same way as do the White House public relations specialists who assist the president in this respect. The president's media coverage is generally positive precisely because of White House efforts to control the news. But the White House does not need to solicit press attention to the extent that a presidential candidate might. Moreover, the president already has a staff in place to assist him in selecting the news content that is disseminated to the media. Therefore, a key element in the success of any modern-day president is the shaping of news coverage so as to ensure a favorable portrayal. Democratic presidential candidates will have to become more skillful in this area as well.

An instructive example is the following description of news management by former White House Communications Director David Gergen: "We had a rule in the Nixon [presidency] that before any public event was put on his schedule, you had to know what the headline out of that event was going to be, what the picture was going to be, and what the lead paragraph would be."[32] Such image-making is especially critical for presidential candidates inasmuch as they are subject to public scrutiny, at least to the degree that their names and campaign themes are recognized by the general public.

This point is illustrated by a frank exchange that took place in 1988 between a reporter and George Bush as president-elect:

Q: Mr. Vice-President, you seem to be dancing around just how much your administration would—will spend on housing.
A: Yes.
Q: Would you talk about that?
A: I wouldn't have phrased it that way, but that's exactly what I was doing.[33]

News management does, however, have the potential to backfire on presidents and presidential candidates. For example, Jimmy Carter (who successfully emphasized his small-town roots, his experiences as a farmer and a small businessman, and his preference for staying in voters' homes during campaign trips) and George Bush (who successfully portrayed his preference for pork rinds, backyard barbecues, and playing horseshoes) both avoided the trap Dukakis fell into by allowing himself to be pictured on television riding in an army tank while wearing an oversized combat helmet.

In the realm of electronic coverage, politicians—even as they attempt to control the news—lose a great deal of say-so about their messages and performances.[34] For example, when they ask that the television camera or tape recorder be turned off, they appear to have something to hide. But when the camera or microphone is on, politicians can no longer separate their interaction with the press from their interaction with the public. The camera unthinkingly records their flashes of anger and their shivers in the cold; it determinedly shadows them as they trip over words or down the stairs. Moreover, words and actions recorded on electronic tape are impossible to deny later. Thus, even while politicians are attempting to structure the content of media coverage, the form of the coverage itself is changing the nature of their political images. The revealing nature of television's presentation of information cannot be fully counteracted by manipulation, practice, and high-paid consultants. Often even a staged media event is more personally revealing than a transcript of an informal speech or interview. When in 1977 President Carter allowed NBC cameras into the White House for a day, the result may not have been what he intended. As John J. O'Connor reported in the *New York Times*, "Mr. Carter is a master of controlled images, and he is obviously primed for the occasion. When he isn't flashing his warm smile, he is being soothingly cool under pressure. But the camera ferrets out that telltale tick, that comforting indication of ordinary humanity. It finds his fingers nervously caressing a paperclip or playing with a pen. It captures the almost imperceptible tightening of facial muscles when the President is given an unflattering newspaper story about one of his sons."[35] Thus, control of television appearances may indeed pose problems for the Democratic presidential candidate. However, experience and advice can largely overcome these difficulties.

CONCLUSION

Television will continue to play a very important role in presidential races in the future. The medium will remain the primary means of communicating political messages; it will continue to set the national political agenda. Hence Democratic presidential candidates must place greater emphasis on disseminating simple and believable messages that are delivered in a composed, yet enthusiastic manner.

The pervasive electoral influence of television has resulted in a paradox that should be of concern to the Democratic party and to Democratic presidential hopefuls: Although the Democratic party has been noted historically for its support of the average blue-collar, working-class individual in America, recent Democratic presidential hopefuls have not come across as credible to this demographic group. By contrast, Republican presidential candidates, traditionally from a white-collar, elitist background, have been perceived on television as being more credible. This paradox should pose a specific challenge to Democratic presidential candidates in 1992 and in the future. Democratic candidates will have to communicate a viable message to all Americans and use television to their advantage in order to win. How can they do this? One way is through skillful use of television as a primary means of communicating a campaign position. And, in most instances, paid political consultants will be the vehicle through which this communication expertise can be achieved. Successful Democratic candidates cannot ignore the medium of television. They simply must be better prepared when the cameras turn their way.

NOTES

1. Robert E. Denton, Jr., *The Primetime Presidency of Ronald Reagan: The Era of the Television Presidency* (New York: Praeger, 1988).

2. David S. Broder, *Behind the Front Page* (New York: Simon and Schuster, 1987), pp. 144-145.

3. Ibid.

4. Marshall McLuhan and Quentin Fiore, *The Medium Is the Massage* (New York: Random House, 1967), p. 8.

5. Lynn B. Hinds, Windt Hinds, Jr., and Theodore Otto, *Cold War as Rhetoric* (New York: Praeger, 1991).

6. Montague Kern, *30-Second Politics: Political Advertising in the Eighties* (New York: Praeger, 1989).

7. Scott Keeter, "The Illusion of Intimacy: Television and the Role of Candidate Personal Qualities in Voter Choice," *Public Opinion Quarterly* (Fall 1987): 344-358.

8. McLuhan and Fiore, *The Medium Is the Massage*, p. 76.

9. Fay Lomax Cook et al., "Media and Agenda Setting: Effects on the Public, Interest Group Leaders, Policy Makers, and Policy," *Public Opinion Quarterly*, 47 (Spring 1983): 16-35; Jerry L. Yeric and John R. Todd, *Public Opinion: The Visible Politics*, 2nd ed. (Itasca, Ill.: F. E. Peacock Publishers, 1989), p. 61.

10. D. L. Protess et al., "Uncovering Rape: The Watchdog Press and the Limits of Agenda-Setting," *Public Opinion Quarterly*, 49 (1985): 19-37; Yeric and Todd, *Public Opinion*, p. 61.

11. Donna R. Leff et al. "Crusading Journalism: Changing Public Attitudes and Policy-Making Agendas," *Public Opinion Quarterly*, 50 (1986): 300-315; Yeric and Todd, *Public Opinion*.

12. Yeric and Todd, *Public Opinion*; Robert McClure and Thomas Patterson, "Print Vs. Network News," *Journal of Communication*, 26 (1976): 23-28; Doris A. Graber, *Mass Media and American Politics*, 3rd ed. (Washington, D.C.: CQ Press, 1988).

13. Mary E. Stuckey, *The President as Interpreter-in-Chief* (Chatham, N.J.: Chatham House Publishers, 1991), pp. 58-59; Arthur Larson, *Eisenhower: The President Nobody Knew* (New York: Scribner's, 1968), p. 165.

14. J. Leonard Reinsch, *Getting Elected: From Radio and Roosevelt to Television and Reagan* (New York: Hippocrene Books, 1988), p. 85.

15. Sig Mickelson, *From Whistle Stop to Sound Bite: Four Decades of Politics and Television* (New York: Praeger, 1989) pp. 151-152; Reinsch, *Getting Elected*,

p. 85.

16. Bill Moyers, *The Thirty-Second President* (video) (New York: PBJ, 1984); Michael Pfau and Henry C. Kenski, *Attack Politics: Strategy and Defense* (New York: Praeger, 1990), pp. 6-7.

17. Dwight D. Eisenhower, "Annual Message to Congress on the State of the Union," *Public Papers of the Presidents* (Washington, D.C.: U.S. Government Printing Office, January 6, 1955).

18. Stuckey, *The President as Interpreter-in-Chief,* p. 59; Dwight D. Eisenhower, "Inaugural Address," *Public Papers of the Presidents* (Washington, D.C.: U.S. Government Printing Office, January 20, 1953).

19. Gerald Pomper et al., *The Election of 1984* (Chatham, N.J.: Chatham House Publishers, 1985), p. 79; Denton, *The Primetime Presidency of Ronald Reagan,* p. 1.

20. Denton, *The Primetime Presidency of Ronald Reagan,* p. 2.

21. Ibid.

22. Ibid.

23. Ibid., pp. 2-3.

24. Sidney Blumenthal, *Pledging Allegiance: The Last Campaign of the Cold War* (New York: HarperCollins Publishers, 1990), p. 292.

25. Ibid., p. 294.

26. Marvin Chernoff, Interview with principal in Chernoff/Silver and Associates (public relations firm), Columbia, S.C., October 7, 1991.

27. Stuckey, *The President as Interpreter-in-Chief.*

28. Richard Davis, *The Press and American Politics* (New York: Longman, 1992); Mickelson, *From Whistle Stop to Sound Bite*; Denton, *The Primetime Presidency of Ronald Reagan.*

29. Interview with Bill Clinton, The Today Show, NBC, October 4, 1991.

30. Sidney Blumenthal, *The Permanent Campaign* (Boston: Beacon Press, 1980).

31. Bruce Itule and Douglas A. Anderson, *News Writing and Reporting for Today's Media,* 2nd ed. (New York: McGraw Hill, 1991), p. 362.

32. Hedrick Smith, *The Power Game: How Washington Works* (New York: Random House, 1988), p. 406; Davis, *The Press,* p. 138.

33. Remarks by Bush and Kemp at a news conference in the Capitol, *New York Times,* December 20, 1977, p. 88; Davis, *The Press,* p. 145; John J. O'Connor, "TV: A Full Day at the White House," *New York Times,* April 14, 1977.

34. Joshua Meyrowitz, "Lowering the Political Hero to Our Level," in Allen J. Cigler and Burdett A. Loomis, eds., *American Politics: Classic and Contemporary Readings* (Boston: Houghton Mifflin Company, 1989), p. 332.

35. *New York Times,* December 20, 1977; Meyrowitz, "Lowering the Political Hero," pp. 332-333.

9

CHARLES V. HAMILTON

Minority Politics and "Political Realities" in American Politics

For more than fifty years, at least since 1936, no single group in the United States has been more committed to a national liberal-progressive policy agenda than African Americans. Though not surprising, this fact has been insufficiently understood and its political implications inadequately appreciated. African Americans have always perceived their interests as closely identified with policies that call for enlightened socioeconomic and civil rights initiatives coming from an activist national government.

Such policies—and the social policy and civil rights agendas they spawned—have clashed at times. Although blacks have always advocated liberal, left-of-center socioeconomic policies, there have been "political realities" to contend with. Thus, for instance, during the New Deal, to which many liberals correctly trace the origins of current-day national structural progressive programs, black liberals had to come to grips with the "political reality" that required them to accept the conclusion that at least two-thirds of the black labor force would *not* be covered by the contributory social insurance system of the Social Security Act of 1935. This was so because the initial coverage did not extend to agricultural and domestic workers, among whom many blacks counted themselves. To be sure, the NAACP and the National Urban League lobbied to no avail to have those workers included. Likewise, blacks had to bite their tongues and accept the fact that the price to be paid for support of a Full Employment Bill in 1945 was *not* to insist on a "fair employment practices" provision against racial discrimination. In fact, blacks were admonished, and the sponsors of the measures agreed, not to raise the racial issue in the late 1940s, though they supported proposed liberal national health legislation. In both instances, the sponsors felt that passage would be difficult enough without the additional burden of the race issue.

THE INHIBITING OF BLACK ACTION

There is further indication that during the New Deal, some blacks were astute enough to recognize that their support of certain policies could be politically harmful. In 1937, then Senator Hugo Black introduced a Wages and Hours Bill designed to raise wages, improve the working conditions of all workers, and regulate child labor. But the bill did not contain a differential geographic wage rate, which, of course, would have hurt southern black workers. Clearly the National Urban League favored the measure, but the organization concluded that "it would be a mistake for Negroes to press too strongly for passage of the [bill]." The bill was "desirable, but inasmuch as the chief opposition to the Bill has come from the South, the Southerners would take advantage of the wide appeal from Negroes—to round up opposition based upon racial animosities."[1] In other words, there were times, more often than is generally known, or at least widely acknowledged, when blacks acquiesced to the "political realities" of the times and agreed not to play the race card, or even to appear out front on an issue. None of this was especially surprising in the years of *de jure* segregation and blatant racism. These were circumstances that, unfortunately, had to be accepted, as painful as that was.

At the same time, blacks were told that the American political system of pluralism was a complex, infinitely slow process, yielding for the most part only incremental changes, even in heightened periods of social policy breakthroughs. To some of us, this was sound, albeit bitter, counsel. You don't get all you want right away. But through the tedious, arduous process of coalition-building, bargaining, negotiating, and compromising, slowly favorable results would be realized. In its own protracted way, the American political, democratic system would yield and deliver deserved benefits to those who kept the faith, played by the rules, and relentlessly pursued the process.

For a brief time, about a decade from the early 1950s to the early 1960s, many progressive blacks (with more than a few white allies) grew tired of this accommodation to "political realities" and decided to insist that equitable civil rights policies *not* be subordinated to the achievement of liberal, progressive social policies. Therefore, during that period they supported the "Powell Amendment" (introduced by Congressman Adam Clayton Powell, Jr., of Harlem), which denied appropriation of federal funds in support of segregated or discriminatory facilities. This meant that proposed liberal aid to education, hospitals, and housing was jeopardized, because southern whites—who wanted the aid but not the desegregation—would not support it. And their support, in the face of definite northern conservative opposition, was needed. "Political realities," again. The liberal Democratic forces were rent asunder by this political dilemma. The civil rights people were being unreasonable, so the charge went. This was not a wise strategy in the long run for a majority of those (both black and white) who really needed the federal aid, the familiar argument was made. Insist on the Powell Amendment and you cut off your nose to spite your face—or something like that. It was the old argument raised during the New Deal and again in the 1940s. We don't like this, some liberals insisted, but—"political realities." And to be sure, the liberal measures failed time and again in the 1950s. (Whether that failure was avoidable under a conservative Eisenhower administration is another matter.)

Of course, these circumstances changed with the passage of the Civil Rights Act of 1964, specifically Title Six. From that point on, there was no need to make a *political* case against *de jure* segregation.

But interestingly enough, the "political realities" saga continued. As the civil rights battle was chalking up impressive victories in the courts, in Congress, and through executive decrees, there remained the daunting problem of poor socioeconomic conditions facing many African Americans. Too many had been left out of the economic mainstream for too long. Too bad that we were now reaping the results of less than *truly universal* social policies from the New Deal on. Although the important Social Security system was, indeed, beginning to incorporate more categories of workers into the first-tier social insurance system (thereby in its own way validating the pluralist theory of incrementalism), the fact was that, by the 1960s, objective conditions had changed substantially. Agricultural mechanization had rapidly transformed farming and sent millions into the cities in search of jobs. And industrial development and modernization were beginning to require new skills from a work force that a racially segregated educational system (in both north and south, incidentally) had not prepared many blacks to obtain.

Though clearly respectable on its own terms, the traditional pluralist political process had problematic consequences—a fact that needs to be acknowledged. If you make the process in one sphere too protracted, if you compromise too much in one arena, you might well be laying the ground work for disastrous consequences in other equally important arenas.

To be sure, at each juncture, with each particular set of policies, one could cite "political realities"—and to do so would be accurate. But whatever else we might know about the complex business of societal development, we surely know that there are *many* real worlds, many "political realities." And they often are not the same for everyone. People have different interests and different experiences, and are therefore politicized differently. Such differences often lead to very different worldviews about what is legitimate in the political realm. (One is reminded of the classic exchange between Dr. Martin Luther King, Jr., and the Birmingham clergymen as depicted in King's "Letter from a Birmingham Jail" in 1963.)[2]

Let's grant that the congressional testimony of the NAACP and the National Urban League in 1935 in favor of *one* federal social welfare system (as opposed to the two-tier system, which also involved a fair amount of state control in the public assistance category) was not, then, "realistic." Let's grant that the very progressive Lundeen Bill (which the Urban League strongly supported) was "too radical"—calling, as it did, for such things as the financing of greater Social Security benefits and coverage out of increased inheritance and gift taxes. And for protection for workers who refused to work as strike breakers. Let's grant that the Murray-Wagner-Dingell Bill of the 1940s, with its "cradle to grave"-like social welfare protection, was simply not going to fly.

But let's also understand *other* realities.

It is fashionable today—in the 1990s—for some conservatives to lament the growing welfare rolls, to talk about a "cycle of dependency" created by liberal social welfare policies. These conservatives rail against generations of the poor and untrained who seem to be content to live on welfare and take no responsibility for their lives. Their chant is loud and clear about a "culture of poverty" and an "underclass" pathology that gives illegitimate birth (in many senses) to a costly dependent class. They place blame squarely on liberal social policy shoulders, asserting that well-intentioned liberal policies have gone awry. But these conservatives are either historically ignorant or hauntingly disingenuous. They appear to be latter-day savants articulating truths no one else seems to grasp. Rather, it is more accurate to suggest—and so today's liberal-progressives ought to remind them constantly—that today's conservatives are late-comers to knowledge of a set of tragic consequences *they themselves* were largely instrumental in bringing about. They should be reminded of the following insight:

> The relief rolls are no substitute. Relief is a dole which robs a person of self-respect and initiative. Unemployment Compensation is more like an insurance against hard times, and as insurance may be accepted with self-respect and self-assurance.[3]

This was the admonition *of the blacks in the NAACP* in 1937! That civil rights organization *then* understood the need for viable progressive legislation that would provide employment for *all* and would be made a part of the "social insurance" system of the Social Security Act, rather than shunting people into the "public assistance" category, which was means-tested and required proof of need. This category surely could lead to a stigma on the recipients. The National Urban League likewise called for "Jobs, Not Alms." (The fashionable cry today among conservatives is to link welfare with "workfare." Blacks decades before were crying for "work.") The blacks were told to wait, not to make a fuss about being left out of social insurance coverage—"political realities." Why? Because the conservatives would not support such a move. How *right* this seemed!

The implications for American politics today should be clear. If there is a concern for truly viable socioeconomic policies that will stem the tide of growing poverty and dependency, the answers hardly lie with the conservatives. The liberal-progressive forces have always been more enlightened about what needs to be done. And the longer we procrastinate, the worse the problems become.

It was the liberals (led substantially, but by no means exclusively, by African Americans) who advocated the A. Philip Randolph Freedom Budget in 1965-1966. It was the conservatives and Republicans who responded: "Politically unrealistic." It was the liberals who called for a *meaningful* Humphrey-Hawkins Full Employment Bill in the 1970s. It was the conservatives (in both parties) who scoffed at this and said: "Too potentially inflationary."

Let there be no misunderstanding here. Each time these enlightened liberal proposals were made, there came the warning that unless action was taken, conditions would deteriorate. Pay now, or pay more later.

The time has come to bite the bullet and adopt *truly universal* programs (especially with a heavy component of gainful employment) for the truly disadvantaged. If we do little or nothing now in favor of the former, we only increase the magnitude of the problems for the latter—and for the country. And then an aroused, indignant public will cry out for harsh, draconian, "penalize the poor" measures and, even more absurd and insulting, for "tough love."

In the 1990s, American politics should be far more honest than it has been about these issues. And an unapologetic liberal-progressive Democratic party ought to be the vehicle for that mission. The Democratic party has no need to redefine its sixty-year mission. It has no need to apologize for raising and arguing for the truly enlightened policies that would benefit *all* Americans. It has only to blame itself if it continues to abdicate to the conservative "political realities" that got us into the fix we are in today. And we can go all the way back to the New Deal. (Most people, disappointingly, go back only as far as the Great Society.) The liberals understood then, and they understand now, what is needed to benefit this vast complex society. They understand but have caved in at crucial points to a conservative "political reality."

We continue to cave in—to our collective, societal peril.

Where will the majority of African American voters be in this scenario? Where they always have been: on the side of those who are more liberal and enlightened. In many respects, they have no choice. They know their interests: Election behavior studies and survey data have indicated this time and again. The point, of course, is not *where* they go but *if* they go—and how far they go. If the liberal-progressives collapse to the center, play some sort of mimicking-the-Republicans, me-too game, if they give every indication of marching to a conservative definition of "political realities," then the black voter turnout will be diminished. Neither is it necessary to make overt, racial appeals to increase that vote. (I would suggest that many blacks voted for Jesse Jackson in 1984 and 1988, not only because of his race but also because he was the most *liberal* contender. Note the distinctively lesser enthusiasm among blacks for governor Doug Wilder's abbreviated presidential candidacy, wherein the governor characterized himself as fiscal conservative.)

DANGERS—AND OPPORTUNITIES—
FOR AFRICAN AMERICANS

African Americans have always understood the dangers of raising the race flag in American politics. (Recall the National Urban League's calculated silence on the favored Wages and Hours Bill in 1938. Blacks understand that to many white people a black face is still a red flag.) This is nothing new to African Americans. They have always understood that there is a universal Social Policy Agenda and a distinctive Civil Rights Agenda. That's the value of understanding the history going back to the New Deal.[4] The Social Policy Agenda has always advocated policies that could be applied to a wide range of Americans, across racial lines—to the poor, to the unemployed, to workers uncovered by health insurance, and so on. These are not race-specific issues, although their impact is clearly greater on some groups than on others. But a poor white family in Appalachia ought to have as much interest in a liberal Social Policy Agenda as a poor black family in Harlem. The policy solutions need not and should not be articulated in racial terms. Avoidance of such terms is not only wise political strategy but fair public policy as well. This is the stance to be adopted by a liberal-progressive Democratic party—uncowed in the future, by contrast to its status all too often over the last two decades. And the challenge is to point up to the American society that these are truly universal programs that must be implemented now, not later—lest we become faced with even more formidable political realities."

As for the Civil Rights Agenda, there is no question (even leaving aside Willie Horton) that the Republicans have played on deep-seated sentiments in the electorate on this issue. President Johnson recognized this vulnerability of the national Democratic party in the South when the Voting Rights Act of 1965 was passed. In addition, there is no question that affirmative action and quotas are issues that send many whites into the Republican camp.[5] At the same time, it would be neither honest nor wise to act as if this country no longer had a problem of racism. I suggest that this issue is not as difficult to deal with politically as some observers have indicated. There are some quite sound studies that indicate the persistence of racial discrimination, especially in employment and housing.[6] The emphasis of the Civil Rights Agenda ought to be on exposing these practices in the most concrete manner.

A study undertaken in 1991 by the Urban Institute effectively demonstrated discrimination in hiring during job interviews in Chicago and Washington, D.C., in 1990. The method of investigation—used also in real estate transactions—was an old one pioneered by such groups as the Congress of Racial Equality (CORE) back in the 1940s. The method was to send in black applicants and compare the treatment given to them with that given to white applicants under as close to identical circumstances as possible. In some instances, the results—especially in the area of rental properties—were conclusive: "No apartment available" was the statement made to blacks; whites applying minutes later were told, "We have a choice for you." Both black and white applicants were test subjects supplied by the investigators.

Unfortunately, such investigative tactics must still be used, and they still provide sound evidence of racial discrimination. This discrimination must not be tolerated. Where evidence is strong, punishment should be severe, including stiff fines, revocation of licenses, and setting of specific tests to monitor future compliance. The latter instance could mean the imposition of quotas. The justification is twofold: punishment for breaking the law, and remedy of the wrong committed against victims of discrimination. There is no quicker or better way to send the message of tolerating absolutely no racial discrimination whatsoever than to be as precise in the remedy as possible. It should also be made clear that this action is the result of *specifically determined* acts of discrimination, and that the remedy (for instance, monitoring future compliance) should span a specific time period. If compliance has not been achieved by the end of this period, even stiffer penalties should be imposed.

CONCLUSION

It is often said that most people want to be "fair," that they simply do not like "quotas," which are viewed as "reverse discrimination." "Fairness" in the abstract is painless. But where the pursuit of fairness occurs in the context of specific evidence of past or current wrongdoing, then the policy of punishment and remediation ought to be equally specific.

If the Democrats leave this issue in the broad realm of "fairness," subject to the negative, zero-sum connotations attached to quotas, then the Republicans will outdo them every time. It is not in the Republican party's political interest to see this issue dealt with in a straightforward manner. Rather, precisely because that party has less to offer most whites and blacks on the Social Policy Agenda, it is likely to capitalize on innuendo, negative inference, and latent and manifest fears in its attempts to exploit the civil rights issue for political advantage. Indeed, the Republicans have little to gain from a Social Policy Agenda of deracialized politics, or from a Civil Rights Agenda of legitimate confrontation of racial discrimination.

Of even more critical significance, however, is the need for a clear distinction between a deracialized politics that addresses the liberal-progressive Social Policy Agenda and a race-specific set of policies aimed at overcoming specifically identifiable acts of racial discrimination. The two agendas carry their own sets of "political realities," and we should not presume that the coalitions available for achieving the goals of one agenda will necessarily be available for achieving those of the other. But if we clearly delineate the two, the various realities can be dealt with more honestly. Equally importantly, the necessary process of coalition-building, bargaining, and compromising can be made more comfortable. Rather than superficially lumping the two agendas together, we must recognize quite different policy requirements for dealing with the distinctly different problems.

Finally, it is my own suspicion that any significant headway we make on the Social Policy Agenda could well mitigate the tensions related to the Civil Rights Agenda. One important reason is that truly universal socioeconomic policies will give *everyone* more options in the society. And as such options increase, there will be less pressure (on both whites and blacks, albeit for different reasons) to use the identification of race as a means of gaining advantage over others.

This is my prediction and my predilection; it is thus also my prescription for a viable liberal-progressive Democratic party in the 1990s.

NOTES

1. Memo to executive secretaries from Eugene K. Jones, April 19, 1938. Library of Congress: NUL Papers, Series XII, Box 1. Quoted in Dona Cooper Hamilton, "The National Urban League During the Depression, 1930-1939: The Quest for Jobs for Black Workers," S.S.W. Dissertation (Columbia University, 1982), pp. 257-258.

2. Letter of Martin Luther King, Jr., To Eight White Birmingham Clergymen, April 16, 1963.

3. NAACP Memo from Charles Houston to Walter White, October 22, 1937. Library of Congress: NAACP Papers, Group I, Series C, Box 406.

4. See Charles V. Hamilton and Dona Cooper Hamilton, "The Dual Agenda: Social Policies of Civil Rights Organizations, New Deal to the Present," unpublished paper delivered at the Annual Meeting of the American Political Science Association, Washington, D.C., September 1991.

5. Thomas Byrne Edsall and Mary D. Edsall, *Chain Reaction: The Impact of Race, Rights, and Taxes on American Politics* (New York: W. W. Norton & Company, 1991).

6. Margery Turner, Michael Fix, and Raymond Struyk, *Opportunities Denied, Opportunities Diminished: Discrimination in Hiring* (Washington, D.C.: Urban Institute, 1991).

10

MARY LOU KENDRIGAN

Progressive Democrats and Support for Women's Issues

If it is to win presidential elections, the Democratic party dare not ignore women's issues. Women are not just another special-interest group. They constitute 53 percent of today's registered voters. In the past, men were more likely than women to go to the polls. Since 1980, however, that trend has been reversed; beginning in that year, voting participation by women has equaled or exceeded that of men. Furthermore, women are more likely than men to vote Democratic. In 1990, women gave Democrats 54 percent of their votes, whereas men gave them only 50 percent.

The gender gap is even more apparent in political attitudes. Surveys regularly show that women are more likely to express liberal views on contemporary issues.[1] Women are also more likely to favor an activist role for government in assisting the disadvantaged members of society, such as the young, the poor, the elderly, and the unemployed. In short, the women's agenda is the agenda of the Democratic party. These female political attitudes provide the potential for mobilizing other women in the electorate to vote Democratic.

In fact, if the Democratic party is going to win elections, it must speak to the concerns of women. But women's issues must be seen in a broader perspective than is usually the case. The various economic and social changes that America has experienced throughout the last two generations have had an especially pronounced impact upon women. In particular, women's lives have been profoundly altered by corporate governmental policies that facilitated the large-scale and probably permanent loss of hundreds of thousands of jobs around which traditional manufacturing industries and communities have been built.

The Democratic party needs to make clear the impact of the postindustrial society on the ordinary citizen. The postindustrial society has produced significant changes in the economy, in the structure of the family, and in the cultural values that define the ways in which we live and experience our world.[2]

The Democratic party will win elections when it is able to form coalitions of precisely those people who have been most affected by the changes of the past twenty years. Families at all but the highest income levels have fared badly indeed during the Reagan-Bush years. They receive a smaller share of total income today than they did at the start of the 1980s. The American standard of living has dropped, both in real terms and in comparison with the rest of the world. Real wages have barely increased since the 1970s. For most families, only the factor of added hours on the job, usually worked by the wife or mother, has kept real incomes from falling during this period. Thus wage levels and wage growth are crucial issues for most families, whose problems in these areas have been worsened by the insensitivities of recent Republican administrations.

The Democratic party must show that it represents the real interests of these families. In doing so, however, it must demonstrate its understanding that family structures have changed dramatically in the past twenty years. The family form changed first when the world moved from an agricultural, rural society to an industrial, urban civilization. At that time, the extended family diminished in importance and was replaced as the dominant family unit by the nuclear family. Today, we are seeing equally fundamental changes in family structure. Family forms have become increasingly diversified. The stereotypical family, with dad at work, mom at home, and two kids, is now in the minority. Married couples in which both parents work are now more common than those with only one worker. The proportion of single-parent families has also increased over the past twenty years.

The postindustrial society is characterized by fewer jobs, more structural unemployment, and a larger number of people in low-paying, part-time work. This kind of work provides no job security, no retirement benefits, and no health insurance. Moreover, in an economy in which even two incomes barely keep a family running in place, the number of single-parent families has dramatically increased in proportion to all families with children; in fact, it has more than doubled, from 12.8 percent (3.8 million) in 1970 to 27.3 percent (9.4 million) in 1988. Another measure of the changing family structure is the number of single mothers who provide for their children's sole support: In the 1980s this number jumped by 40 percent.[3]

THE DEMOCRATIC INTEREST

As noted, the people most affected by such changes are actual and potential Democratic voters. And the Democratic party can win elections only when these citizens recognize that the Democrats understand the problems they are facing and can come up with programs that will ease their burdens.

The privileged are better able to adapt to these changes, the impact of which will fall most heavily on the most vulnerable members of society—on women, children, and men of color. More than half the children in households headed by single women are impoverished, and unemployment disproportionately affects women and men of color. Even relatively well-off women are far more worried about the economy than are their male counterparts.

As Progressive Democrats must make clear, there will be no economic recovery that automatically solves the problems of the emerging society. On the contrary, long-term solutions are needed to address such deep-seated problems. These are hard economic times—not simply the downside of an economic cycle; they reflect the shift from a manufacturing to a service economy, from an industrial to a postindustrial society. Hence, improvements in the economy will not necessarily help the most vulnerable members of the society. The stock market may well go up at the same time the income of the ordinary citizen continues to go down.

In effect, the Democratic party must sound the call for a new War on Poverty; but it must also communicate its awareness that the poverty we confront today threatens the working and middle classes, too. Self-preservation, and not merely altruism, must mobilize its energies. The kind of jobs being created by the postindustrial society, unless consciously directed by democratic institutions, will scarcely provide even full-time workers with a wage sufficient to raise them out of poverty. Since 1980, poverty has increased in numbers and intensity. There are over 300,000 homeless people in the United States. One of every two children living in poverty is from a single-parent home, and that parent is almost always a mother. Children are the poorest group in our society; more than one in five live in a household whose income is below the poverty level ($12,700 for a family of four).

Furthermore, the impact of these conditions threatens a much larger proportion of our population than in the past. The working poor make up about one-third of all persons age 16 and over who live in poverty. These are the more than 6 million persons whose family incomes are below the official poverty level, even though they have worked or looked for work for at least half a year. The role of government, though always important, has become critical for this growing segment of our population.

Government must become involved in efforts to make working conditions more humane. In years past, the Democratic party has come up with new ways to use government creatively in order to improve the life of the ordinary citizen. It must do so again. In the process, it must make clear to the average voter that it is simply continuing the tradition of the Democratic party that developed Social Security, unemployment compensation, workmen's compensation, and the laws protecting the rights of unions to organize. These overwhelmingly popular programs provide both the heritage and the political base upon which a victorious Democratic coalition can be constructed—but only if the contemporary concerns of America's women are taken into account.

More people than ever will need government assistance to acquire higher wages and easier access to family care services such as child care, aid for ill or disabled family members, and assistance in completing high-school education and moving beyond high school. Jobs that pay more than the minimum wage need to be created. And discrimination, or lack of access, in education must be combated, because poor parents are disproportionately undereducated. Job-training programs will also be necessary, as the postindustrial society will require many workers to make several job changes. Indeed, workers must retrain for the kinds of skills that the economy requires. And basic equal employment opportunity is necessary to provide equal access to better jobs.

Women have been more aware than men of the role that government has played in opening the doors of economic and educational opportunity for them. In order to maintain and strengthen their support, Progressive Democrats must advocate strong affirmative action programs, equity in pay, government subsidy of daycare, and family and medical leave protection. They must also emphasize the government's role in providing benefits that were presumed to go along with "good" jobs in the industrial age—that is, unemployment, job-training, health care, and retirement benefits. Women clearly have a stake in all such programs.

One of the realities of the postindustrial society is that women must work. (Ideally, they must *want* to work.) In recent years, women have joined the labor force in steadily increasing numbers. In the 1950s, 33 percent of all women were employed; by the 1980s, that figure had risen to 50 percent. Today, a majority of married women, even those with children under 6 years of age, are working outside the home. And more than half of all mothers with infants, toddlers, and preschoolers are now employed.[4]

The most dramatic change in women's labor force participation since the end of World War II has been the entry of mothers with young children into the job market. Such women work because they are the single heads of households or because their income is needed to help pay the mortgage and provide for other costs of living in the postindustrial society. As we approach the year 2000, the level of women's participation in the labor force will continue to rise.

Meanwhile, men's real earnings have not recovered to their 1973 level. Women are bringing more income to their families, and their earnings account for a rising proportion of total family income. Among married couples at the bottom and middle of the income distribution, only the increased hours of work by the wives have kept total family incomes from falling in real terms.

Families headed by single women are at a particular disadvantage for two reasons: They face wage discrimination in the work force, and child rearing places an added burden on their chances for success in the economy.

A strong commitment to affirmative action by the Democratic party is a key to winning the support of women on these crucial economic issues. Because low wages disproportionately affect women and minority workers, combating race and sex discrimination in the labor market is critical.

To win the female constituency, then, the Democratic party must be able to explain why pay-equity (comparable worth) programs are essential in today's workplace. "Equal pay for equal work" will do little to close the earnings gap if most women continue to work jobs different from those held by men. Yet sex-linked occupational segregation would disappear only if fully two-thirds of all employed women and men changed jobs—clearly unrealistic. A much better alternative is the pay-equity strategy for raising the wages of underpaid jobs and providing employment to poor single mothers. The intent of this strategy is to remedy the systematic underevaluation of "women's work" in the marketplace.[5]

Women are still much more likely than white men to be earning low wages. And the major cause of this economic inequality is the sex-segregated job market. Half of all working women are in occupations that are over 70 percent female, and more than a quarter are in occupations that are over 95 percent female. Overall, 80 percent of employed women work in female-dominated occupations.

Thus we have a dual or segmented labor market. Women and minorities work disproportionately in low-paying industries and small firms. And in this "pink-collar" ghetto of female-dominated jobs, women work for low wages in weak or nonunion firms—in dead-end jobs with few benefits.

Occupational segregation stems from many sources: from discrimination, from cultural conditioning, even from the personal desires of the women themselves.[6] Socialization pressures and overt sexism have led many women to choose jobs traditionally thought of as "women's work." Indeed, many women have been conditioned to believe that these usually low-paying, low-status jobs are the *only* proper jobs for them.

At the same time, many employers have been unwilling to invest resources in on-the-job training designed specifically for women. They have also resisted placing women in training or management positions that will lead to higher pay. Not surprisingly, perhaps, the index of sex-based segregation in the labor market has remained about the same since 1900.

THE KEY TO ECONOMIC EQUITY

If women are to achieve economic parity, it is essential that they enter the nontraditional job market. A major example is provided by the role that women are playing in the military today. Of course, no career has been more closely identified with the essence of "machoism" than the military. And it has often been argued that military ventures and force are the essential core of politics. Furthermore, the extension of the vote to blacks after the Civil War and to 18-year-olds in our own times was defended on the grounds that citizens who were mature enough to risk their lives for their country were responsible enough to participate in its democratic processes. To the degree that this argument is valid, it demonstrates that women must be involved in military ventures or they will always be victims of male power. If women wish to be treated similarly to men in public life, they must be present in significant numbers in the military and they must also work to eliminate the provisions excluding women from combat.

Although the number of women in the U.S. military is still modest, their increased participation during the past twenty years has been dramatic. The United States military began recruiting women in large numbers when it abolished the draft in 1973. Since then, the percentage of women has grown steadily, particularly in key support, medical, engineering, and intelligence specialties. Women constitute roughly 11 percent of the 2 million members of the armed forces. Perhaps the pictures of military women returning from the Persian Gulf will continue to convince both men and women that it is also appropriate for women to deliver mail, read electric meters, work for the highway department, and participate in police work and fire fighting.

Beyond the issues of affirmative action and pay equity, women are least likely to have any of the benefits traditionally seen as part of the job package tied to a good job. Women remain disproportionately employed by smaller and less capital-intensive firms, which in turn lack the stability and resources to provide employment security. Women are less likely to get on-the-job training, less likely to have continuous work experience, and more likely to drop out of the job market. Women are less likely than men to get another job after a period of unemployment.

It follows that issues of unemployment compensation, health care, and retirement benefits are of increasing concern to women as they become a permanent part of the labor force. Programs in these areas pioneered by the Democratic party before the time when most women worked outside the home, though they have served our country well, need to be rethought in order to account for the new reality of women in the economy. Women make up about two-thirds of "discouraged workers," a term that refers to unemployed people who have ceased looking for work and are therefore not counted in official unemployment statistics. Yet the unemployment insurance program is structurally biased against these workers.[7] In the late 1970s, three-fourths of the unemployed people were covered by unemployment compensation benefits. Today, approximately one-third of those who are unemployed qualify for unemployment compensation benefits. About half of the states do not make unemployment insurance benefits available to part-time workers. At the same time, three-fourths of the jobs that have been created since 1980 have entailed part-time work. Clearly, unemployment compensation programs must be developed to deal with the problems of unemployment in this postindustrial society.

Meanwhile, women and others most in need of health benefits are least likely to have them. Thirty-four million Americans have no health insurance. Twelve million of those are children. Fewer than 60 percent of workers in households with children have employer-provided health benefits. Only 28 percent of low-wage workers in households with children have health benefits. Clearly, universal access to comprehensive health care must be guaranteed for all Americans.

Fifty percent of those who are employed in the United States receive retirement benefits from their place of employment. Social Security provides not only retirement income but also replacement income for workers who are long-term disabled (i.e., for six months or more). But Social Security payments are dependent on years of employment and wage rates, two areas in which women are disadvantaged—both because of labor market discrimination and because of the time they must spend outside the labor force in family care. In fact, this time outside the labor force conveys no eligibility for either unemployment insurance or Social Security. Clearly, these benefit programs are in need of major revision.

CHANGING NEEDS

In addition to the benefits traditionally provided by jobs, there are benefits that are increasingly needed by workers today as a result of the changes wrought by the postindustrial society. For instance, as two-income families become the norm, daycare becomes an important concern. Clearly, the Democratic party must let women know that it is strongly committed to federal funding and regulation of a comprehensive daycare program.

Such a concern is self-evident in the case of single-parent households. According to the U.S. Census Bureau, there are currently more than 1 million single fathers in the United States. In addition, most children have mothers in the workforce. By the year 2000, two-thirds of preschool children and three-quarters of older children will need child care. The lack of effective and affordable child care seriously limits the ability of women to work—a problem that is becoming increasingly pressing as we approach the year 2000.[8] The resources, facilities, and personnel for this service, which are profoundly important to both our economy and our "general welfare," are a legitimate public obligation.

Child care is so expensive that a government subsidy or a negative income tax has become a necessity. It is the fourth largest expense for most families, after housing, food, and taxes. Working parents spend about 10 percent of their annual income on it; and poor families, 25 percent. Currently, child care arrangements cost on average $3,000 per year per child. Americans spend between $75 billion to $100 billion a year on private care.

As these arrangements vary in quality, some kind of government regulation is also necessary. Child care should be regulated and monitored for health and safety, much like food processing and airplanes, because parents simply cannot undertake this task efficiently. Currently, states set standards for safety, staff-child ratios, and health issues. But it is estimated that unregulated homes outnumber regulated ones by an average of 3 to 1.

We also need infancy-care leave for one or both parents, a policy of every industrialized nation except the United States and South Africa. In this area, not much is to be expected from the Republicans. Despite his advocacy of a "kinder and gentler nation," President Bush vetoed the Family and Medical Leave Act (FMLA). This act would have entitled employees to take a reasonable amount of short-term family or medical leave without risking termination of employment.

The Democratic party should make an issue of the fact that President Bush vetoed that bill. The costs borne by workers because of childbirth, illness, and dependent care are staggering, amounting to over $100 billion annually.[9] A national leave policy would dramatically reduce such costs, because having the right to return to one's job would reduce unemployment and loss of earnings for workers who must be absent.

Sixty-seven percent of working women do not have any maternity leave, and those who do have it usually get four months or less—unpaid. For women, childbirth and child care are important factors in their absences from work. Unlike unemployment, illness, and disability, family care is not yet recognized as a reason for absence that makes wage replacement necessary—yet it clearly is. Some thought might usefully be given to extending temporary disability insurance programs, or unemployment insurance, to absence for family care.

Most of the economic and social policies stressed above are genuine "family issues" and, as such, are especially important to women. It is a tragedy that Republicans have been allowed to define "family" issues as part of the conservative agenda. Some years ago, George McGovern lamented that he, a husband and father of five, had been attacked for his stand on "family issues" by a Republican Senate challenger who was a bachelor with no personal record or responsibilities in this domain. But in politics, the rule is "define or be defined." Democrats must show that these economic and social issues form the central core of the "family" agenda for any serious political party, and thereby recapture a label and an issue that have been demagogically used by their conservative opponents.

Although it is important to view women from the same perspective as other vulnerable members of society, there are some issues that are of intensely personal (as opposed to merely sympathetic) concern to *all* women. Common gender brings together women of quite diverse economic interests. And women can more readily perceive the dimensions of sexism as well as its role in both past wrongs and present injustices. The Democratic party must make clear its commitment to use government to eliminate all those practices that challenge women's competency while also trivializing and victimizing them.

Especially when women enter nontraditional jobs, such as the legal profession, the military, or higher education, the problems of sexual harassment are severe. The Democratic party must let women know that it finds such behavior unacceptable and will back legislation to assist women in eliminating them. The consciousness recently raised in the struggle against sexual harassment increases the probability that the electoral support of middle-class women will be won, even though pressures of class and status militate in another direction.

THE ABORTION HIGH GROUND

A second important battleground on which Democrats can seize the high ground from Republicans involves the issue of abortion. Over the last few years the Republican party has played politics with women's bodies; now *Roe* v. *Wade* is in danger of being overturned. If that should occur, 14 million women in thirteen states face a high risk of not being able to obtain a legal abortion. The Democratic party must strongly defend *Roe* v. *Wade* and all government policies necessary to protect reproductive rights for women. It must also endorse the right of federally financed family-planning clinics to give women advice on abortion.

Abortion policies affect a woman's most intimate human right: the right to determine and control her own body. If democracy is based on human rights and the individual freedom to determine the decisions that affect one's life, then the right to abortion as well as the broader concern of reproductive rights are crucial to the practice of democracy. Women's bodies and their capacity for pregnancy require this specification. Otherwise, the liberties and natural rights that Locke's *Second Treatise on Civil Government*, Jefferson's Declaration of Independence, Mill's *On Liberty*, and the entire American tradition postulated as inhering in every *man's* right to his life and the fruits of the labor of his body, would indeed belong only to *males*.

It also follows that, if biology is not to determine women's destiny, then women must control reproduction to the degree that such control is scientifically possible. One of the most important issues of the abortion controversy has been that raised by feminists in regard to personal autonomy. How much power can anyone have who does not have control over her (or his) own body?

Certainly, the state must recognize and protect citizens' autonomy in determining whether to terminate a pregnancy. But this freedom is purely negative if it ratifies merely a woman's "legal" right to an abortion. In order to be truly able to choose an abortion freely, a woman must possess the ability to have and raise a child if she wants to. She therefore needs available and high-quality prenatal care, a living wage, and affordable and high-quality daycare. Hence the federal government must fully fund the

Women, Infants, and Children Supplemental Feeding Program, which currently reaches only two-thirds of those who are eligible. It is clear that the choice of abortion, as a "real" freedom, must go beyond the removal of archaic, paternalistic legal prohibitions.

POLITICAL POWER: THE KEY TO WOMEN'S ISSUES

Finally, in order to vindicate their economic, social, and personal rights, women need political power. Lincoln defined democracy as government of the people, *by the people*, and for the people. If women do not have political power, then social changes and government policies will come at their expense. Certainly, greater equality includes the removal of obstacles to greater participation in public life. The lack of representation by women in policymaking means that public policy is not as effective as it might be in creating more equality. When women are not involved in the shaping of policy, the right questions are frequently not asked.

The Democratic party must commit itself to electing more women to office and appointing more women to positions of responsibility. In spite of the increased number of women who vote, the 1990 election did not bring a major increase in the number of women officeholders. For instance, women hold only 30 seats in the 101st Congress. There are 2 women in the Senate and 28 women members of the House of Representatives—the largest number of women ever to serve in Congress. Women hold 5.6 percent of the 535 seats in Congress: 2 percent of the 100 Senate seats, and 6.4 percent of the 435 House seats. And there are still only 3 women in the governor's job. Can this be seen as progress for women? If the present rate continues, forty years from now there will only be 53 women in Congress (approximately 11 percent of the total).

Democrats must demand increased political participation by women. Feminists of both sexes must become involved in the development of policies, in their implementation, and in the evaluation of their effectiveness. What counts, however, is not simply participation but significant participation. One can have marginal impact on the political system even while participating in it. The goal is to be influential. When feminists are influential, a difference can be made. [10]

Congress must move women into leadership posts, which are currently filled exclusively by white males. Nor do women chair any of the standing congressional committees. This lack of effective influence by women was apparent in the haphazard and ultimately disastrous handling of the serious issues raised during the hearings by the Senate Judiciary Committee on the Supreme Court nomination of Clarence Thomas.

Women bring to government both backgrounds and perspectives that are different from those of men. Women in high places have elevated the importance of family issues in the workplace and in policy considerations. They have also contributed to collaborative problemsolving. They have empowered others by sharing their power. And by prizing consensus rather than conflict, they have fostered group cohesion and responsibility for ideas and decisions.[11]

CONCLUSION

If the Democratic party is going to win elections, it must appeal to the 50 percent of the population that does not vote. It must also mobilize all of the eligible voters who are struggling to deal with the changes of the past twenty years. Toward that end, it must make the moral claim that everyone should have access to food, clothing, shelter, medical care, education, and opportunities for further self-development. It must also demand that the gap between the haves and the have-nots, if not entirely eradicated, must at least be narrowed.

Public policy must be directed toward lessening the obstacles of race and gender. African Americans should have no more obstacles than the average white person. The average woman should have no more obstacles than the average male. The desired outcome is the elimination of all internal and external barriers to the attainment of full personhood by all women and minorities.

Such a program would win presidential elections and create the largest gender gap in favor of the Democratic party yet recorded.

NOTES

1. Keith T. Poole and Harmon Zeigler, *Women, Public Opinion, and Politics: The Changing Political Attitudes of American Women* (New York: Longman, 1985).

2. Suzanne Berger, Michael L. Dertouzos, Richard K. Lester, Robert M. Solow, and Lester C. Thurow. "Toward a New Industrial America," *Scientific American* 260, no. 6 (June 1989).

3. U.S. Bureau of the Census, *Money, Income, and Poverty Status in the United States* (Current Population Reports, Series P-60, no. 168, 1989).

4. Howard Hayhge, "Family Members in the Work Force," *Monthly Labor Review* 113 (March 1990): 17.

5. Sara M. Evans and Barbara J. Nelson, *Wage Justice: Comparable Worth and the Paradox of Technocratic Reform* (Chicago: University of Chicago Press, 1989).

6. Mary Lou Kendrigan, *Gender Differences: Their Impact on Public Policy* (Westport, Conn.: Greenwood Press, 1991).

7. Diane Pearce, "Toil and Trouble: Women Workers and Unemployment Compensation," *Signs* (Spring 1985): 439-459.

8. Irene Nyborg Andersen and Pamela Guthrie O'Brien, "The Child-Care Patchwork," *Ladies Home Journal*, November 1989, pp. 199-208.

9. Roberta M. Spalter-Roth and Heidi I. Hartmann, *Unnecessary Losses: Costs to Americans of the Lack of Family and Medical Leave* (Institute for Women's Policy Research, April 1990).

10. Kendrigan, *Gender Differences*.

11. Susan J. Carroll, *Women as Candidates in American Politics* (Bloomington: Indiana University Press, 1985).

11

RICHARD SANTILLAN AND
CARLOS MUÑOZ, JR.

Latinos and the
Democratic Party

On November 8, 1988, Vice-President George Bush received a significant
share of the Latino vote, which contributed to his presidential election
victory over Democratic nominee Governor Michael Dukakis of Massachusetts. Estimates of the actual percentage of Latino votes for Bush nationwide range from 40 to 55 percent. Yet, regardless of the actual figure, the
unmistakable fact remained that the Republican party had continued to make
important inroads among Latino voters, who in the past usually had been
viewed as faithful supporters of Democratic candidates.

The growing support of Latino voters for Republican presidential
contenders during the 1980s caught many Democratic leaders by surprise.
However, a close examination of this electoral trend reveals that the GOP
had been methodically chipping away at the formerly solid block of loyal
Democrats for nearly four decades. This increasing Latino support cannot
be dismissed as a mere political fad; rather, it must be seen as the result of
a long-term effort by the Republican party to establish a new relationship
between the GOP and Latino voters. This ongoing Republican initiative has
been, in large part, a direct political response to the increasing importance
of the Latino vote in several key electoral vote states.

This chapter is divided into two main sections. The first part examines
the erosion of Latino support for the Democratic party over the past several
decades, especially among Mexican Americans and Puerto Ricans.
Politically speaking, the Democratic party continues to view the Latino
community as a homogeneous interest group whereas the GOP treats the
Latinos as a socially diversified community. As a result of these opposing
political frames of reference, Republican candidates have been more

politically flexible than their Democratic counterparts in keeping pace with the rapid demographic changes taking place within the Latino community. Latino voters, moreover, have developed an electoral pattern of switching back and forth between both parties depending on the personalities of the candidates, the strategies and public relations involved, and the amount of attention committed by the candidates to Latino issues.

The second part of this chapter discusses what the Democrats must do in order to recapture the confidence and elective support of Latino voters. The Democrats have a choice. The 1990s can bring either continued neglect and false promises or a significant change that transcends cosmetic accommodation and truly integrates diverse Latino concerns into the party program.

POLITICAL TUG-OF-WAR

Prior to the Great Depression of the 1930s, large segments of the Mexican American community identified with the Republican party. At that time, the GOP was considered to be more socially progressive than the southern-based Democratic party on the issues of civil rights, electoral reform, women's suffrage, and regard for family-oriented farms and small businesses. Abraham Lincoln is believed to have campaigned among Mexican American voters in California during the presidential election of 1860. In New Mexico, the Republican party was known as the Hispano party until the 1930s. And in California as well as Colorado, nearly half of the Mexican American elected officials between 1860 and 1910 were Republicans.

The Great Depression, however, was widely viewed as marking the turning point for Latino support for the Democratic party. Herbert Hoover, the Republican president at the time, believed that the solution to the economic crisis was reduced federal spending. Among the drastic actions he took was federal implementation of the Repatriation Program, under which thousands of Mexicans (including numerous U.S. citizens) were forcefully deported from the United States. Many of the Mexican Americans who remained in the country experienced increased prejudice and discrimination; and they also suffered severe social and economic hardships resulting from a lack of steady work.

The election of Democrat Franklin Delano Roosevelt and the inauguration of his New Deal were viewed by many Mexican Americans as a refreshing alternative to Hoover and his unfair domestic policies. Thus born was the idea that the Republicans were for the rich and the Democrats were for the common people. In the 1930s many Mexican Americans found employment in various federal job programs, which further deepened their attachment to the Democratic party.

Certain sectors of the Mexican American community did not, however, have to depend on the federal government for work. In particular, Mexican American farmers and businesspeople who were self-employed had less reason to shift their political allegiance. As a consequence of this economic self-reliance, Mexican Americans in parts of Arizona, New Mexico, and Colorado tended to remain loyal Republicans over several generations. The majority of these Mexican American Republicans continue today to identify with the moderate wing of the party.

By contrast, both World War II and the Korean War consolidated Mexican American support for the Democratic party, largely because of the nationalistic pride of the nation and the distinguished service record of Mexican Americans in those conflicts. Furthermore, the G.I. Bill, which was passed during a Democratic administration, made it economically possible for many Mexican American veterans to attend vocational school, acquire new job skills, and purchase homes outside the Mexican community. These new-found social opportunities, along with new civil rights legislation, further cemented the political bond between the Democratic party and the Mexican Americans residing in the Southwest and the Midwest. During the presidential campaign of 1952, however, the GOP took its first systematic steps to woo back Mexican Americans and other Latinos after an absence of twenty years.

The presidential campaigns of 1952 and 1956 matched two very different men. General Dwight D. Eisenhower had been a professional soldier all his life, whereas Adlai Stevenson was a career politician. In California, Mexican Americans formed a group called Latin-American Veterans and Volunteers for Eisenhower-Nixon. Finding Mexican American men who would support Eisenhower during the Korean War was not difficult. Many of these veterans were convinced that Eisenhower's military experience and leadership could help end the war in Korea. Mexican American involvement in the two Eisenhower campaigns was primarily defined by local efforts in California, Texas, New Mexico, and Illinois. In contrast, there appear to have been no organized Mexican American outreach programs in either of Stevenson's campaigns in California or other key states. Thus, in the early 1950s, the GOP moved slightly ahead of the Democratic party by recognizing Mexican Americans as part of its overall presidential strategy. In the next two presidential campaigns, however, the Democratic party recaptured the political momentum from the Republican party and further tightened its electoral grip on the Mexican American community.

The presidential races of 1960 and 1964 were political disasters for the Republican party because of divisive philosophical and platform disagreements between moderates and conservatives within the party. This disunity contributed to the Democratic victories of John F. Kennedy in 1960 and Lyndon B. Johnson in 1964, and represented a major setback in Republican efforts to reach out to Mexican American and Puerto Rican voters. The division within the leadership of the GOP also resulted in a lack of unity among some Latinos, who were no longer inclined to back one Republican candidate. For instance, conservative Cuban Americans, a small but rapidly emerging new group inside the GOP, partly blamed the moderate Eisenhower-Nixon administration for losing Cuba to the Communists and, therefore, were attracted to Goldwater's staunch anticommunism. Furthermore, a sizable group of moderate Republican Mexican Americans in the Southwest and some Puerto Ricans on the east coast supported Rockefeller in both 1960 and 1964. Many Mexican American and Puerto Rican Republican leaders were deeply impressed with Rockefeller's knowledge of Latin American culture and his fluency in Spanish.

Senator Kennedy possessed several distinct cultural advantages over Nixon that attracted Mexican American voters in California and elsewhere. These advantages included his Catholic, immigrant background, the ability of his wife to speak basic Spanish, and the large and extended families within the Kennedy clan. In addition, Kennedy's war record as a hero appealed to many newly established Mexican American organizations, the majority of which had been founded by World War II veterans. Most important, the 1960 Democratic convention was hosted by the city of Los Angeles, which provided the Mexican American leadership access to Kennedy's campaign staff. The political dialogue that ensued eventually led to the creation of "Viva Kennedy" clubs in thirteen states in the Southwest, the Midwest, and on the east coast.

Nixon never really had adequate opportunity to incorporate Mexican American and other Latino groups into his 1960 campaign, largely owing to the aforementioned rift inside the Republican party. Active participation by Mexican Americans was pretty much limited to the "Arriba Nixon" clubs located in southern California.

Many of the internal factors that had seriously undermined the Republican party's Latino outreach program in 1960 surfaced once again in the 1964 presidential race. Nevertheless, Goldwater won a bitter victory over Rockefeller at the 1964 Republican convention held in San Francisco. A Californian, Manuel Ruiz, Jr., was asked to direct the national Latino effort for the Goldwater-Miller ticket. Several groups were formed in California, including the Mexican-American Committee for Goldwater-Miller, Latin

Americans for Goldwater, Hispanic Citizens for Goldwater, and Latino Youth for Goldwater.

In contrast to the 1960 Kennedy campaign, Mexican American support for President Johnson in California and elsewhere can best be described as politically soft, even after the establishment of a national "Viva Johnson" campaign. The tragic assassination of President Kennedy in November 1963 had dampened Latino interest in the 1964 contest, and the expected Johnson victory, unlike the close race in 1960, seemed to minimize the national importance of the Mexican American and Puerto Rican vote. As predicted, President Johnson won in a massive landslide over Barry Goldwater.

In retrospect, it can be seen that the Kennedy and Johnson "Viva" movements of the early 1960s introduced a new era in the evolutionary development of Mexican American politics in the United States. Whereas the GOP's Latino efforts were primarily limited to a few scattered states in the 1950s, the Kennedy and Johnson campaigns viewed the Latino community as a national constituency from coast to coast. President Johnson, for example, established the Inter-Agency on Mexican-American Affairs, the first federal agency designed to provide policy guidance to congressional lawmakers and the White House concerning the needs of Mexican Americans.

Ironically, both the Kennedy and Johnson administrations eventually came under political fire from a growing list of Mexican American Democratic leaders for a host of reasons, including the failure to make higher-level appointments of Mexican Americans, a string of broken campaign promises, the lack of adequate federal funds to remedy the pressing problems plaguing the barrios, and the breakdown of communication between the White House and some Mexican American national organizations. The Johnson administration, as a result of this political pressure, hosted a national conference on Mexican American issues in El Paso, Texas, in 1967. The Democratic party clearly designed the conference to diffuse this volatile situation involving the Mexican American leadership, particularly with the 1968 presidential election just around the corner. But its perceived neglect was viewed by some of the party's strongest Mexican American supporters as a "taking the Mexican American vote for granted" syndrome.

By dropping the Mexican American political football in the mid-1960s, the Democrats had given the GOP a second chance to narrow the partisan gap in the contest for Latino votes. As the beneficiary of this newfound political fortune, the Republican party wasted no time in taking the initiative; in 1966 it established its now-famous "Southwest Strategy." The Republican leadership theorized that as Mexican Americans moved upward on the economic ladder, they would increasingly identify with the economic views of the GOP because of their higher social status. The 1966 campaigns of Ronald Reagan for California governor and John Tower for the U.S. Senate in Texas were viewed as political litmus tests regarding this GOP assumption concerning Mexican American middle-class voters. Both candidates appeared before numerous Mexican American civic groups and stressed the work ethic and entrepreneurial spirit of the Mexican American culture—and both won. Reagan and Tower each received nearly 30 percent of the Mexican American vote in their campaigns in California and Texas, which greatly contributed to their victories—including the upset of an incumbent Democratic governor in California. Several key Mexican American Democratic leaders had warned their party for many years about such Republican efforts and had stressed the need to counteract them. Their pleas for support and funds for a viable Mexican American strategy had fallen on deaf ears at Democratic headquarters.

As expected, the GOP was ecstatic over its success in attracting a high percentage of middle-class Mexican American voters in such critical states as California and Texas. Convinced that it had established a political beachhead among middle-class Mexican Americans, it moved rapidly after 1966 to widen its geographical base for the upcoming 1968 presidential election.

This presidential campaign was the next logical opportunity for the GOP to field-test its "Southwest Strategy" nationwide. Several state directors were hired to coordinate "Viva Nixon" operations including those in the key states of California, Texas, Florida, and Illinois. The Democratic party, meanwhile, found itself seriously divided between the hawks and the doves regarding the war in Vietnam. Rank-and-file Mexican American Democrats were correspondingly divided in 1968 and 1972 by age and ideology.

The campaigns of Humphrey and McGovern did establish "Viva" outreach programs, and both candidates promised to appoint Mexican Americans to key positions in their administrations. In reality, however, these campaign promises by the Democrats in 1968 and 1972 were merely token gestures. Further hurting the Democratic party's chances was the emergence of La Raza Unida party in the late 1960s and early 1970s. In California, members of La Raza Unida publicly jeered several Democratic leaders. The incident received widespread news coverage throughout the nation, in part because Democratic leaders were not accustomed to unfriendly Mexican American crowds. Meanwhile, the Republican party was spending considerable amounts of money and time in an effort to attract the Latino vote nationally, particularly in connection with the 1972 election.

The Democratic party failed to recognize the Republican party's inroads into the Mexican American community and, again, simply dismissed the notion that a new realignment was taking place in the sunbelt states. In the 1970s the GOP took further political advantage of Democratic inaction and significantly expanded its Latino electoral base by introducing a series of innovative tactics designed to fine-tune the "Southwest Strategy." Its first tactic under the Nixon administration was the much-heralded appointment of Mexican Americans to head the U.S. Treasury, the Office of Economic Opportunity, and the Small Business Administration.

As a second GOP strategy in 1971, the Inter-Agency on Mexican-American Affairs was renamed the Committee on Spanish-Speaking Affairs. This name change was obviously designed to broaden Nixon's political base in the Puerto Rican and Cuban communities. A third move was the GOP's offer to subsidize Mexican American redistricting activities in the early 1970s with technical resources and financial assistance. The Republican party clearly understood redistricting to be an issue that had historically strained the delicate relationship between Mexican Americans and the leadership of the Democratic party. The traditional Democratic practice had been to fragment the Mexican American community into as many districts as possible in order to ensure Mexican American votes for Anglo incumbents. Having recognized this inherent conflict, the GOP took advantage of the situation by offering to help Mexican American organizations spearhead redistricting battles in California and Texas. As a fourth tactic, the Republican National Committee established the Republican National Hispanic Assembly (RNHA) at both the national and local levels—including in California, Texas, Florida, New York, and Illinois. The establishment of the RNHA within the Republican party structure was another clear signal to the Latino community that the GOP seriously viewed it as an integral part of the national political scene.

President Gerald R. Ford was sworn into office after the resignation of Richard Nixon in August 1974. Throughout most of his political life, Ford (unlike Nixon, Goldwater, and Rockefeller) had minimal social interaction with Latinos. His already slim chance to win over Latino voters was seriously crippled by several factors, including outright political blunders. As in the early 1960s, the GOP was divided between moderate and conservative factions. Not surprisingly, this ideological bickering inside the party leadership created disunity among Latino Republicans, even though Ronald Reagan had established strong links with the Republican Latino community nationwide while serving as governor of California between 1966 and 1974.

The Democratic party took advantage of this Republican infighting by repeating Reagan's primary campaign charges against Ford in the general election. On the Democratic side, Jimmy Carter (unlike previous Democratic presidential candidates) enjoyed overwhelming support from a broad base of Latino voters, including some second-generation Cuban Americans. The Carter campaign established a national Latino effort with state offices in more than twenty states, thereby completely eclipsing the Republican Latino effort; and as a result, Carter captured nearly 85 percent of the Latino vote nationwide (including in California). This landslide victory in Mexican American and Puerto Rican precincts dealt a serious blow to the Republican "Southwest Strategy," which had already been left in a shambles by national GOP internal battles and the effective Latino outreach program established by the Democrats. Some Democratic leaders went so far as to declare the "Southwest Strategy" to be political history. Unfortunately for the Democratic party, this political obituary was premature as Ronald Reagan commenced in 1979 his initial successful try for the White House.

Reagan was clearly the political beneficiary of three decades of Latino outreach efforts by the GOP. The Reagan campaigns of 1980 and 1984 borrowed several successful strategies from past Republican campaigns. These included Republican endorsements by disgruntled Latino Democrats, a direct appeal to the Cuban community and to middle-class Mexican Americans, the use of Latino film and television personalities in political advertising, and efforts to reach out to the Latino business sector.

Reagan's appeal to Latino votes in general and Mexican American votes in particular was primarily based on ideology rather than on campaign pledges of more Latino federal programs and appointments. His particular strategy focused on three main themes. The first of these centered around religious issues. The Reagan camp repeatedly endorsed prayer in public schools, supported tax credits for private educational institutions, and expressed opposition to both abortion and federal funding for family-planning programs. In part, these issues were selected by the GOP to take advantage of the perceived religious cultural conservatism among many Latino Catholics. The second theme revolved around the virtues of patriotism and the necessity for a strong national defense. Reagan appealed to the Cuban community by making anti-Castro speeches and playing up the Soviet threat in Central America. He also praised and honored several Mexican American Medal of Honor winners at the White House. Along the campaign trail, moreover, he depicted the Democrats as being soft toward communism.

The final Reagan theme involved lauding Latino culture as supported by the twin pillars of the work ethic and the entrepreneurial spirit—the same successful theme he had used during his 1966 campaign for California governor. Mexican American Democrats found themselves almost politically voiceless in the two elections of 1980 and 1984 because of their fragmentation among numerous camps including those of Edward Kennedy, Jimmy Carter, Walter Mondale, John Anderson, Jesse Jackson, and Jerry Brown. As a consequence of this internal political squabbling, both Carter in 1980 and Mondale in 1984 were unable to launch an effective Latino campaign. In contrast, Reagan gained the highest voting percentage among Latinos of any Republican presidential candidate since the 1930s.

By the end of Reagan's second term, however, this unprecedented Latino support had begun to slip away. A growing number of Latino Republican leaders were now openly expressing extreme disappointment over Reagan's poor record of Latino appointments, including the total absence of Latinos in his cabinet. And it was no secret that many Mexican American and Puerto Rican Republicans couldn't wait for the Reagan era to end so that they could support Vice-President George Bush in 1988.

Like Reagan in 1980 and 1984, Vice-President Bush did not, however, openly speak out on specific Latino issues such as bilingual education, the English-only movement, voting rights legislation, immigration, and Central America. Instead, he focused on the general themes of a strong defense, the war against crime and drugs, and the need for a "kinder and gentler nation."

The Dukakis campaign, too, lacked a strong national Latino effort. Most of his campaign's Latino outreach was spearheaded by elected and appointed Latino Democratic officials; but that strategy somewhat backfired because many of these officials were busy with their own elections and thus had neither the time nor the resources to devote a full-scale effort to the Dukakis campaign. In addition, many key Latinos nationwide had supported the primary campaign of Jesse Jackson, who they believed was speaking directly to the issues confronting the Latino community. Subsequently, many of Jackson's Latino supporters were angered by the way the Dukakis campaign treated Jackson after the Democratic convention and chose not to participate in the Dukakis fall campaign, thus clearly hurting the Democrats' efforts in the Mexican American and Puerto Rican communities.

The Democrats also neglected to take political advantage of Bush's blunder when he referred to his Mexican American grandchildren as the "little brown ones." In fact, Latino Republicans were able to defuse this potential embarrassment by declaring that Bush's comments were but affectionate in nature.

LATINOS AND THE DEMOCRATIC PARTY: 1992 AND BEYOND

The historical relationship between Latinos and the Democratic party has been tenuous at best. The party leadership has failed to prioritize issues of specific relevance to Latinos. And ignorance of Latino realities continues to permeate all levels of the Democratic party apparatus, from rank and file to leadership at the local, state, and national levels. Only in those southwestern states such as Texas, California, and New Mexico where there is a visible Mexican American presence in terms of elected and appointed officials as well as high demographic profiles is there real awareness of Latino needs, issues, and realities. (Latinos now number over 22 million nationally.) More generally, however, Latino concerns are relegated to secondary symbolic responses. Indeed, Democratic party candidates tend to offer mere lip service to Latino concerns and issues—and then only when they happen to be campaigning in Latino barrios during election time.

The sole instance in recent party history where Latino issues (such as bilingual education and immigration) played a significant part in a presidential candidate's platform was during Jesse Jackson's candidacy in the primary elections of 1988. None of those issues, however, were likewise incorporated into Dukakis's presidential campaign. In fact, the Dukakis campaign never placed any particular priority at all on developing a strong, well-funded, and well-supported staff to mobilize the Latino vote. The party leadership apparently assumed that it could count on the Latino vote simply because of Dukakis's immigrant background and his ability to speak some Spanish. Perhaps it further assumed that the Latino vote that had gone to Jackson during the primary elections would automatically transfer to Dukakis. No doubt some of it did, but many who voted for Jackson did not bother to vote again in the November election.

CONCLUSION

What will it take for the Democratic party to make itself relevant to Latinos? First, it needs a new progressive leadership that understands the complexities of the Latino experience in the United States. And, second, it must develop a vision of a multiracial and multicultural democracy for the twenty-first century that goes beyond the traditional liberalism forsaken by the Democratic party since the emergence of Bush's "New World Order."

Latinos, or "Hispanics," are wrongly perceived as a heterogeneous white ethnic Spanish-speaking minority group—a misperception especially underscored by the U.S celebration of the 1992 Columbian Quincentenary. The term "Hispanic" emphasizes the white European culture of Spain because it refers to "lovers of Spanish culture." Latinos referred to as "Hispanics" are therefore being promoted as Americans who are direct descendants of the Spaniards, who in turn colonized and brought European civilization to the Americas. In reality, however, the majority of Latinos are "mestizo,"—a multicultural and multiracial people whose collective experience is rooted in the indigenous cultures of the Americas, Africa, and Asia. Very few are descendants of Spanish immigrants.

The Democratic party leadership has historically been ignorant about the complexities of the Latino experience in the United States. As noted, Latinos represent a multitude of different cultural groups, each with its own unique history and class realities. All may have the Spanish language in common, but not all share the same degree of racial and class inequality.

After Native Americans, Mexican Americans are the oldest inhabitants of North America. They make up 70 percent of the Latino population in the United States. The majority constitute a working class that for the most part remains a continuing source of cheap labor. They are an indigenous mixed-race people who became "Americans" through the military conquest of the Mexican nation in 1836 and again in 1846-1848. Those wars resulted in the loss of half of Mexico's territory to the United States; what was then northern Mexico became the southwestern United States.

Further complicating matters is the fact that Mexican Americans are products of contemporary Mexican immigration into the United States. Some can therefore trace their roots to the 1400s, when the Spaniards colonized New Mexico; others are aware of their families' entry into the United States during the Mexican Revolution of 1910-1920; and still others are children born of more recent Mexican undocumented immigrant workers.

The other 30 percent of Latino peoples are comprised (in order of largest to smallest populations) of Puerto Ricans, Cuban Americans, Central Americans, and other Latin Americans. Puerto Ricans are the poorest of all Latinos. They became colonial subjects and U.S. "citizens" after the United States waged war against Spain in 1898. (The United Nations continues to classify Puerto Rico as a colony of the United States, although the U.S. government classifies it as a U.S. commonwealth.) Cuban Americans are mostly products of the anti-Communist immigrants who fled to the United States after the 1959 Cuban Revolution. They are the most affluent Latinos, although a small poverty sector has become visible in the last ten years. Central Americans, notably Salvadorans, are the more recent immigrants. Most are in the United States as a consequence of political repression and civil war in their homelands. Most are also of poor working-class status. Immigrants from other Latin American nations, too, have come to the United States from diverse class backgrounds and situations.

With the exception of Cuban Americans, the vast majority of Latinos are part of the U.S. working class. But the diversity of cultures and ideologies they represent makes it difficult to mobilize them effectively according to one racial or ethnic political consciousness. Ideologically, for example, Cuban Americans are far more conservative than Mexican Americans. The former vote Republican for the most part and often are members of the U.S. middle class, whereas most Mexican Americans are working class and have traditionally voted Democratic (although, as noted, an increasing number have voted Republican in recent elections).

There is only a slim chance that the Democratic party will become a party that represents the majority of Latinos in the United States in 1992. The party leadership has decided to place the issues important to the middle class at the forefront of party concerns. But issues of racism, sexism, multicultural and multilingual education, workers' rights, immigrants' rights, public and mental health (e.g., AIDS, drugs, alcoholism), and many more affecting the daily lives of Latinos and people of color as a whole are not even being discussed, much less debated, during the 1992 presidential campaign.

If the Democratic party is to lead the nation in the future, it must go beyond "seeking common ground with the President and the Republicans,"[1] to quote House Speaker Thomas Foley. Indeed, it must seek common ground with those who have been victimized by the domestic and foreign policies of the Reagan-Bush New World Order. A new party leadership is needed with the courage to reprioritize the party's agenda. The human needs of the most oppressed members of the working class—people of color, the poor, women, gay and lesbian people, youth, and the homeless—must replace the needs of the corporations. The party cannot lead if it does not accept two realities: that the United States is a multiracial and multicultural nation, and that people of color will be the majority population in the twenty-first century.

NOTES

1. Thomas Foley, in *The Democratic Party Response to President Bush's 1992 State of the Union Address*, January 28, 1992.

PART THREE

A Politics of Substance

12

SAMUEL BOWLES, DAVID M. GORDON,
AND THOMAS WEISSKOPF

A Democratic Economic Policy

As communism crumbles and U.S. capitalism continues to fail to meet the basic needs of Americans, economic democracy is an idea whose time has come. It makes economic sense. It is consistent with deeply held values. And the steps necessary to implement economic democracy could garner the support of substantial majorities of U.S. citizens. This is our argument.

By a democratic economy we mean an economy that guarantees to all citizens basic rights to an economic livelihood; that offers to all citizens opportunities for participation in making the economic decisions that affect their lives, either directly or through elected representatives; that puts an end to the economic dependency of working people on the whims of their employers; and that eliminates the economic dependency of women on men and removes racial, sexual, and other forms of discrimination throughout the economy and in access to jobs and housing. We mean, in short, an economy in which citizens and workers can much more nearly become the authors of their own histories.

Our support for such an alternative system is based on two important considerations: We believe that greater democracy and greater equality are desirable goals per se, and we believe that a more democratic and more egalitarian economy would dramatically reduce the enormous waste in our present economic system. We think that rightwing economics—which

---

Adapted from Samuel Bowles, David M. Gordon, and Thomas Weisskopf, *Beyond the Waste Land: A Democratic Alternative to Economic Decline* (Garden City, N.Y.: Anchor Press/Doubleday, 1983), pp. 187-217. Published by permission.

appeared so self-confident throughout the 1980s—will eventually be seen for what it really is: a program to enrich the wealthy at the expense of everyone else, justified by outdated economic ideology. But we cannot counter something with nothing. The development of a democratic and egalitarian alternative is long overdue.

We favor a fundamental restructuring of both the political and the economic systems in the United States. But such changes do not come overnight; they can result only from long-term changes in the political-economic environment. In the meantime, the crushing cost of mounting poverty will not wait; the effects of environmental degradation are already hitting home; the thawing of the cold war opens up new opportunities and calls for new initiatives in both domestic and foreign policy.

Because none of us can afford to wait until more fundamental political change occurs, we seek to steer a deliberately realistic course, stressing gradual and feasible steps for improvement rather than outlining a complete blueprint for an ideal new economic and political order. Nothing we propose here has not already been applied in one form or another, either on a small scale in the United States or on a national scale elsewhere in the world—and with good effect.

The democratic economics we advocate is nonetheless uncommon in the realm of conventional policy discourse in the United States. The prevailing debate swings largely between the poles of rightwing and centrist policy approaches. The differences between the two are not great, as we shall see, and neither offers real solutions to our economic problems. It is time to expand the range of policy alternatives.

Initially we outline the basic objectives and underlying logic. Then we turn to the manner in which a democratic program would address the macroeconomic issues of deficits, productivity growth, and investment. Finally, we consider how to overcome some potential barriers to the implementation of a democratic economics in the United States.

To have both appeal and promise, an economic program must pursue a compelling set of objectives, address the emergent realities it will confront in its period of testing and application, and build upon a coherent and practicable economic logic. From each of these three angles, we examine here a democratic economics for the year 2000.

THE OBJECTIVES OF A DEMOCRATIC ECONOMICS

First, a democratic economics seeks sustainable improvements in living standards. Expanding knowledge and advancing productive skills will permit an improvement in people's well-being—whether through enhanced free time or greater access to goods and services. But these gains must also be sustainable; they cannot be bought on time. Gains in living standards today must be consistent with maintaining our natural surroundings so that our immediate material pleasures do not impose environmental nightmares on our children and succeeding generations. Similarly, material improvements based solely on borrowing from the rest of the world are unsustainable; neither we nor our children can continue to run up a tab with others around the globe.

Second, a democratic economics should enhance democracy and community at home and cooperation abroad. The political life of our society—ranging from family relations to global peace—hinges primarily on economic policy choices. Some kinds of economic policy come with a heavy price tag; by promising economic gains at the expense of escalating racial injustice, or increasingly unaccountable power in the hands of the rich, or intensifying global inequality and international rivalry, rightwing approaches tear at our social fabric and invite domestic and international conflict. We believe that a democratic economic program can achieve its objectives through a reduction in conflict, not through its exacerbation—by securing basic democratic rights and by making power democratically accountable to those affected. If a democratic program can foster not only sustainable improvements in living standards but also deeper democracy, stronger communities, and enhanced global cooperation, it will be doubly blessed.

Third, a democratic economics seeks greater fairness. Most people will differ on exactly what constitutes economic justice, but few will disagree about the unfairness of the rich having more than they can reasonably spend while others forgo such fundamental necessities as health care, housing, and nutrition. We think that an economic program should place an especially high priority on improvements in the living standards and economic rights of those with the most pressing material needs. By these standards, it makes more sense to measure the economic effectiveness of such an economic program by the growth rate of the average income of middle- and lower-income households than by the growth rate of total income per capita. As we saw during much of the 1980s, the latter is perfectly consistent with rapid increases in the incomes of the very rich alongside stagnating or deteriorating living standards for everyone else. Such an outcome cannot be tolerated by a democratic economics.

CHANGING ECONOMIC REALITIES

At first blush, these objectives may seem remote from the headline-grabbing economic issues of the day in the United States—particularly the twin deficits of the federal government budget and foreign trade. Yet the manner in which we address these deficits in the short term will commit the United States to an economic trajectory whose consequences over the longer term will be more or less sustainable, more or less fair, and more or less conducive to democracy and community at home and to global cooperation abroad. We cannot easily assess the potential impact of any economic program, much less that of a democratic economics, unless we face some new economic realities that will characterize the world of the twenty-first century. Among these new realities, which will radically alter certain critical assumptions of prevailing economic policy debates, three are particularly important.

The End of Pax Americana

The United States must learn to live with the end of its global empire. We never advertised our empire to the degree that the British celebrated theirs, but the era of Pax Americana was no less imperial than the age of Pax Britannica. In the early 1950s, "we" were Number One while the rest of the world was weaker, poorer, and often falling further behind. Where necessary we got what we wanted by shaking the iron fist, whether for Middle Eastern oil or global markets. American power underwrote the American standard of living.

This landscape now has the nostalgic feel of a 1950s movie. Few realists doubt that the age of Pax Americana has ended, at least temporarily. But the idea of empire dies hard, and its legacy continues to inform our economic policy. Democrats and Republicans alike still pursue the vain project of restoring American primacy. Advocates of "preparedness" prefer the military route back to global domination, while those favoring economic means focus on revising U.S. international "competitiveness."

The military route is hardly promising. In a heavily armed and polycentric world, military dominance is not possible and its pursuit is a recipe for war. Nor does it guarantee national security, because the interventions and arms build-ups it requires would impose huge costs on the United States, thus hastening our economic decline and exposing us to increasing risk of international retribution or isolation.

Advocates of an economic route to restored global power would agree that the economic costs of the military strategy are unsustainable. But in their preoccupation with competitiveness, they mistake keeping ahead of the Joneses with economic well-being. Like strategists of military dominance, advocates of competitiveness fail to address the two most fundamental challenges of today's global economy: first, how to coordinate the macroeconomic policies of the leading economies and, second, how to foster the growth of living standards throughout the world. Both are essential to maintaining the stable growth of world markets, to reversing the trend toward north-south polarization, and to reducing global tensions and national rivalries. Neither of these challenges will be addressed as long as we adopt a zero-sum approach to the global economy—promoting better-than-thy-neighbor policies in the mistaken belief that the best way to defend jobs in Detroit is to impede their creation in Guadalajara. But we are unlikely to reject this global version of the zero-sum illusion as long as "preparedness" and "competitiveness" frame our global objectives.

The End of Pax Patriarcha

Unlike "empire," which haunts our political conscience but is seldom invoked from the electoral podium, "the family" (always in the singular) is what "we" are repeatedly urged to protect. But "the family" as an economic institution is undergoing such rapid change that its traditional economic tasks—income redistribution and child rearing—are in danger of abandonment. This is the second new economic reality that any economic program must face.

The traditional family, with breadwinning husband and homemaking wife, was once the standard. But today fewer than one in five adults lives in ways that fit this description.[1] The economic stakes involved are staggering. Even today, more income is redistributed between men and women within the family than by the welfare state.[2] And the unpaid domestic labor of child rearing and housework exceeds by a factor of four the labor employed in the entire goods-producing sector of the U.S. economy.[3] Indeed, domestic production and redistribution constitute our "infra-economy."

As a result of changes in that infra-economy, the means by which women and children gain access to material necessities is undergoing a profound shift. Among the increasing number of women who are not married, more and more depend entirely on their own earnings. The result is an increase in the numbers of well-off single males and hard-pressed single women—often mothers with sole responsibility for raising children.[4]

As a further consequence, much of the exchange that characterized the traditional family—income sharing in return for full-time child raising—is no longer occurring. The income is not being exchanged, and the children are not receiving adequate care and nurturance. The odds that the traditional family could be reinstated—with women pulling back out of the labor force and returning to economic dependence upon their husbands—are about as high as for the restoration of U.S. global domination. Neither is in the cards, and neither is an objective worthy of a free society. Economic policy must urgently find ways of replacing the economic functions that traditional family households fulfilled before entire new generations of women and children are committed to penury and economic marginality.

Natural Limits

The third new reality facing economic policymakers is the closing of the environmental frontier. Long after the western frontier reached the Pacific, the conception of infinite expansion in a world without natural limits continues to shape our conception of the good life. Bigger is better. America's manifest destiny, according to the prevailing logic, centers on economic growth of an annual rate of 3 percent, with gross national product per capita doubling every generation.

But the insistent pursuit of ever-multiplying goods is threatening an increasingly endangered natural environment. We are thus running up yet another deficit—the environmental deficit. We are using up our natural environment, literally running down our stocks of clean air and water, open spaces, and livable environments. The environmental deficit is the additional amount we would have to spend today—in public programs as well as in the private costs of design and production of more ecologically sound consumer goods and production technologies—to prevent further deterioration of our natural surroundings. Dealing with this deficit, with the sharply rising economic and human costs of environmental degradation, poses a third stiff challenge to economic policy for the year 2000 and beyond. "If the world does not seize the opportunities offered by the promise of change," Lester R. Brown writes, "the continuing environmental degradation of the planet will eventually lead to economic decline."[5]

THE LOGIC OF A DEMOCRATIC ALTERNATIVE

Our democratic alternative to conventional economics builds on two fundamental premises:

■ Democratic rather than "free market" approaches are needed to address the continuing imbalances and instability of the U.S. economy in the context of changing global, family, and environmental realities.

■ Democracy and fairness in the economic realm depend upon and reinforce democracy and fairness in the political realm.

The first premise contrasts sharply with the basic premise of rightwing economics, which insistently touts the virtues of unadulterated, "free market" exchange. The second premise contrasts just as sharply, for rightwing economics has promoted both domestically and internationally not true democracy but hierarchical control, not fairness but inequality. This promotion of hierarchy and inequality incurs high costs and has ruinous effects.

The premises of democratic economics build on much more than wishful thinking. We argue that they build on a coherent and compelling political-economic logic. We review here four main economic and political rationales to support our preference for democratic over free market approaches and policies that promote fairness and participation rather than inequality and hierarchy.

Market Failures

"Free" markets often fail. There can be little question that reliance on markets for the allocation of goods and services effectively provides information about and coordinates the activities of the millions of people who constitute any complex economy. But in many crucial areas, markets will misallocate resources unless their operations are significantly modified by governmental intervention.

Ideology aside, this is hardly a controversial proposition. As economists have long recognized, Adam Smith's "invisible hand," which is commonly thought to guide the market allocation of resources toward socially beneficial ends, cannot perform its magic when there are significant spillover effects of "externalities." These externalities occur whenever the costs or benefits of a given economic activity are not fully registered in the price of its inputs and outputs. Factory smokestacks spewing soot on neighboring homes provide a classic textbook case of such negative externalities. Far from being exceptional, as is often suggested in the textbooks, negative externalities are ubiquitous in a modern economy.

Much of the waste burden of the U.S. economy results precisely from these kinds of market failures. Indeed, the emerging global, family, and environmental realities further dramatize the weaknesses of exclusive reliance on the free market. In each of these areas, policies based solely on the private calculus of profit and loss generate economically corrosive results:

1. Although rightwing ideological trumpets resoundingly herald the virtues of free trade, no nation (including the United States) allows its pattern of international exchange to respond solely to the profit-and-loss motives of its major capitalist players. Trade in goods and services with other nations is inherently political; among other characteristics, it requires the use of distinct national currencies, the value of which is greatly influenced by national monetary and fiscal policies. More directly, many of the United States' most successful exports—military equipment and agricultural commodities, for example—are actively promoted by the U.S. government.

2. The family is no less a locus of profound market failures. Sentiment aside, there are good economic reasons why societies of all ideological hues largely eschew the profit motive when it comes to providing for the education, care, and love of children; any advanced society relies far too heavily on the skills and spirit of its future generations to risk the abandonment of children because their education and nurturance appears to be "unprofitable."

3. In the absence of strong environmental, health-and-safety, and consumer-protection regulations, basing the choice of technologies, plant location, and product design uniquely on the private profit-maximization calculus predictably leads to environmental destruction, unhealthy workplaces, and endangered consumers. Further, some of the most pressing investment needs in the United States today—for more adequate education, for basic research, and for modernization or at least restoration of our transportation system—simply will not be met through market incentives. On the contrary, substantial public-sector involvement is required.

Market allocation of most goods and services is essential, but exclusive reliance on "free" markets courts economic disaster. Markets are necessary, but political guidance for and regulation of those markets are equally necessary.[6]

State Failures

We need to rely on economic regulation and on income redistribution by a democratic state. But such reliance cannot and should not lead to blind faith in or reverence for everything the government does. Like markets, government interventions often fail to achieve desired results. To parallel the conception of "market failures," we refer to "state failures" when government intervention fails because the structures of governance do not fulfill necessary conditions for broadly beneficial policy impacts.

Democratic decisionmaking is one of the most fundamental of those conditions. When the institutional structures governing state interventions make it difficult for those affected by such decisions to acquire sufficient information and political influence to be able to hold government decision-makers accountable, special interest groups with privileged access both to the relevant information and to the key decisionmakers generally prevail.

The result is often the adoption of policies designed to maximize the income of those closest to the legislators and bureaucrats—to the detriment of economic management as a whole. Despite the long and bountiful traditions of democracy in the United States, our government features many examples of deliberately undemocratic structures of government decision-making that shield the political elite from the general citizenry and foster the average citizen's dependence on business elites. Observe, for example, the fourteen-year terms of the Board of Governors of the Federal Reserve System, which were designed both to secure and to help perpetuate disproportionate influence over the Fed's decisions by big financial interests. (It is to this lucrative connection that we owe the disastrous recession of the early 1980s.)[7] Or witness the cozy relationship between the Nuclear Regulatory Commission and the nuclear power industry, a relationship produced by the long and systematic campaign by the latter to maintain control over government decisions about nuclear power. (It was only when this political monopoly was broken by rising public concern and antinuclear activists that the astronomical risks and massive monetary costs of nuclear power were exposed.)

In short, we should be concerned about state failures as much as about market failures. But these concerns should encourage us to strengthen the democratic character of the state, not to dismantle it. Government interventions can be much more effective than they have been over recent decades in the United States, but that outcome will require much more effective mechanisms for holding the government accountable to all of the people, not just to a wealthy or well-placed few.

The Garrison State

Cooperation and reciprocity are generally less costly than conflict and domination. By increasing economic inequality, the rightwing program has exacerbated social tensions. Taking this course inexorably promotes tendencies toward the garrison state. An ever-increasing fraction of the nation's productive potential must be devoted simply to keeping the have-nots at bay. The global "big stick" principle has a comparably high price tag, whereby a mounting fraction of the labor force is not producing goods for consumption or for investment but, instead, is either producing military goods or working for the Pentagon.

Not only is the garrison state economically expensive, but the political and moral costs of its logic are pervasive and incalculable. The economic costs may be illustrated by the proliferation of what we call "guard labor" and "threat labor."

In any society a significant number of people do not produce goods and services directly but, rather, enforce the rules—formal and informal, domestic and international—that govern economic life. The presence of some guard labor in an economy is hardly an indictment of an economic system; it is a fact of life that rules are necessary and that they do not enforce themselves. But some rules are harder to enforce than others, and some economic structures must rely more heavily on guard labor than others. In the workplace, for example, large expenditures on surveillance and security personnel are needed to enforce rules that workers often perceive as invasive, unfair, unnecessary, and oppressive.

It should come as no surprise that the amount of guard labor in the U.S. economy is mammoth. We include the following enforcement activities in our estimates of guard labor: workplace supervisors; police, judicial, and corrections employers; private security personnel; the armed forces and civilian defense employees; and producers of military and domestic security equipment. By our estimates, guard labor in 1987 constituted 22.5 percent of nonfarm employment plus the armed forces.[8]

Added to this burden is another category of unproductive labor in an inegalitarian society—the wasted activities of what we call "threat labor." Employers in conflictual workplaces rely on the threat of job dismissal to intimidate their workers and exact greater labor intensity from them. The more hierarchical and conflictual the workplace, the more important the presence of this threat becomes. And the greater the reliance on this threat, the more important it is that unemployed workers clamor outside the workplace for jobs, thus making the threat of dismissal credible. We include three groups in our estimate of threat labor in the United States—the unemployed, "discouraged workers," and prisoners. In 1987, threat labor made up another 10.4 percent of nonfarm employment plus the armed forces.[9]

Collectively, more than 34 million people occupied roles as either guard or threat labor in 1987, constituting almost a third of nonfarm employment plus the armed forces. The burgeoning garrison state accounted for an increase of 7.6 million in total guard and threat labor between 1979 and 1987. This is equivalent to three-fifths of the 12.6 million total increase in nonfarm employment (plus the armed forces) during that same period. Had those additional workers been put to work in more productive employment in the investment-goods sector, rather than as new recruits to the battalions of the garrison state, U.S. net investment would have reached more than double its actual levels in 1987.

Growth for Growth's Sake

We need to rethink the economic growth ethic. In a world that is beginning to bump up against the environmental wall, it is simply infeasible to define the good life as having ever more goods. The problem is not our desire to better our lives, nor is it growth as such. Indeed, the growth of productivity—output per hour of labor, or per unit of some other input—is a reasonable objective. But the growth of productivity is not the same thing as the growth of output. The main benefit of productivity increases might well be the expansion of our free time rather than a greater outpouring of goods. Or it might result in the implementation of resource-saving technologies. Moreover, not all outputs are equally damaging to the environment: The provision of basic human services such as education and health has relatively benign ecological impacts in comparison with the production of energy-intensive manufactured goods.

In deliberating over economic policy we must therefore grapple with the basic question: Growth of what, and for whom? Essential to the response are the following guidelines. We must begin by recognizing that our well-being is based primarily on our security, health, dignity, and freedom, and that goods are a means to these ends, not the other way around. Next, a painful reality: Meeting the pressing needs of the less affluent, here and throughout the world, will require real income distribution; we can no longer comfort ourselves with the ecologically unsustainable premise that if the outpouring of goods is increased, "a rising tide will float all boats." And, finally, the necessary restructuring of our way of life will require common deliberation, changing values, and planning: Dealing with the environmental crisis haphazardly through the "free" market only courts economic and political disaster.

BEYOND THE TWIN DEFICITS

We have argued that policies promoting the objectives of a democratic economics should rely on two basic premises: Market allocation needs to be supplemented with democratic political intervention into the economy, and such political intervention must promote fairness and democratic participation. And we have justified these premises by means of four rationales: the pervasiveness of market failure, the economic benefits of general democratic accountability, the high cost of unfair and hierarchical economic strategies, and the need to rethink the growth ethic.

The principal elements of our proposals are highlighted in Table 12.1, which outlines the primary policy thrusts of a program for a democratic economy. Such a program is both practicable and appealing. Indeed, it could begin to move the U.S. economy into a new economic era.

The Contemporary Economic Content

But these principles of a democratic economics may appear to be rather far removed from contemporary economic policy debate in the United States. No doubt our democratic and egalitarian economic approach does not figure prominently in economic reports, the daily papers, or the nightly news. Attention is far more likely to be given to the federal budget deficit, or the trade deficit, or our problems in keeping up with the Japanese. Yet our approach can help to illuminate the nature of the various problems faced by the U.S. economy. Even more important, it can point to ways to overcome these problems in the future.

We turn first to the twin-deficits problem of the federal government budget and international trade imbalance. Next we consider the underlying problem of productivity growth. And then we tackle the related problem of investment stagnation. In each discussion we explore the ways in which a democratic economic program would help solve these problems, and we contrast our approach with more conventional rightist and centrist policy approaches.[10]

The most common indictment of rightwing economics is that the nation, after a decade under its auspices, still cannot make ends meet. Since the early 1980s the United States' current account trade balance has been consistently negative, adding to our international debt at a rate of more than a hundred billion dollars a year in the late 1980s.[11] And the Reagan presidency, which came to power on a wave of promises to close the federal budget deficit, concluded with the federal budget awash in red ink.

TABLE 12.1 Program for a Democratic Economy

Program Themes	Program Proposals
Right to economic security and equity	Public Jobs programs Significantly higher minimum wage Reduced workweek and work sharing Pay equity and renewed affirmative action Expanded child care, family leave programs Lower real interest rate
Right to a democratic workplace	A worker's bill of rights Labor law reform to promote democratically controlled unions Plant closing legislation Public support for profit sharing and workers' cooperatives Workers' right to know
Right to chart our economic futures	Democratization of Federal Reserve Board Investment bank for democratic allocation of capital Managed trade for balanced growth Expanded infrastructural investment Local communities' environmental bill of rights Local right-to-know legislation
Right to a better way of life	Dramatically reduced military spending National health insurance program Closing of nuclear power plants; expansion of public support for renewable energy Expanded public support for low-cost, decent housing Expanded public support for education Increased tax rates on upper-income brackets

But the twin deficits are not merely an indictment of the political illusions of supply-side economics or of the economic temerity of Republican administrations that refuse to raise taxes to balance the budget. Much more fundamentally, they should be understood as a symptom of the "trickle-down" economics upon which both rightist and centrist policy approaches rely. The unwanted twin deficits are results, not causes, of the failures of rightwing economics.

The Federal Budget Deficit

This deficit did not arise from adverse circumstances or bad luck; it was created by the rightwing program of military build-up, tax cuts for the wealthy, and high interest rates. The changes in the composition of federal revenues and expenditures during the 1980s help to clarify the sources of this persistent deficit: Between fiscal year 1981 and fiscal year 1988, tax revenues (other than social security payments) fell from 15.7 percent of gross national product (GNP) to 14.0 percent, as a direct result of generous tax cuts that largely benefited corporations and the wealthy in the early 1980s. Meanwhile military spending rose from 5.3 percent to 6.1 percent of GNP and federal interest costs rose from 2.3 percent to 3.2 percent. At the same time, nonmilitary, noninterest federal expenditures fell from 11.4 percent of GNP to 9.2 percent.[12]

Among the categories of nonmilitary, noninterest expenditures that declined in importance, particularly hard hit were education, which fell from 1.1 percent of GNP to 0.7 percent; energy and natural resources programs, which fell from almost 1 percent of GNP to just over 0.3 percent; and transportation and community development expenditures, which together accounted for well over 1 percent of GNP in 1981 and fell to under 0.7 percent in 1988.

The net result of these changes was not a reduction in the size of government expenditure as a fraction of gross national product—an outcome the rightwingers had steadfastly promised their supporters. In fact, government expenditure as a proportion of GNP reached 20 percent in 1979, climbed to 22 percent in 1981, and remained at 22 percent in 1987.[13] Hence, these changes dramatically increased the interest-payment and military-cost components of the government's spending package at the expense of other program categories. Indeed, many observers believe that the tax cuts and resulting deficit pressure were welcomed (and perhaps even sought) by rightwingers, who needed a club with which to batter the domestic social programs they had been unable to cut during the 1970s. Milton Friedman clearly had this in mind when he justified the 1981 tax cuts: "We know full well that Congress will spend every penny—and more—that is yielded by taxes. A cut in taxes means a cut in spending. There is no other way to get a cut in spending."[14]

Whatever the motivation for the tax cuts and military build-up, the responsibility for the deficit lies squarely at the feet of the architects of rightwing economics. The rightwingers' insistence on "trickle-down economics" motivated and justified huge tax cuts for corporations and the wealthy—tax cuts that depleted federal revenues. Their determination to wield the global big stick generated rapidly rising military expenditures. And their determination to enforce the rule of the invisible hand and the discipline of the whip underlay their continuing reliance on high real interest rates to enforce market discipline. These unprecedented real interest rate levels, in turn, help explain the rising costs of interest payments on the federal debt.

It may sound quaint, but the way out of this mess is through the front door. Indeed, restoring the tax rates of the late 1970s and rolling back the military budget could begin a process of deficit reduction that would allow interest rate reduction and the eventual restoration of the programs cut during the 1980s. The numbers fit together quite compactly. For example, Jesse Jackson's 1988 presidential campaign offered a carefully constructed budget program whose entirely practicable proposals, if implemented, would have cut the federal budget deficit by 1993 to barely more than a third of its projected levels.[15] The package would have achieved its target deficit reductions primarily through a combination of higher revenues from tax increases on the wealthy and reduced military expenditures. These two strategies created enough room for maneuver to have permitted, by 1993, both an annual increase of close to $100 billion in productive domestic expenditures and a projected annual reduction in the federal deficit of $85 billion.

Much of the Washington debate on federal deficit reduction has tiptoed around the underlying problems. Developed here is a more meaningful and promising approach, in two steps. First we seek to clear up some of the fog generated in recent policy discussions, specifically by reviewing several reasons for which deficit reduction itself should not be such an obsessive preoccupation of national economic policymaking. Then we argue that the budgetary deficit should indeed be reduced and summarize the principal differences between our approach to deficit reduction and the approaches of rightists and centrists.

The first and probably most important corrective to recent discussions about the federal deficit involves repeating the simple conclusion that the deficit results from, but did not cause, the disappointing effects of rightwing economics. Rightwing forces won almost all of their political battles and were almost fully able to implement their rightwing economic program; so they cannot claim, as a result, that the deficit resulted from a failure to implement their economic agenda. Indeed, as we have just noted, the rapid growth of the federal deficit during the 1980s flowed directly from the application of the rightist economic reliance on trickle-down economics, the discipline of the whip, the invisible hand, and the global big stick.

To say that the deficit is a symptom of policy failures rather than their cause does not mean, however, that it isn't a problem in its own right; controlling the fever of a sick infant is advisable even if it does not address the causes of the illness. But deficit reduction will not itself address the underlying imbalances and instability of the U.S. economy; we should shed the illusion that deficit reduction is somehow a panacea for all that ails our economy heading into the 1990s.

Second, borrowing, even on a massive scale, may be productive and is often necessary. Had the budget deficits of the 1980s financed programs such as an expansion of basic research, human-resource development, environmental protection, and transportation network modernization, there would be much less reason for concern: Borrowed money productively spent is not burdensome to repay.[16]

Third, deficit spending is often necessary to maintain aggregate demand, and a policy of rapid deficit reduction could by itself produce a major recession and a significant increase in unemployment. If the deficit-reduction strategy had the initial effect of reducing demand and thus lowering business capacity utilization and hence the rate of profit, the reduction in government demand stimulation would almost certainly be augmented by a reduction in investment.

Rightwing economics emphasizes two principal solutions for the federal deficit problem: First, supply-side strategies will provide enough of a boost in revenues that tax-rate increases will not be necessary to help close the deficit. ("Read my lips!" George Bush insisted during the 1988 presidential campaign in reaffirming his commitment not to raise taxes.) Second, rather than raising taxes to reduce the deficit as we wait for the supply-side harvest, advocates of rightwing economics argue that we should cut spending on what they characterize as "wasteful" government programs.[17]

Centrist economics emphasizes two main policy planks as well: Because of centrists' concerns about the low levels of savings in the United States, they argue that the federal deficit must be drastically reduced as soon as possible and that this imperative requires raising taxes. (It was on this alluring promise that the Mondale 1984 presidential campaign foundered.) They further insist that those tax increases should concentrate primarily on taxes that would discourage consumption and thus encourage savings—such as targeted excise taxes, a national sales tax, or a value-added tax—in order to promote investment.[18]

Democratic economics proposes to reduce the federal deficit as much as may be necessary, under specific political and economic circumstances, by restoring some of the tax cuts that benefited the wealthy in the early 1980s, by cutting military spending substantially, and by pushing down real interest rates.

The Trade Deficit

Like the federal budget deficit, the problem of the U.S. foreign trade deficit has been exacerbated by a decade of rightwing economics. This acute problem has one key source: The U.S. economy has been losing competitiveness internationally throughout the period of economic stagnation. The reason is that productivity growth in the United States has been much slower than in major competing economies. Between 1966 and 1988, for example, U.S. output per hour in manufacturing relative to that of major competitors declined by roughly 40 percent.[19] This lower productivity might not have resulted in a growing trade imbalance, however, if the United States had been willing to allow a continuing devaluation of the dollar over the same period. And, in fact, a devaluation did occur following the move to flexible exchange rates in 1971 (until the onset of the Cold Bath in 1979); as a result, the trade deficit was kept in check.[20] But after the inauguration of hardball economics in 1979, the value of the dollar soared as a consequence of the buoyant demand for dollars by foreigners seeking to cash in on high U.S. interest rates. The high value of the dollar, in turn, made U.S. goods prohibitively expensive in many world markets and made imports a bargain for U.S. buyers. As the value of the dollar continued to soar, the trade deficit fell through the floor. Compared to the values of the currencies of our major trading partners, the dollar's value increased by 59 percent between 1979 and 1985; as a result, the U.S. trade deficit on current account increased from $1 billion in 1979 to $144 billion in 1987.[21] Only a surge in the productivity of the U.S. economy could have countered the effects of the dollar's rise, but this was not forthcoming.

What to do? Rightists build on three planks. They have insisted on a "free trade" regime, promising that international competitive pressure, operating through the invisible hand, would force sluggish U.S. manufacturers to see the entrepreneurial light.[22] And they have looked for opportunities to brandish the global big stick in search of more favored access to markets abroad. But they have also insisted on keeping real interest rates high to prevent the economy from "overheating." The first two planks have had virtually no success, whereas the third plank has continued to keep demand for the dollar high and prevented enough devaluation to balance the trade accounts.

Centrists counter with three proposals of their own. First, rather than relying on "free trade," they believe the United States should follow the example set by other countries and seek to "manage" its trade, using government subsidies, credits, and selective tariffs to spur U.S. industries to sharpen their competitive edge. Second, they favor efforts to gain market access abroad through vigorous export promotion rather than through the military big-stick approach, hoping to encourage rapid development of a few specialized "sunrise" industries in which the United States could enjoy growing competitive advantage. Third, they hope and pray that progress toward federal deficit reduction is rapid enough to allow interest rates to come down over the medium term.[23]

Advocates of democratic economics share with centrists a commitment to "managed trade" but insist that government efforts to manage trade must aim at a balanced promotion of industrial competitiveness to ensure national economic security rather than international dominance. Rather than waving the global big stick or pushing aggressive export promotion, a democratic program would pursue cooperative bilateral and multilateral trading arrangements that would seek not only to advance U.S. trading interests but also to promote balanced development around the globe. And rather than representing "a unilateral attempt to capture advantage at the expense of other nations," Robert Kuttner writes, "managed trade can have positive sum benefits for the system as a whole in the form of technological innovation, stabilization, and diffusion of productive wealth."[24] Finally, a democratic program insists on immediate reductions in real interest rates through some combination of vigorous political pressure on the Federal Reserve Board and an actual reduction in its political independence.

SUSTAINABLE PRODUCTIVITY GROWTH

The twin deficits are symptoms of underlying problems in the U.S. economy. The key to solving those underlying problems lies in a reinvigoration of what we term "sustainable productivity growth"—increases in hourly output that take into account not only the paid inputs used up in the production process but all inputs including the natural environment. Any economy experiencing a boom in sustainable productivity growth would have little difficulty reducing and eventually eliminating its domestic and international deficits alike.

The productivity slowdown began during the 1960s with the erosion of bosses' power over workers. It continued in the 1970s under the additional weight of a Cold Bath policy, which resulted in slack aggregate demand and sagging investment. The recovery of productivity growth during the long 1980s expansion was tepid. Old problems were not redressed and new problems appeared.

More specifically, stagnating real spendable earnings in the 1980s gave workers little basis for positive work motivation. But where the carrot failed, the stick prevailed: Higher unemployment and drastically reduced unemployment insurance coverage in the 1980s gave the threat of job termination real teeth. Yet the unemployment that so effectively scared workers into submission also spelled low levels of capacity utilization and a diminished incentive for businesses to invest. With lagging investment and growing workplace resentment over the anti-union policies from the Oval Office and the anti-labor attitudes from the boardroom, the prospective advantages of enhanced capitalist power over workers were offset by the macroeconomic burdens of rightwing strategies.

The productivity doldrums were exacerbated by the shift of labor out of the high-productivity industrial sector of the economy and into services: Between 1979 and 1987 the goods-producing sector of the economy lost a million jobs, whereas services added 14 million.[25] Although this shift reflects some longer-term trends, it was accelerated by the overvalued dollar; less expensive imports made the production of internationally traded goods vulnerable to global competition but had much less impact on services, whose outputs are for the most part neither imported nor exported.

At the same time, the labor force became increasingly segmented. This outcome was fostered both by the erosion of the real value of the minimum wage, which languished at a constant nominal value of $3.35 an hour throughout the Reagan administration, and by the Reagan Justice Department decision to turn a blind eye toward discriminatory hiring practices. These policies, along with a substantial amount of immigration, generated a burgeoning pool of low-wage labor. This in turn reinforced the expansion of low-wage/low-productivity sectors of the economy: retail trade, especially bars and restaurants.[26] Throughout the 1980s, then, the chickens came home to roost from an industrial policy—featuring an overvalued dollar and depressed wages—that systematically channeled labor from high-productivity to low-productivity sectors.

A democratic strategy to enhance sustainable productivity would build upon four principal strategies: It would seek to foster a positive motivation and commitment toward work; it would aim to reverse the shift of labor from high- to low-productivity sectors; it would strive to develop a more skilled and committed work force; and it would enforce environmental sustainability.

Carrots Instead of Sticks

There is no substitute for positive work motivation: In contrast to the carrot, the stick is costly to wield and, in some jobs, is actually counterproductive. This is true of the increasingly complex types of team production required in the service sectors of the economy, and it is especially true of the information-intensive branches. Where jobs are routine and easily monitored (as on an assembly line), the stick works. But only a tiny minority in the U.S. labor force is made up of assembly-line workers. Where the quality of the job is subject to subtle variations that are often difficult to detect, and where work is done in groups so that individual inputs are hard to monitor, the carrot is indispensable. More and more jobs in the advanced economies share these latter characteristics.

The most certain route to a positive work motivation is self-evident: Give the worker a stake in the job. According to this logic, the person who does the work should participate in its design and own the results of his or her labor. But most modern technologies, which require relatively large groups to work together, preclude individual ownership of separate production units. The closest approximation to the ideal of self-ownership and self-direction, therefore, is an economy of firms each no larger than necessary to take advantage of the economies of scale offered by the relevant technology, and each owned and democratically controlled by those who work in them.

Shifting Toward High-Productivity Jobs

Reversing the shift toward low-productivity sectors clearly requires a reversal of the policies that have been primarily responsible for this perverse development in the 1980s: the overvalued dollar and labor market segmentation. A reduction in interest rates would help to reduce the value of the dollar, for it would diminish the demand by foreigners for dollar-denominated financial instruments such as U.S. Treasury bills. The reduced amount of external borrowing would of course require some compensating combination of spending cuts or tax increases in domestic budgets (which we earlier reviewed in our discussion of the federal budget deficit).

Reducing labor market segmentation would require a substantial increase in the real value of the minimum wage, active pursuit of anti-discrimination policies, unionization in low-wage sectors, and other strategies designed to equalize wages by pushing from the bottom up. The logic of this high-wage route to enhanced productivity is straightforward: High wages contribute to productivity growth not only by offering workers a carrot but also by forcing employers to modernize or "get out of the kitchen." The main problem in the U.S. economy is not low-productivity workers but low-productivity jobs. When a skilled machinist laid off from a tool-and-die plant takes a job at McDonald's, the worker's hourly output falls dramatically. But the fault is not the worker's; the problem is the job. Low-productivity jobs exist and proliferate because the abundance of low-wage workers—often victims of discrimination or those unable to exercise legal rights due to immigrant status—makes it possible for low-productivity businesses to make profits. By shifting workers from low-productivity to high-productivity jobs, a high-wage strategy coupled with a full-employment program would increase productivity in the economy as a whole, even if it had no effect whatsoever in each sector of the economy.

Such a shift would obviously have its costs. Workers previously employed in low-productivity jobs would be temporarily unemployed; many would need to be retrained.[27] Although some high-productivity businesses could expand production using previously idle capacity, others would have to invest in new plants and equipment. But the productivity gains would vastly outweigh the retraining and capital costs involved.[28]

Our proposal of wage equalization from the bottom up is modeled on the "solidarity wage" policy of the Swedish labor unions. One study has concluded that the spread of wages between higher- and lower-paid workers in Swedish trade unions, representing nearly 80 percent of all employees, "declined by almost half in the 15 years" between 1959 and 1974.[29] This narrowing of the wage gap helped promote productivity growth during those years; between 1960 and 1973 productivity growth in Sweden's manufacturing sector soared at a rate nearly twice that of the U.S. economy.[30]

Supporting High-Productivity Workers

Although we argue that the principal productivity problem in the U.S. economy involves low-productivity jobs rather than low-productivity workers, we agree with many others who argue that the United States must reverse trends toward depletion of our stock of human resources.

The means by which we should pursue such a commitment are hardly mysterious: The United States needs to invest a higher proportion of time and resources in the education and training of both the currently working population and of future generations. Regarding this imperative we agree with the many centrists who pay special attention to the need for a better-skilled work force.[31]

Our concern in this area is aimed rather more at the purpose of reinvigorating education in the United States. Many propose such an effort primarily on instrumental grounds—as a means of making the U.S. economy more competitive. But we regard education as an end in itself. Learning is a public good. Higher education, in particular, is a process that everyone should be able to enjoy and whose fruits redound to society as a whole. A better-educated citizenry is a more informed and ultimately more intelligent citizenry. And a better-educated work force is more capable of participating in and helping manage a democratic economy. Dramatically expanded participation in higher education strikes us as yet another precondition for a democratic economy. Elite and expensive education reflects and reinforces an elite and unequal society; universal and democratic education is essential for popular participation in shaping our society.

Making Productivity Growth Sustainable

We come now to the issue of sustainability. Just as we seek to prevent businesses from making profits from underpaid labor, so we seek to foreclose their opportunities to enrich themselves by fouling the planet. Economic policy must ensure that those making production decisions concerning plant location, waste disposal, technologies of production, and product design—private businesses and worker cooperatives alike—consider the real costs of production including environmental and worker-health costs. Of course, such policy will not eliminate pollution. But it would at least end the subsidy of pollution that we now tolerate by allowing businesses to make free use of nature.

No less important than changes in national policy are policy initiatives to give local communities and working people the information and the political means to chart their own environmental policies. Two legal changes would be instrumental in this regard. First would be to establish (by an act of Congress) the absolute right of local communities, through referenda, town meetings, or elected municipal governments, to bar the disposal or transshipment of hazardous or environmentally destructive materials and to reject the location of nuclear power plants. Communities would of course be free to bargain away these rights, but at a price to be paid by the potential polluter—thus ensuring that the potential cost of the project as assessed by the citizens affected would become part of the profit-and-loss calculation of the relevant businesses. Second, Congress should legislate a community right-to-know law requiring businesses operating in a locality or transshipping goods through a community to provide full information on the nature of any hazardous substances that they intend to use or transport.

COMPARING APPROACHES TO
THE PRODUCTIVITY PROBLEM

We are now in a position to compare with rightist and centrist strategies our proposal for solving the productivity problem. All of these approaches place a strong emphasis on improving the rate of investment in order to boost the rate of growth of capital intensity; they also deal with the problems of business efficiency and labor intensity.

Rightwing economics proposes two primary strategies: Rely primarily on business deregulation to help encourage improved business efficiency; and rely on the stick of low wages and high unemployment to push workers to increase their work intensity.

Centrist economics is caught between the rightwing and the democratic approaches. On the one hand, it shares with democratic economics a commitment to industrial policy, the carrot instead of the stick to provide positive worker motivation, and sustained commitment to a more skilled work force.[32] On the other hand, it insists on a trickle-down approach by which savings and profits must drive investment and productivity growth—thus requiring, among other constraints, relatively slow rates of real wage growth and continued hierarchical control over basic decisions about production. We call this approach "profit-led productivity growth."[33]

Democratic economics, like the centrist approach, would push for industrial policy, the carrot of positive worker motivation, and investments in the skills of our current and future labor force. In sharp contrast to centrist trickle-down economics, however, we stress the critical importance of "worker-led productivity growth" to strengthen worker incentives and "wage-led productivity growth" to push businesses to invest in high-productivity jobs.

REVITALIZING INVESTMENT

Sustainable productivity growth will require more than worker owner-ship, democratic participation, a high-wage industrial policy, and a deepening and democratization of environmental regulation. In short, it will also require investment.

Maintaining a high level of investment is not unlike securing a high level of quality and intensity of work. Just as the worker is ultimately the one who determines what he or she will or will not do at work in a capitalist economy, it is the capitalist who will ultimately determine the course of private investment. And just as the boss cannot literally force the employee to work harder but has to provide the necessary incentives, we cannot force the capitalist to invest; only bright profit prospects, low interest rates, and a high level of utilization of existing stock will do the job.

Public Investment

Broadly defined, public investment includes all the publicly financed activities that contribute to future output, including education, health, research and development, environmental protection, public energy production facilities, roads, bridges, and other infrastructure. In a profession that agrees on very little, there is a surprising consensus among economists on the centrality of at least some of these forms of public investment in the process of productivity growth. As shown in a variety of statistical studies, for example, improvements in the education and health status of the population as well as in technology account for a sizable fraction—often well over half—of the productivity growth experienced in the U.S. economy during the twentieth century.[34]

Though difficult to estimate (for obvious reasons), the size of the public capital stock exceeds that of the private capital stock by a considerable margin: Bridges, roads, and sewers alone represent a stock equal to roughly half of the private capital stock, and the stock of publicly financed human capital (education and health) dwarfs not only the publicly financed physical infrastructure but the private capital stock as well.[35]

Moreover, public investments are likely to stimulate private investment. The adequate provision of an educated and healthy labor force, modern transportation and communication networks, research and development, and energy are essential to low-cost production in the private sector and, hence, to profits as well. David Alan Aschauer of the Federal Reserve Bank of Chicago estimates that a 10 percent increase in the public capital stock of roads, bridges, sewers, and other components of the public infrastructure would increase the private rate of return by 12.6 percent.[36] Although most economists point to the danger that public expenditures will "crowd out" private investment, the truth is that public expenditure—if devoted to human-resource development, research, and infrastructure—is often an indispensable precondition for private investment.

The reign of rightwing economics has resulted in a substantial run-down of public capital stock since the late 1970s. The most obvious policy response to this looting is simply to stop it—by reallocating funds away from military uses and toward the construction of specifically those elements of capital stock that we need for future sustainable increases in living standards. Even prior to the 1980s the United States had a significantly lower level of government investment than most other major capitalist nations. In 1980, for example, government investment in the United States was 1.8 percent of gross domestic product. But for Japan, the figure was 6.3 percent; for Germany, 3.6 percent; for Canada, 2.8 percent; for France, 3.0 percent; and for Italy, 3.4 percent.[37] Simply redressing the 1980s deterioration of public capital stock would still leave the United States well behind its major trading partners.

Private Investment

For all the importance of public investment, private investment remains central to the U.S. economy. Our analysis of the persistent stagnation of investment during the 1980s suggests some of the elements of a progressive strategy to enhance private investment. The paradox of investment during the 1979-1988 business cycle is that the after-tax rate of profit recovered substantially during the long expansion after 1983, but the rate of investment did not. This paradox is readily explained: Investment stagnated despite higher profitability because of the extraordinarily high real interest rates and the low levels of capacity utilization that the rightwing economic game plan imposed throughout much of the decade.

A strategy to revive investment would therefore need to include lower interest rates, which both spur consumer demand and directly enhance the incentive to invest. Lower interest rates also encourage a lower value of the dollar, thereby stimulating exports, discouraging imports, and consequently boosting the net export component of aggregate demand. And, of course, major renovation of public capital stock over the longer run stimulates private investment.

No less important than stimulating the amount of private investment is the need to alter its character. We have already discussed the necessity for countering environmentally destructive investments or other investments with significant negative externalities. But a second pressing need is to slow down the socially wasteful hypermobility of capital, which, in seeking greener pastures in union-free low-wage and environmentally unprotected havens, often wreaks havoc on communities. In this connection, legislation requiring advance notice of plant closings and the payment of extended health benefits and generous severance pay has been shown to reduce the destructive impact of such moves and, possibly, to discourage plant closings as well.[38]

Three institutional changes would also further be warranted, to help promote a democratic investment strategy. First, it is essential that the relevant decisionmaking bodies be rendered democratically accountable. In the case of investment, democratic control over the Federal Reserve System must be established, perhaps through the election of its Board of Governors by the members of the House of Representatives to four-year terms, to coincide with the term of the president.

A second important change would involve the formation and adequate funding of a national cooperative bank to provide worker-owned cooperatives with the necessary start-up and working capital. Federal and local governments currently subsidize various forms of ownership on the basis of their contribution to the social fabric, with home ownership and the family farm constituting the most important examples. An equivalent commitment to workplace democracy makes sense on both political and efficiency grounds.[39]

Third, the laws governing the investment of pension-fund monies must be changed to allow the owners of the funds to determine, democratically, the investments they would like to make. Under present law, a union pension fund is prohibited from using its pension funds to generate jobs for union members, barring exceptional circumstances. This law should indeed be changed; many union members and other pension-fund participants would benefit from control over the assets that they technically own.[40]

CONCLUSION

How, then, does our investment strategy differ from rightwing and centrist approaches? Advocates of rightwing strategies emphasize two

TABLE 12.2 Major Differences in Policy Approaches

	Rightwing	Centrist	Democratic
Federal deficit	No tax increases Cut government spending	Raise taxes across the board Increase regressive taxes on consumption	Raise taxes on wealthy Cut military spending Lower interest rates
Trade deficit	Free trade Brandish global big stick Keep interest rates high Restore U.S. as Number 1	Manage trade; encourage trade specialization Vigorous export promotion Wait for lower interest rates Restore U.S. as Number 1	Manage trade; reduce trade specialization Cooperative trade agreements Promote lower interest rates Seek global economic security
Sustainable productivity growth	Deregulate business Use stick with workers Tolerate environmental abuses	Industrial policy, training Use carrot with workers Profit-led productivity growth Moderate regulation of environmental abuse	Industrial policy, training Use carrot with workers Worker-led and wage-led productivity growth Aggressive regulation of environmental abuse
Revived investment	Deregulation and investment	Curb consumption to boost savings Foster public investment	Augment wages to stimulate demand Foster public investment Democratize investment institutions

planks. They want to stimulate private investment through deregulation and tax incentives, especially lower capital-gains taxation. And they want to get the government out of the investment business to whatever degree possible, thus tacitly endorsing the continued deterioration of public capital stock.

Centrists oppose deregulation, however—both because they believe in the need for a more interventionist government and because they are skeptical about the usefulness of tax incentives to stimulate investment. They therefore press for curbs on wages and consumption as a way of fattening profits and savings, in order to provide the necessary funds for investment. In sharp contrast to rightwingers, moreover, they strongly support the importance of renewed public investment. Both private and public investment would be supported within the current structure of relatively centralized private and public decisionmaking institutions.[41]

Democratic investment strategists share with centrists a commitment to revitalized public investment. But they differ from the centrist approach in their emphasis on the need to democratize investment institutions—for example, through reduced independence for the Fed, direct credit support for democratic enterprises, and greater latitude for worker influence on pension fund investment decisions. See Table 12.2 for our summary of the principal differences among rightwing, centrist, and democratic approaches to current and critical issues in macroeconomic policy.

In short, we believe that a democratic economics has substantial promise as a programmatic approach to achieve sustainable improvements in living standards, stronger democracy, enhanced community at home and cooperation abroad, and greater fairness.

NOTES

1. *Statistical Abstract*, 1989, pp. 449 and 469; and 1987, p. 439.

2. A conservative estimate of the extent of income redistribution within the family may be calculated as follows: In 1987 the median family income for husband-wife families was about $35,000, of which the wife's contribution was about $10,000. (These figures are drawn from *Statistical Abstract*, 1989, p. 448.) If the income is used equally within the family, the husband and wife each enjoy an income of $17,500; the increase in the wife's income ($7,500) is the redistribution (from the husband) in this family. In 1987 there were 51.8 million husband-wife families, accounting for a sum total redistribution of $388 billion. In the same year the sum of income security (welfare) payments was $123 billion. Because our estimate of intrafamily redistribution does not include redistribution from adults to children, it is a very substantial underestimate (these intergenerational transfers are analogous to the Social Security system). Nonetheless, our estimate exceeds the sum of income

security and social security payments by the federal government (payments which, in fiscal 1987, amounted to $331 billion, according to *Economic Report*, 1990, Table C-77).

3. In 1988, 25 million workers were engaged in goods production (*Economic Report*, 1989, Table C-43). If they all worked a full year (1,750 hours), their hours of labor would total 43.8 billion. According to household time-budget studies, men work an average of 11 hours a week and women an average of 29 hours a week at housework, including child rearing (see Victor Fuchs, "His and Hers: Gender Differences in Work and Income, 1959-1979," *Journal of Labor Economics* [July 1986]). This amounts to a total of 165.4 billion hours, even counting only housework done by those above the age of 24 (almost exactly three-quarters of this domestic labor is done by women). The population figures on which this calculation is based are drawn from *Statistical Abstract*, 1989, p. 15.

4. See, for example, Mary Jo Bane, "Household Composition and Poverty," in Sheldon Danziger and Daniel H. Weinberg, eds., *Fighting Poverty: What Works and What Doesn't* (Cambridge, Mass.: Harvard University Press, 1986), pp. 209-231.

5. Lester R. Brown, "The Illusion of Progress," in Lester R. Brown et al., *State of the World 1990* (New York: Norton, 1990), p. 16.

6. An enlightening discussion of the interplay between markets and politics, which argues the necessity of both, is provided in Charles Lindbloom, *Politics and Markets: The World's Political-Economic Systems* (New York: Basic Books, 1977).

7. For a discussion of the influence of financial interests on the Fed, see William Greider, *Secrets of the Temple: How the Federal Reserve Runs the Country* (New York: Simon & Schuster, 1987).

8. The full estimate of guard labor includes those in "supervisory occupations": police, judicial, and corrections employees; private security guards; and military personnel on active duty, civilian employees of the Defense Department, and those in defense-related employment. The data for those in supervisory occupations are based on the percentage of employees defined (in U.S. Department of Labor, *Dictionary of Occupational Titles*, 4th ed. [Washington, D.C.: U.S. Government Printing Office, 1977]) as having "supervisory" or related "relations with people." The data for police, judicial, and corrections employees are drawn from U.S. Department of Justice, *Criminal Justice Statistics* (Washington, D.C.: U.S. Government Printing Office, various years), and from *Historical Statistics*, numerous series. The data for private security guards are taken from *Statistical Abstract*, various years, and *Historical Statistics*, series D589 and D591. Finally, the data for military personnel on active duty, civilian employees of the Defense Department, and those in defense-related employment are drawn from *Statistical Abstract*, 1989, p. 335. (More detailed definitions, sources, and calculation methods, pertaining to business-cycle peaks from the mid-1960s through the late 1980s, are available in a supplementary memorandum upon request from the authors.)

9. The category of threat labor includes the unemployed; "discouraged workers," who would be considered unemployed if they had not dropped out of the labor force because they could not find work; and prisoners. The total number of unemployed

are taken from *Economic Report*, 1990, Table C-33. The definition for the number of discouraged workers is drawn from *Statistical Abstract*, 1989, p. 395; data are based on U.S. Bureau of Labor Statistics, *Labor Force Statistics Derived from the Current Population Survey*, 1948-1987, BLS Bulletin no. 2307 (August 1988), Tables A-22 and A-25. Finally, the number of prisoners is taken from U.S. Department of Justice, *Sourcebook of Criminal Justice Statistics 1988* (Washington, D.C.: U.S. Government Printing Office, 1989), Table 6.31. As with the calculations on guard labor, more detailed definitions, sources, and methods for the estimates of threat labor are available in a supplementary memorandum upon request from the authors.

10. We identify rightwing approaches with the "conservative" economics that dominated economic policy in the United States during the 1980s. We associate centrist approaches with the clustering of corporatist and neoliberal prescriptions (which possess strong bases in both the Republican and Democratic parties) that during the 1980s posed as the principal alternatives to the rightist regime. For further definition and elaboration of this centrist perspective, see our discussion of corporatism ("top-down economics") in Samuel Bowles, David M. Gordon, and Thomas Weisskopf, *Beyond the Waste Land: A Democratic Alternative to Economic Decline* (Garden City, N.Y.: Anchor Press/Doubleday, 1983), ch. 9.

11. Data on the United States' international investment position and balance-of-payments status are given in *Economic Report*, 1990, Tables C-101 and C-102.

12. These figures and those in the next paragraph are taken from Office of Management and Budget, *Historical Tables*, Tables 2.4 and 3.3; and *Economic Report*, 1990, Tables C-76 and C-77.

13. *Economic Report*, 1990, Tables C-79 and C-1.

14. *Newsweek*, July 28, 1981.

15. See Frank Clemente, ed., *Keep Hope Alive: Jesse Jackson's 1988 Presidential Campaign* (Boston: South End Press, 1989), pp. 73-92.

16. For an effective presentation of this side of the argument, see Peter L. Bernstein and Robert L. Heilbroner, *The Debt and the Deficit: False Alarms/Real Possibilities* (New York: Norton, 1989).

17. See Aaron B. Wildavsky, *How to Limit Government Spending* (Berkeley: University of California Press, 1980), especially for the argument about the need to cap revenues and curb or reduce government spending.

18. One of the pillars of the centrist approach to the deficit has been the Brookings Institution, many of whose economists have repeatedly called for tax increases as part of a deficit-reduction strategy and have often advised Democrats to incorporate such economic advice into their campaign platforms. See, for example, Henry J. Aaron et al., *Economic Choices 1987* (Washington, D.C.: Brookings Institution, 1986), especially chs. 3 and 4.

19. This percentage is based on unpublished data from the U.S. Bureau of Labor Statistics, Office of Productivity and Technology.

20. The data on U.S. exchange rates and the U.S. trade balance are drawn from *Economic Report*, 1990, Tables C-109 and C-102.

21. See Ibid. A decline in the value of the dollar after 1985 helped to reduce the trade deficit from its peak of $144 million in 1987, but it was still well over $100 million at the end of the 1980s.

22. For a reasoned advocacy of adherence to free trade, see Robert Z. Lawrence and Robert E. Litan, *Saving Free Trade: A Pragmatic Approach* (Washington, D.C.: Brookings Institution, 1986).

23. One of the core advocates of a centrist approach to industrial policy and managed trade has been *Business Week*. See Business Week Team, *The Reindustrialization of America* (New York: McGraw-Hill, 1982), especially pp. 134-139; and "The Hollow Corporation," *Business Week*, March 3, 1986, pp. 57-85. See also Kevin P. Phillips, *Staying on Top: A Business Case for a National Industrial Strategy* (New York: Random House, 1984).

24. Robert Kuttner, *Managed Trade and Economic Sovereignty* (Washington, D.C.: Economic Policy Institute, 1989), p. 24.

25. *Economic Report*, 1990, Table C-43.

26. *Statistical Abstract*, 1989, p. 392.

27. Most elaborations of a democratic economics would seek to emulate the "active labor market" programs of the Swedes, who have managed to keep unemployment rates remarkably low throughout the period of global economic stagnation—specifically, by providing immediate worker retraining, location assistance, and, when necessary, supplementary public employment in periods of transition. For a useful recent discussion of these policies, see Bob Rowthorn and Andrew Glyn, "The Diversity of Unemployment Experience," in Stephen Marglin and Juliet Schor, eds., *The Golden Age of Capitalism* (Oxford: Oxford University Press, 1990).

28. We provide some arithmetical examples to illustrate this point in Bowles, Gordon, and Weisskopf, *Beyond the Waste Land*, pp. 281-282.

29. Rudolph Meidner, *Employee Investment Funds: An Approach to Collective Capital Formation* (London: Allen & Unwin, 1978), p. 30.

For an extension of the same data throughout the 1980s, see Douglas A. Hibbs, Jr., "Wage Compression Under Solidarity Bargaining in Sweden," in I. Persson-Tanimura, ed., *Generating Equality in the Welfare State: The Swedish Experience* (Oslo: Norwegian University Press, 1990).

30. Productivity growth in Sweden in the years between 1960 and 1973 was 6.4 percent annually; in the United States it was 3.3 percent. Over the entire period from 1960 to 1988, productivity growth in Swedish manufacturing was 4.5 percent annually, whereas in the United States it was 3.0 percent (see U.S. Bureau of Labor Statistics, "Output Per Hour, Hourly Compensation, and Unit Labor Costs in Manufacturing, Fourteen Countries or Areas, 1960-1988," Office of Productivity and Technology, August 1989).

31. See, for example, the Cuomo Commission on Trade and Competitiveness, *The Cuomo Commission Report* (New York: Simon & Schuster, 1988), pp. 122-127.

32. These inclinations are well illustrated in Ibid., chs. 6 and 7.

33. One of the clearest examples of a centrist emphasis on the need to fatten

profits and savings in order to stimulate productivity growth is presented in George N. Hatsopoulos, Paul R. Krugman, and Lawrence H. Summers, "U.S. Competitiveness: Beyond the Trade Deficit," *Science*, July 15, 1988, pp. 299-307.

34. See Edward F. Denison, *Accounting for U.S. Economic Growth, 1929-1969* (Washington, D.C.: Brookings Institution, 1974); and Edward F. Denison, *Trends in American Economic Growth, 1929-1982* (Washington, D.C.: Brookings Institution, 1985).

35. Figures for the public capital stock in roads, bridges, and sewers are drawn from David Alan Aschauer, "Is the Public Capital Stock Too Low?" *Chicago Fed Letter*, no. 2. October 1987. The human capital stock may be conservatively approximated by the present value of the sum of all direct public expenses on the education and health of the current population. The considerable magnitude of the public capital stock may be suggested by the fact that the gross fixed nonresidential private capital stock per capita ($26,000 in 1987) is considerably less than the direct cost of putting one student through elementary and high school (*Statistical Abstract*, 1989, pp. 140 and 532).

36. Aschauer, "Is the Public Capital Stock Too Low?" p. 3.

37. Philip Armstrong and Andrew Glyn, "Accumulation, Profits, State Spending: Data for Advanced Capitalist Countries, 1952-1981," Oxford Institute for Economics and Statistics, May 1984.

38. Nancy Folbre, Julia Leighton, and Melissa Roderick, "Plant Closing Regulation in Maine: 1975-1982," *Industrial and Labor Relations Review* (January 1984): 185-196.

39. See, for example, the proposals for a National Investment Program and an American Investment Bank among Jackson's 1988 campaign documents, in Clemente, *Keep Hope Alive*, pp. 93-94.

40. On potential democratic uses of pension funds, see Jeremy Rifkin and Randy Barber, *The North Will Rise Again: Pensions, Politics and Power in the 1980s* (Boston: Beacon Press, 1978); and Teresa Ghilarducci, *Labor's Capital: The Economics and Politics of Employee Pensions* (Cambridge, Mass.: MIT Press, 1992).

41. Perhaps the clearest recent statement of a centrist approach to revitalizing investment is provided in Benjamin Friedman, *Day of Reckoning: The Consequences of American Economic Policy Under Reagan* (New York: Random House, 1988).

13

JAMES A. NATHAN

A New World Order
That Means Something

In Operation "Desert Storm," the Bush administration was given one of history's greatest victories. But the object of war is not just the banishing of an adversary or the destruction of an enemy's society. Rather, as the great theoretician of war Clausewitz knew, war's purpose—if it is to have any meaning at all beyond battlefield success—is the construction of a "better kind of peace." Yet George Bush's boyish enthusiasm for arms is unmatched by any eagerness to plan for what follows the fight.

"We must lead," the Bush administration insists. Though the words trip with the steady cadence of the rains, policies effervesce and dematerialize. There was to be an energy policy. But it's gone now. There was to be a permanent U.S. presence in the Gulf. But the Saudis lost interest. There was to be a program to defang Saddam Hussein, to eliminate his weapons of mass destruction, to break the aggressive and repressive menace of his "Republican Guards." But the money ran out for international inspectors, and the Saudis objected to Saddam being undone if the cost were taken in the coin of regional "instability."[1] There was to be an arms-control accord in the Middle East—suppliers' agreements that might, in Mr. Bush's words of May 1991, exercise "collective self-restraint." But forbearance was forgone. In June 1991 Defense Secretary Richard Cheney opined, as he announced some of the largest arms sales in years, that any control of arms to our major associates in the Gulf would be "counterproductive."

PROWESS AT ARMS IS NOT ENOUGH:
THE PANAMA FLOP

From Panama to the Gulf, the president has shown a competence at war, even a worrisome streak of bellicosity; but he has evinced little sense of

what the consequences of victory might bring. The president invaded
Panama to rid the Panamanians of a man the president personally detested,
Manuel Noriega—a man whom the CIA (when Bush was its director) paid
hundreds of thousands of dollars. Noriega was a drug-trafficker, Bush
asserted, although this is yet to be proven in court. And he was an arms
smuggler, although this could never have been much of a revelation to Bush,
inasmuch as Noriega was smuggling arms during the time he was on the
Bush-Reagan payroll.

After reducing Panama's GNP by over 30 percent with an embargo and
an invasion, and after the deaths of hundreds of Panamanians (and twenty-
seven American soldiers), the United States can be certain of nothing except
that Panama is not now less free from drugs and drug money. Indeed,
Panama, as the *New York Times* put it in mid-1991, continues as a drug
exporter's "free for all."[2] The General Accounting Office estimates that
more than twice the amount of cocaine is now being shipped from Panama
compared to the time when General Noriega was in charge. And some of
the most prominent members of Panama's ruling Endera family—the
relatives of the president whom the United States installed to take Noriega's
place—are said to be heavily involved in drug trafficking and money
laundering. U.S. anti-drug enforcement aid to Panama barely reaches 1
million a year—not even as much as it cost to transport Noriega and bring
him to inconclusive trial.[3] As a result, young, inexperienced Panamanian
anti-drug and customs units go without any planes whatsoever, and make do
with but one speed boat. A few years after "Operation Just Cause," it
seems George Bush has simply lost interest.

THE GULF WAR ABUSE OF VICTORY

On November 4, 1990, Secretary of State James Baker told the U.S.
First Cavalry division in Saudi Arabia, "I think that most Americans are
home wherever our principles are. And that's what this crisis is all about:
it's about the defense of the values that made the United States of America
the finest country in the world." To be sure, apprehension of the ethics of
the United States association with Saddam came late in the day. The United
States had supported Iraq against Iran since 1983 with $500 million in
sensitive technology transfers and with satellite intelligence. When an Iraqi
missile hit the U.S. frigate *Stark*, killing thirty-seven American sailors, the
administration blamed Iran—the "villain in the piece," as Ronald Reagan put
it.[4]

A week after the administration had been warned by the Defense Department and the CIA that an Iraqi attack on Kuwait was imminent, and only three days before Iraq's invasion, U.S. Assistant Secretary for Near Eastern Affairs John Kelly appeared before Congress. His testimony hardly indicated an American interest in the issue of "aggression."

> *Representative Lee Hamilton (D-Ind.)*: "Do we have a commitment to our friends in the Gulf in the event they are engaged in oil or territorial disputes with their neighbors?"
> *Kelly*: "As I said, Mr. Chairman, we have no defense treaty relationship with any of the countries. We have historically avoided taking a position on border disputes. . . ."
> *Hamilton*: If Iraq, for example, charged across the border into Kuwait, for whatever reason, what would be our position?"
> *Kelly*: "That, Mr. Chairman, is a hypothetical or a contingency. . . . I cannot get into the realm of 'what if.'"
> *Hamilton*: "In that circumstance, is it correct to say . . . that we do not have a treaty commitment which would obligate us . . .?"
> *Kelly*: "That is correct."

It took a post-invasion meeting with Margaret Thatcher to steel the president sufficiently to stand up to Saddam. But when the penny dropped about "aggression" in the Gulf, the lesson was hardly generalized, for the Bush administration barely seemed to notice the de facto annexation of Lebanon to Syria (one of the United States's coalition partners in the Gulf) a few months later. Nor was the issue of Iraq's aggression ever related to the classic American concern not only that enemies be defeated but that a *just* political outcome result from the use of American arms.

Democracy in Kuwait seemed a kind of taboo to the Bush administration.[5] The president refused to meet with any of the Kuwaiti resistance forces lest they jeopardize the restoration of a repressive Emir. And when the Sabah family and its retainers were free to return, Kuwaiti native resistance was systematically disenfranchised while putative collaborators and "outsiders," some of whom had been in Kuwait for generations, were brutalized and driven out of the country.

Nor was President Bush much interested in a democratic Iraq if it meant that a weak Iraq might be "exploited" by Iran. Hence he ordered a cease-fire twenty-eight hours ahead of the schedule suggested by his commander-in-place, General Norman Schwarzkopf. As a result, 57,000 elite Iraqi troops and 700 top-of-the-line T72 tanks escaped, only to proceed with their own vision of Gulf "stability." Saddam's forces smashed the very uprising that Bush himself had called for.

"On background," a high administration official revealed the Bush administration's new thinking: "We were not going to leave the world's second largest oil exporter without some means of self-defense."[6]

LETTING THE GREAT TREE FALL:
OR, ABSENT AT THE CREATION

All during the languid collapse of Soviet power, the Bush administration, like the simple-minded protagonist, Chauncey Gardner, in Jerzy Kosinski's great novel, *Being There*, just "liked to watch." CIA and other professionals had warned for over a year that the Soviet Union was not just coming apart but was ripe for fascism and civil war. Bush conveyed the warnings to his "friend," "Misha" Gorbachev, but let events take their course.[7] The Soviets were frozen out of the International Monetary Fund (IMF)—an organization with 157 members, including such countries as Burma and Albania—until a month before the August 1991 coup. Most-favored-nation trading arrangements were denied until after the coup, when Gorbachev was on the way out.

No Soviet concession was quite right. Even nuclear, chemical, and strategic arms agreements that might have drawn down the numbers in Soviet arsenals (whether or not Gorbachev stayed in power) were stalled. The problem, the Bush administration said, was that the Soviets had accepted the same far-reaching verification procedures that the United States had proposed several years earlier. Too many Soviets wandering around U.S. defense plants would "tax the FBI's resources."

Once Gorbachev was finished, Secretary of State James Baker finally committed the United States to a partnership with the new Commonwealth of Independent States: "We will help them move along that path of democracy and economic freedom," he vowed.[8] But while President Bush pledged that "nobody will starve," there was only an abundance of inaction. After all, Bush said, "We've got a lot of domestic demands. And we've got to sort it all out."[9]

U.S. foodstuffs were sent. But they didn't benefit many people, except indirectly as animal feed. Only a fraction of the consumables promised in the late fall could be delivered before harsh weather came and went. Large amounts of the food that did make it off the docks found its way to the black market.

The Bush food plans offered no real mechanisms for food distribution or market transformation. For the desperate pensioners living on fixed incomes of several dollars a month, and for the tens of millions of unemployed, the promise of U.S. food last winter was a chimera.

There were alternatives. U.S. forces or NATO forces might have been used for food distribution.[10] The Pentagon had staffed out the suggestion, using as a guide its experience in the spring 1991 "Operation Provide Comfort" with the Kurds.[11] NATO forces might have softened the impression of NATO irrelevance and satisfied European apparent wishes for successful common undertakings. But the Bush administration, already famous for caution, earnestly courted a reputation for a kind of circumspection that bore a closer resemblance to paralysis than to any kind of prudence.

TOMORROW AND TOMORROW: PLANNING VERSUS PROCRASTINATION

Thomas Jefferson was wont to speak of the thousandth generation. But the Bush administration has been firmly fixed on its own priorities concerning the next election—and with "Whatever it takes" to win, as the president candidly confessed to David Frost at the start of 1992.

It was not always thus. Historically, the defeat of armies and simple prowess at arms has never been enough for Americans. Our greatest presidents have known that unless our adversaries were rehabilitated, conflict would simply be repeated.

Much of Europe is critically dependent on the former Soviet Union. A total collapse in the East could draw the industrialized world, Europe first, into a depression. Thirty percent of Germany's natural gas is Soviet in origin. Twenty percent of Germany's oil comes from the Soviet Union.[12] The former Soviet Union owes $33 billion to German banks alone, at a time when international liquidity and savings for investment are already drying up.[13]

Perhaps a million people drifted west out of the Soviet Union in 1991,[14] and if widespread civil war or anarchy comes, many millions more may flee.[15] The prospect of new Berlin Walls going up, just further east, or bread lines in a Europe already plagued by double-digit inflation is an augury, says Library of Congress expert John Hardt, not just of recession but of depression as severe as any seen this century—unless something is done to shore up the new Russia and its Commonwealth.[16]

The past few years can be seen as a great vindication of the idea of America. We can and should help cement the fact of freedom rather than assuming that freedom without reduction in freedom's ways will, by itself, prevail. We can provide freedom's expertise. At the end of 1991, at long last, President Bush pledged 500 Peace Corps volunteers to the former Soviet Union's new republics.[17]

The recruitment and training of business school graduates and young technicians of all kinds will take another two years. But 500 young people, in an area much larger that the United States, will hardly be enough. The Soviets need business expertise and marketing skills (which exist in abundance in the United States), and there is an ample reserve of retired Americans who would be willing to lend a hand now. In short, the emerging democracies of Eastern Europe and the Commonwealth of Independent States need a critical mass of American volunteers with legal, financial, and communication skills that can buttress the great transformation of world society.

The risks of inaction are grave indeed. Already there are disturbing reports of the sale of nuclear artillery shells from bases just north of the Mongolian border as well as Iraqi and Libyan offers to rocket scientists and nuclear weapons designers. Five thousand people in the former Soviet Union have a background in the design of nuclear weapons, and most are now in search of new work.

We can send experts in factory conversion. Tank factories can produce tractors, and laser laboratories can produce medical goods. And we can send special Pentagon "recruiters" to sweep up nuclear weapons technicians, as the U.S. Army did with German rocket scientists in 1945 at the end of the war in Europe. Scientists from the former Soviet Union could help the United States clean up the hundreds of billions of dollars in environmental damage that our nuclear program has created in this country. Indeed, we could create a kind of job bank for unemployed weapons engineers that might discourage would-be Dr. No's from shuttling off to North Korea or Tehran.

At the same time, basic and applied research in this country ought to be re-funded with an eye toward keeping our own weapons designers and nuclear arms specialists employed and occupied in civilian pursuits. After World War II, special tax write-offs and tax incentives were common features of a government policy that, in fact, solved many cold war needs. Our needs now are no less great. Specialists skilled in rocketry and weapons targeting could work on weather forecasting. And nuclear engineers could do environmental research and reclamation.

Now we are facing perhaps the last chance to destroy all of the former Soviet Union's weapons for some $2 billion. We can destroy their tactical weapons alone for some $500 million. Better to try to gather up and store or destroy Soviet weapons than to arm ourselves to deter against their use. But as of this writing, no weapons of any kind have been destroyed. The Bush administration is waiting for a sign that the moment is opportune—that is, that it won't be punished at the polls by the isolationist admirers of Pat Buchanan.

THE NEW ENVIRONMENT FOR MILITARY POWER

The new nuclear threat is now confined to the barely imaginable (given that there are now multiple fingers from four different republics on "the button" in the former Soviet Union). Atomic attack, perhaps on a close American ally or American asset, is possible still, but both the scale of the threat and its likelihood have dimmed dramatically. Other threats to our security are more time-urgent and diffuse. American embassies and citizens may be seized or ransomed. Drug lords and war lords could rampage. The need now isn't for a massive globe-encircling war-fighting machine, but for a well-honed constabulary force on watch and adequate reserve forces to meet any contingency, including a Desert Storm II.

We need to retain and augment the mobility of our forces. The U.S. Air Force should emphasize lift and tactical support, rather than hugely expensive planes that carry limited loads. And we must acquire a better mine-clearing capacity. Currently, the United States has eighteen Korean-era minesweepers but only one modern minesweeper; accordingly, a huge carrier task force—designed to fight (within eyesight of Soviet shores) Soviet carriers that never were built—has had to rely on allied navies.[18] Twice in Gulf operations—in 1987 and again in 1990-1991—we lacked adequate mine protection and had to ask the Europeans for help. We also need better sea-lift. The U.S. Navy will not always be able to count on rusting merchant reserves and the kind of in-country support we received from the Saudis. We need, but do not have, the wherewithal to get water, food, and supplies for several combat divisions to any part of the world and to sustain these forces for months.

As we draw down the numbers of our forces, we need to be careful about standing down reserves. Careful consideration of readiness and sustainability of reserve forces can make the difference, if another test comes.

In this transition to an international order characterized by different threats, we should also be concerned about maintaining our vital industrial base and protecting jobs. In particular, we should be wary of "dumping" huge numbers of our military service people and civilian defense personnel on the job market. Currently only six hours of preparation for the civilian job market are given to our fighting forces.[19] We can do better. Reductions in force should be gradual and talented personnel should be retained, as much as possible, in the reserves and in the guard, for emergencies.

THE COLD WAR'S OVER:
WHO'LL TELL THE PRESIDENT?

Cold war habits linger. NATO war plans are little changed, save that the name of the enemy, the USSR, has been scratched out, and new twin evils—Russia and "instability"—have been penciled in.[20] Each day, $438 million is parsed out for the armed defense of Europe, against contingencies and threats so vague and surreal that nobody in the Defense Department is able to name them.

To be sure, American power is an essential ingredient of American security. But forces designed to counter the Soviet threat—massive carrier task forces, penetration bombers, huge numbers of land-based intercontinental ballistic missiles (ICBMs)—simply do not make any sense now. Yet, clearly, some weapons of retaliation are necessary as long as nuclear knowledge exists, as long as nuclear programs are proliferating, and as long as successor states in the former Soviet Union retain them.

We can dramatically reduce the number of our deterrent weapons and the means to produce them through reciprocal actions. The Congressional Budget Office (CBO) estimates that the savings realized from such action—reducing U.S. warheads to, say, 1,000 warheads—could exceed $261 billion over the next fifteen years.[21] And even halving current arsenals according to the formulas worked out in 1986 by Presidents Gorbachev and Reagan would generate savings of over $9 billion a year.

THE MULTILATERAL IMPERATIVE
IN DEFENSE AND PEACEKEEPING

NATO

NATO's present size is far in excess of any conceivable current threats from the East. NATO is not really needed to deter nuclear attack. That threat is now minuscule. And each of the national nuclear forces of France, Britain, and the United States is sufficient by itself to deter any nuclear lunacy from the East.

NATO, as President Bush has insisted, can help to stabilize the East. But merely being there won't do very much good. NATO has to engage the East where it is possible, and suffuse tensions with an active presence where it is not. Otherwise, like the Knights of Malta or the Women's Christian Temperance Union, NATO might go on for a great while, but its relevance to the politics of our time will atrophy and fade.

Europeans are searching for common undertakings. But the United States has sought to inhibit alternative European security institutions. Although the United States demands primacy in Europe, the Bush administration has kept its distance from the real threats to the Europeans' security in the Balkans and further to the east. For over a year, the CIA had warned of a civil war in Yugoslavia.[22] But even though a NATO solution could have been an effective way to separate warring peoples, a NATO solution was taken off the table by the Bush administration. When the inevitable war occurred and one part of Yugoslavia, Serbia, made war on another, Croatia, the Bush administration's "policy" was to boycott all of Yugoslavia, as if both parties were equally culpable.[23]

By standing aside while the UN and the European community founders over the issue of Balkan chaos, the United States has only encouraged Europe to go it alone. But NATO could become more engaged with the UN and could, as well, help reintegrate the former countries of the Warsaw Pact into the West.

We can offer the more solid fledgling democracies a real spot in collective defense. Why not offer Hungary, Poland, and Czechoslovakia the security of NATO membership? Why not offer Russia some kind of NATO association in return for a stand down of nuclear forces or a dual NATO-Russian key to NATO nuclear forces?[24]

If NATO becomes more active and the United States shares global responsibilities with its allies, suggest the respected Harvard analyst William W. Kaufman and John D. Steinbruner of Brookings, then the United States could save some $800 billion over the next ten years.[25] In turn, significant savings in defense would help lower budget deficits, reduce interest rates and the cost of capital, stimulate capital formation, create more jobs, stimulate growth, create investment, and provide needed money for other critical national needs.

But NATO can't be everything. To attain a new world order that means something, we should wager on a new kind of multilateral international environment. The United States should stop pouring cold water on allied suggestions for new multilateral military institutions, like the ones the Australians have made in Asia and the Germans and French have offered in Europe. The traditional dominance of the United States in NATO, ANZUS, and the UN might have been prestigious and comfortable, but there is some question as to whether current conditions suit institutions fashioned toward old threats and cold war patterns of power. New collective security mechanisms, shared more broadly with others, make sense. First, we might need them, inasmuch as our resources and bases seem destined to diminish. Second, isn't it time others paid their share? And third, are we afraid that others might get a piece of the leadership limelight in the new world order?

Given the drawdown of U.S. defense procurement, multilateral defense is a necessity. The two new great powers in world affairs, Japan and Germany, should be invited—indeed, urged—to join the UN Security Council. Currently, both are cutting back on defense, yet the United States stations some 50,000 soldiers in Japan[26] and will spend over $100 billion in Germany to defend that country against 233,000 troops, whom the Germans are subsidizing so that they can go home peacefully to what was once the Soviet Union instead of squatting in idleness in Germany.

The United States, Japan, Germany, and the rest of the G-7 countries can pull their fair share of weight. If Japan and Germany—two non-nuclear powers—join the otherwise nuclear-dominated UN Security Council, a powerful message would be sent to the effect that economic leadership, and not just military competence, is the stuff of leadership in international politics. Some observers are bound to argue that both the Japanese and German constitutions inhibit more activity in world affairs, especially in potential multilateral peacekeeping efforts. Indeed, if this is the case (and the contention is very much debatable), the United States should argue that those constitutions written by U.S. military authorities, largely at the end of World War II, ought to be changed.

Japan and Germany are no longer vanquished states to be tutored in democracy. In a real sense, they are like ourselves, victors of the cold war and, as such, have an obligation to contribute to a stable world. If Japan and Germany are reluctant to take their share of global responsibility, the United States should rethink the extensive military services that it renders to both of them. We have selflessly defended both of the losers of World War II throughout most of the cold war. Notable American self-sacrifice has brought the vanquished to great prosperity. It is time for these new victors to bear equitably the burdens of post-cold war reconstruction.

A Revitalized United Nations?

Not too far down the road, even with strengthened military reserves, U.S. forces won't be able to do it all alone. No matter how skillful our military forces, greater international support will be needed if they are to be effective. We can crow, as the Bush administration has done tirelessly, that we are the world's sole remaining superpower.[27] But the plain fact is that in the next five years we will need, more than ever before, the active participation of friends and allies.

Although UN Resolution 678 cited the UN Charter to authorize the American and allied collective international action against Iraq, the suggestion of our allies that we might use meaningful cooperative procedures, established by the UN founders, was being finessed. Under the UN Charter, the Security Council may approve the use of force either by member-states or through the military staff committee. Unity of command need not have been sacrificed, as the Council could have delegated the leadership of the effort to General Schwarzkopf. The UN Security Council Staff Committee could have helped clarify the objectives of the war—and enforce the peace. It could have lent legitimacy to an effort to bring Saddam Hussein himself to justice.

Use of the UN Military Staff Committee of the Security Council might have helped establish a basis for UN relief efforts in Iraq. The terms of surrender might have been more sustainable and less leaky. Although the United States agreed to fill the Military Staff Committee with high-ranking personnel, the Bush administration rejected the principle that the Committee could become an integral part of the thirty-one nation American-led effort in the Gulf. That was a pity.

After the war was over, in July 1991, George Bush along with his G-7 partners began to note that the UN might have as active a role in settling disputes as had been hoped by its founders. As their final communiqué read: "We commit ourselves to making the UN stronger, and more effective, in order to protect human rights, to maintain peace and security for all, and to deter aggression. . . . The UN's role in peacekeeping should be reinforced and we are prepared to support this strongly."

Embarrassingly, the facts behind the rhetoric speak not to a real commitment to the UN but to boiler-plated boosterism without meaningful support. In fact, the United States currently owes the UN $485 million in arrearages. And the United States has been the last of the G-7 countries to provide money promised to the IMF for emergency help to the former Soviet Union. UN-led peacekeeping efforts have seemed to pile success on success. But the U.S. share of these efforts will cost some $300 million more; and, like some Chapter 7 bankrupt firm, the Bush administration has promised to pay what it owes incrementally—eventually. Outgoing UN General Secretary Perez de Cuellar spoke a melancholy coda to American leadership: "It is a source of profound concern to me that the same membership which deems it appropriate to entrust the United Nations

Secretariat with unprecedented new responsibilities has not taken the necessary action at the same time to see that the minimum financial resources are provided."[28]

The cancellation of one B-2 bomber or one Sea Wolf submarine, both useful only to fight the Soviets in a global nuclear war, could yield far more in terms of peace if the money were transferred from bloated war-fighting inventories to starved peacekeeping. That is a far less humiliating and more appropriate method of financing peace than "Operation Tin Cup"—the shakedown of allies and associates before Operation Desert Storm, undertaken, one has the impression, so that the president and the Congress would not be inconvenienced by the Constitution.

A New Respect for Human Rights?

There are two positions in international law. The first clearly condemns genocide and mass brutality. The second enjoins states to respect each other's territorial integrity, no matter what atrocity may be perpetrated within a "sovereign" state's frontiers.

The second definition of international conduct has prevailed. With no effective force to stop them, Idi Amin killed 10,000 civilians a week, Pol Pot starved and massacred a million or more in Cambodia, and Ethiopia's Mengistu created a massive famine. The Security Council took no action. In the cold war, despots could do what they wanted within their own borders.

In reaction to the plight of the Kurds, however, France and England sponsored Resolution 688. Resolution 688 recognized that there is, first, a relationship between internal repression and international peace. It allowed that massive human rights violations are of concern to the Security Council. With Resolution 688 in hand, the United States and the international community were able to undertake "Operation Provide Comfort." More than 10,000 U.S. troops saved more than 100,000 Kurds, who had been hard-pressed by Saddam's rockets, gas, and forced march into oblivion.

President Bush told the Congress in March 1991 that, "[f]or all that Saddam has done to his own people, to the Kuwaitis, and to the entire world, Saddam and those around him are accountable." But then, inexplicably, the Bush administration rejected the very same actions that Bush had forwarded in the heat of war. It seems that the idea of a peacetime trial for Saddam's criminal acts against his own people was dropped by the White House at the urging of Bush's Saudi and Syrian allies, who feared that these principles, once established, might then have a relevance to their own situations.

To push forward the issue of postwar multilateral action against Saddam, Britain's John Major and German Foreign Minister Hans Dietrich Genscher called for a convening of an International Court of Justice to try Saddam Hussein on the basis of the Nuremberg principles.[29] The Senate urged Bush to establish an office charged with promoting an international tribunal.[30] But Bush finessed the suggestion, claiming that the "most important thing" wasn't justice but "to get Saddam Hussein out of there." In fact, there is the worst of both worlds in Iraq: Saddam remains, and the world stays silent, blocked by the Bush administration's moral inertia.

An *in absentia* trial of Saddam, even if he were not brought to the dock himself, would have shrunk him several sizes, not only at home but throughout the Arab world as well; and it would have alerted future despots of the risk of engaging in monstrous crimes.

The principle of collective humanitarian intervention is one that could serve international order in the future; and it is one that should be backed, as the *Wall Street Journal* has enjoined, by "muscular leadership."[31] We should now insist that genocide is a punishable crime.

Only in recent months has the United States even mentioned that it might be a good idea to bring the Khmer Rouge (the group responsible for the murder of over 1 million of its countrymen) before an international tribunal.[32] Prior to the fall of 1991, the United States, lamentably, helped an armed Khmer Rouge back into a position that allowed it to compete for power in the framework of the UN settlement. Henceforth, a great good can be accomplished by a real and consistent U.S. stance on "crimes against humanity."

THE PERILS OF AD HOCERY: WITHOUT VISION YOU DON'T GO ANYWHERE

An unfortunate impression made by the Bush administration is that the United States is led by spleen and personal politics rather than by some epiphanic "new world order." Confident in his place among the fraternity of power players at home and overseas, George Bush wings it. When warned that an Iraqi build-up would lead to an inevitable invasion, the president asked Arab leaders if his own analysts could be right. Bush's collection of informants—various sheiks, emirs, potentates, ersatz princes, and presidents—thereupon assured him that Saddam could not possibly turn on an Arab brother. So Bush turned aside his professionals and listened to his "friends."

Normally, the national security adviser to the president or the secretary of state plumbs the bureaucracy for options, papers, advice, and expertise. But access to Bush's narrow national security team was so closed that his secretary of defense learned of upcoming summits from press conferences, and his chairman of the Joint Chiefs was certain that a peaceful "containment" option, which might have "strangled Iraq," was never considered by those with experience in the area. Indeed, a "strangulation" short of war might have stopped Saddam's nuclear capability and prevented the post-bellum chaos and ecological mayhem that transpired.

Instead, the war remedy seems to have been chosen not through reasoned decisionmaking, but by a kind of towel-snapping, insouciant coterie of insiders, impervious to professional counsel. In short, Bush sought advice from those with whom he was at ease and comfortable. When the Iraqi war was won, not one professional in Persian Gulf politics was brought into the Bush inner circle. Postwar planning for the future of Kuwait and the region was begun only after the war was over. The professionals in the State Department and CIA were frozen out.[33] And when Ambassador Robert Strauss issued anguished calls decrying the lack of White House attention to the imploding former Soviet Union (a "Goddamn outrage," he said), his concerns were met by a deafening silence.[34]

Bush's foreign policy was informed by instinct and viscera rather than by vision and design. Mentioning Saddam twenty times in his address announcing the onset of the war,[35] the president deliberately mispronounced and burlesqued the Iraqi leader's name each time, making it sound to the Arab-speaking ear like "shoe-shine boy." In order further to get the man's goat, the president also said that the dictator was going to get "his ass kicked."[36] (Even Bush's defense secretary, Richard Cheney, took pains to tell a *Washington Post* reporter that he was repelled at this kind of language as inappropriate and unworthy of a president.)[37] Like some eighteenth-century monarch, in pondering the option of war or peace, the personal pronoun tripped easily off Mr. Bush's tongue. "I've had it"; "Consider me provoked"; "I am more determined than ever before in my life"—these have been his usual reactions to the external affairs of the nation. But the splenetic and profoundly personal elements of American foreign policy were in opposition to Bush's own calls for creating institutionalized mechanisms to control international violence.

The Arms Trade

The buzzword for the 1990s, in the Bush administration, has been to assume an "affirmative arms export" posture—apparently the only kind of affirmative action the administration will willingly support at all.[38] Hence, in one of the first and perhaps most symbolic acts of the Bush administration, the old Office of Munitions Control was abolished and its duties transferred to the State Department. Whereas the usual business of diplomats had formerly been negotiations, their new mission in the Bush years, on which each senior field officer has been told he will be graded, is to become a partner to arms exports.

For the first time, the Bush administration has started to use scarce Export-Import Bank money—funds previously restricted by law to civilian projects—in order to promote the commercial sale of arms. We've come a long way when arms are seen as just another export, like soybeans or auto parts.

In public Mr. Bush has given ringing declamations on the virtues of arms control. As he told Congress, just after the Gulf war, "[i]t would be tragic if the nations of the Middle East and the Persian Gulf were now, in the wake of war, to embark on a new arms race." And on May 29, 1991, President Bush told graduating U.S. Air Force Academy officers that "[n]owhere are the dangers of weapons proliferation more important than in the Middle East."

But no sooner had the president proclaimed an aim of creating a "general code of responsible arms transfers" than a new wave of arms sales commenced. The truth, of course, was that no significant amounts of Egyptian or Israeli arms were consumed in the Gulf War. And the small states of the area could not possibly be made secure by new arms. By themselves, the Saudis and the Emirates, no matter how lavishly provisioned, could hardly provide for their own defense against regional predators. Only American power in concert with that of others would be able to save them if they were threatened by the worst. Meanwhile, American arms hardly make our Gulf client-states more secure. On the contrary, U.S. arms can more safely be predicted to fuel regional arms races and insecurity than to produce any putative form of armed "stability."

In the future, we ought to know exactly what arms transfers are supposed to do. Approval and disapproval of sales should be undertaken by both houses of Congress. And a kind of defense proliferation and arms control impact report, modeled on environmental impact requirements, should accompany significant arms transfers.

Real agreements for tracking new weapons systems transfers and for monitoring and controlling quantitative and qualitative increases could dampen arms competition and the cycle of hostility and violence in the Gulf area. But eighteen months ago, the president vetoed legislation to mandate the publication of the names of companies engaged in supplying lethal technologies to any region of the world and tried, with some success, to water down a Japanese-sponsored idea of a UN arms exports registry.

The Bush administration claims it is giving nearly $18 billion of foreign aid this year, but the truth is that over 50 percent of that figure is dedicated to military transfers to the Third World. What is left over tends to go to aid relief, the Peace Corps, and narcotics control. Security assistance ought to be separated from foreign aid and linked to creditworthiness and human rights concerns.

Military assistance rarely adds up to long-term development. In fact, military "aid" can be deleterious inasmuch as it diverts some of the most technically competitive members of a developing country's work force.[39] The new arms trade may not be of much long-term benefit to American arms contractors either. The quarterly balance sheet of U.S. defense contractors might be improved; but as the Congress's Office of Technology Assessment has noted, the "overall benefits are not so clear cut"; "[i]ncreasingly, . . . transfers [of] defense technology to other countries results in more foreign-made defense components being imported into the United States."[40]

A New Competitiveness and a New Foreign Policy

During the cold war, over 30 percent of graduate engineers and some 60 percent of all government-funded research had a defense implication. We will be the poorer if this long, arduous, and immensely expensive investment dissipates now. And we ought to be able to recapture and redirect it.

Government-funded research in the defense of America has already energized our civilian industrial base. But the Bush administration opposes an industrial and infrastructure investment policy. A wise defense industrial policy would assist in the transfer of defense products in order to modernize our civilian economy. A civilian initiative could help create new industries to absorb the talents and overcapacity left by a reduction in direct defense spending.[41]

We also need an intelligent export policy. The Bush administration has embargoed American telecommunication equipment as "defense sensitive," because the newest generation of American gear can't be wiretapped; the Bush administration would rather have an intelligence edge than sales. Moreover, the continued U.S. embargo of fiber optics to the former Soviet Union, at worst, inhibits the success of democracy in the Soviet Union —and, at best, concedes the market to others.[42]

The Bush administration faces the worst of all foreign policy planning worlds. If Russia and the Commonwealth of Independent States survive without American capital and goods, then the benefactors will be the German and the Japanese. And if the Commonwealth's experiment in democracy and capitalism flops, then the United States will be called to man the ramparts again, either economically or militarily. It would be a great irony to wind up still poor and forced to pass the hat again to defend our economic competitors from the effects of a Slavic-Eurasian collapse that we did nothing to impede because we were still caught up in old cold war fights.

POSTERITY UP IN SMOKE?

Jefferson, Adams, and the other great framers of our republic were obsessed with the idea of posterity. Washington used the word nine times in one speech.[43] Our competitors also look to more than the next election and the next quarter's balance sheet. Japan, for instance, is preparing a hundred-year plan to combat global warming and, as a consequence of government policy, has realized a 500 percent increase in industrial fuel efficiency in twenty years. But no energy policy resulted from the great opportunity the Gulf War presented. Instead, George Bush (remember the environmental president?) proposed opening the coastal plain of the Arctic National Wildlife Refuge, the outer continental shelf off the east coast, the Florida coast, and southern California to oil exploration.[44] Most energy experts agreed that Bush's energy "policy" would not only wreak extraordinary environmental damage but would also fail to bring about energy independence.[45]

Indeed, the Bush administration has not been willing to look for a cure for U.S. petroleum heavy use—the world's greatest oil addiction and a condition that lay at the heart of the Gulf conflict. The best energy policy would have been to charge a user fee for energy, making the tax deductible from income when long commutes are necessary for employment, as is often the case in the West. Instead, Bush just watched. When oil prices rapidly doubled after Saddam's invasion, levying a de facto tax estimated to be between a low of $45 billion and a high of $200 billion on the American people, Bush refused to release U.S. reserve stocks of oil to push back the price. The strategic petroleum reserve, built at a cost of $15 billion, could have cushioned most of the price shock. At a minimum, $180 per person was extracted from the economy. Much of this money was remitted overseas.[46]

Even the idea of higher fuel standards was labeled "extreme" by Bush, notwithstanding the fact that American car manufacturers seem to have a corner on some of the most energy-efficient engines (namely, powerful and efficient two-stroke engines) and lightweight carbon fiber car body technology.

In sum, we might have defeated Saddam once; but without a U.S. energy policy, Saddam or those who would do Saddam one better will have their revenge. If our present energy dependence continues to deepen, we will need the sheikdoms and potentates of the Gulf more than they need us.

An Environmental Policy Elsewhere

The Bush administration is ignoring tomorrow. In the developing areas of the world, population growth outstrips resources, and unemployment exceeds 44 percent. But the administration waits for the international market to work its wonders and opposes UN birth control programs. The Bush administration is reluctant to contribute to the UN population fund, lest family planning include any mention of abortion.

The National Academy of Sciences, an organization of America's foremost scientific talent, warned in early 1991 that the world could warm some 9 degrees in the next century, with catastrophic results for the Third World and the world's agriculture. The remedy, the National Academy of Sciences said, would be to reduce greenhouse emissions up to 40 percent. Net costs to the U.S. economy, if any at all, would be "very low."

But the White House has held that the Academy's report was "inconclusive," "not so solid," and that a better "understanding" must be reached before the United States agrees to sign on with Europeans, Japanese, Canadians, Chinese, and members of the former Soviet bloc to remedy a "hypothetical" worry. No matter what the issue—arctic preservation, global warming, ozone, fisheries—the hallmark of the Bush administration has been disinterest. Posterity will have its day—on someone else's watch.

The American Example and American Foreign Policy

No foreign policy program can be more productive for global peace than our own example as a free people. We cannot expect to abandon law and order at home or abroad and at the same time erect new standards of international conduct. Yet, although the Bush administration speaks of a new world order based on a respect for international law and order, the president has asserted that either the FBI or the U.S. armed forces can seize suspects of crimes overseas without obtaining a warrant from or even the consent of foreign governments.

No matter how satisfying it may be to apprehend malefactors, the president has in fact authorized a new standard whereby the United States can, at will, kidnap suspects and lawbreakers anywhere in the world. It is not surprising that the Iranians have already cited this opinion, written by William P. Barr, the U.S. attorney general, as its own justification to mark for death those authors and other fugitives from Iranian justice who break Islamic law.

The Bush administration, while citing the Barr ruling to justify actions against drug dealers in Mexico and Manuel Noriega, has refused to let Congress review the Barr brief and its recommendations. Congress, which makes laws, has been denied Executive Branch interpretation of the laws and barred from knowing Executive Branch interpretation of the numerous treaties regarding extradition, "sovereignty," and "sovereign immunity" that Congress has approved over the last 200 years.[47]

The Constitution and War

The Gulf War could have been conducted with a real legal warrant, rather than with the take-it-or-leave-it, last-minute vote offered the Congress. Leading members of both houses begged the president to take the matter of authorizing the use of U.S. troops to Congress first, as the Constitution demands. Congress would have debated, to be sure, but few doubted that defensive measures would have been authorized—and that, when and if the blockade failed, offensive measures would have also been passed. But the constitutional process, Mr. Cheney and Mr. Bush argued, would send the "wrong signal to Saddam."[48] The argument offered by the White House was that, when confronted by the aggressions of a lawless despot, a government could reject the legacy of Jefferson, Washington, and Adams on the grounds of expediency and, instead, adopt Saddam's own lawless ways.

It was a strange way to get to a "new world order"—that, presumably, would be faithful to upholding international law—by being cavalier about the great constitutional foundations of our laws at home. Finally, with the chairman of the Joint Chiefs insisting that Congress authorize offensive actions before the first shot was fired, the administration yielded to the Constitution's form, if not its logic.

CONCLUSION

The great successes against our communist foes were wrought by a forty-five-year-old bipartisan effort. Long-term interests can be realized only with a bipartisan concord and comity. Finger-pointing divisiveness, looking for the partisan edge with an eye only to the next election, squanders tomorrow. "No one . . . doubts us anymore," Bush told a flag-waving South Carolina crowd in March 1991.[49] That may be. Our reputation at arms is secure. But the future is at risk. Tomorrow will be better only if we have its shape in mind. We need to work together. We need vision. And we can secure a better tomorrow.

NOTES

1. Roger Highfield, "Cash Crisis Halts Iraq Nuclear Inspections," *Daily Telegraph* (UK), December 11, 1991, p. 11; and John J. Flaka, "UN Inspectors in Iraq Running Out of Funding," *Wall Street Journal*, December 16, 1991, p. A10.

2. Joseph B. Trester, "Cocaine Is Again Surging Out of Panama," *New York Times*, August 13, 1991.

3. "US Invasion Brings Panama Slim Dividends," *London Financial Times*, December 29, 1990, p. 6.

4. Meanwhile, in private, Ollie North was selling Iran arms, while the United States, in public, was trying to get the Allies to refrain from arming Iran. When pressed to explain it all, one administration official said, "You had to have been there."

5. "Bush Gives Praise to Kuwait After Meeting Emir," *New York Times*, October 2, 1991, p. A5.

6. Patrick J. Sloyan, "Bush's Decision to End War Early Spared the Nuclear of Hussein's Armored Force," *Baltimore Sun*, June 23, 1991, p. 3.

7. "Gorbachev: I Ignored Bush's Warning of Coup," *Chicago Tribune*, November 13, 1991, p. 20.

8. "September 4, 1991, Briefing, Secretary of State Baker," *New York Times*, September 5, 1991, p. A8; "President Bush's Remarks Cited as President Continues to Exercise Caution on the Soviet Union," *Wall Street Journal*, August 27, 1991, pp. A1 and A14.

9. "Baker Briefing on United States Policy Toward the Soviet Union," *New York Times*, September 4, 1991, p. A12; and "Soviets Again Seek US Food Aid," *Washington Post*, October 23, 1991, p. A40.

10. Karen Elliot House, "Atlanticist Aid: Using NATO to Feed Russia," *Wall Street Journal*, November 6, 1991, p. 18.

11. Melissa Healy, "US Studies New Role for Troops in a Changed Europe," *Los Angeles Times*, September 22, 1991, p. 8.

12. Mathew L. Wald, "Soviet Oil Industry Outlook Is Called Dismal by Experts," *New York Times*, March 22, 1991, p. D1.

13. Steven Greenhouse, "Report Critical of Drop of Savings," *New York Times*, June 10, 1991, p. D2; Keith Bradsher, "Monetary Fund Warns of Shortage of Savings," *New York Times*, September 30, 1991, p. A4.

14. Francis Harris, "European Barrier to Soviet Instability," *Daily Telegraph* (UK), April 19, 1991, p. 11.

15. Phillip Resvin, "600,000 Left the Soviet Union in 1990: East-West Ties Are Fraying at the Edges," *Wall Street Journal*, February 22, 1991, p. A8; Celestine Bohlen, "Moscow Predicts 1.5 Million Will Move West," *New York Times*, January 27, 1991, p. 4; Marc Fisher, "West Europeans Brace for Predicted Mass Migration from East," *Washington Post*, September 22, 1991, p. A1.

16. Telephone conversation with the author, April 1991.

17. Bill McAllister, "Peace Corps Plans to Send 500 to Ex-Soviet States," *Washington Post*, December 31, 1991, p. A11.

18. Eric Schmitt, "Gulf Is Swept for Mines in the Aftermath of War," *Washington Post*, March 19, 1991, p. A14.

19. As Patricia Hines (Deputy Assistant Secretary of the U.S. Army) suggested in the *Wall Street Journal* of January 10, 1992, more thought could be given to using the 50,000 or so officers who soon will be let go from the armed services to help alleviate America's shortage of qualified high school teachers. Eighty percent of the major or above officers who will be entering the civilian job market have at least one master's degree, almost all have experience in public-speaking, and many have had classroom experience as teachers. A presidential initiative pushing alternative teacher certification for this "windfall of talent" would help see that our nation's investment is recouped where it is needed the most.

20. William Drozdiak, "NATO Finds New Role with Soviet Threat Gone," *Washington Post*, November 2, 1991, p. A1.

21. Barton Gellman, "Deep Nuclear Arms Cuts Seen Saving $261 Billion," *Washington Post*, October 28, 1991, p. A4.

22. Jim Hoagland, "What Price Unity?" *Washington Post*, May 14, 1991, p. A19.

23. "US Imposes Sanctions Against All of Yugoslavia," *Washington Post*, December 7, 1991, p. A19.

24. David Remnick, "Yeltsin Pleads for Membership in NATO," *Washington Post*, December 21, 1991, p. A1.

25. William W. Kaufman and John D. Steinbruner, *The Post Cold-War Defense Program* (Washington, D.C.: Brookings, 1991).

26. Fred Kaplan, "Should the US Retreat from the Pacific?" *Boston Globe*, July 14, 1991, p. 69.

27. See, for instance, Robert M. Gates, "American Leadership in a New World," Address to the American Newspaper Publishers Association, The White House, May 17, 1991, p. 7.

28. Paul Lewis, "UN Asks Billion for Peacekeeper Fund," *New York Times*, November 25, 1991, p. A3.

29. William Droziak, "Europeans Seek Trial of Saddam for Genocide: EC Asks UN to Explore Nuremberg Option," *Washington Post*, April 16, 1991, p. A12.

30. Richard L. Berke, "Senate Passes Legislation Urging Tribunal for Iraqi War Criminals," *New York Times*, April 19, 1991, p. A9.

31. "George Bush's United Nations," *Wall Street Journal* [Editorial], April 15, 1991, p. A14.

32. Elizabeth Becker, "Breakthrough in Cambodia," *Washington Post*, October 27, 1991, p. C7.

33. See George D. Moffet III and Jane Friedman, "US Failure to Deter Iraq Blamed on Policymaking," *Christian Science Monitor*, March 22, 1991, p. 4; and author interviews with senior State Department officers.

34. Elisabeth Rubinfein, "Ambassador Strauss Sharply Criticizes Abandonment of Plan to Aid Moscow," *Wall Street Journal*, November 19, 1991, p. A17.

35. "Transcript of the Comments by Bush on the Air Strikes Against Iraqis," *New York Times*, January 17, 1991.

36. Cited by Rowland Evans and Robert Novak, "Bush's New Order," *Washington Post*, December 28, 1990, p. A19.

37. Cheney recoiled at the president's choice of words—see Bob Woodward, *The Commanders* (N.Y.: Simon & Schuster, 1991), p. 282.

38. Mark Sommer, "Weapons—America's Best Export?" *The Christian Science Monitor*, July 18, 1991, p. 18.

39. William Armbrauster, "US Should Revamp Foreign Aid, End Military Programs, Study Says," *Journal of Commerce*, May 17, 1991, p. 1.

40. "Global Arms Trade: Commerce in Advanced Military Technology and Weapons" (Washington, D.C.: U.S. Government Printing Office, 1991); and Memo from Les Aspin, Chairman of the House Armed Services Committee, "A New Budget Deal?" U.S. House of Representatives, Committee on Armed Services, September, 15, 1991, p. 2.

41. John Burgess, "Council Warns of Technological Slide," *Washington Post*, March 21, 1991, p. B11.

42. Stuart Auerbach, "AT&T Export Curbs Hamper Soviet Reform," *Washington Post*, September 25, 1991, p. A16.

43. The observation is original to Henry Steele Commanger; it is cited in Jessica Mathews, "Our Leaders Used to Care About Posterity," *Washington Post*, June 27, 1991, p. A23.

44. "Net Cost of Energy Bill Is Put at $7 Billion," *New York Times*, October 25, 1991, p. A9.

45. William J. Broad, "As Nations Meet on Global Warming, US Stands Alone," *New York Times*, September 10, 1991, p. B8.

46. See, on this point, Representative Phillip R. Sharp (D.-Ind.), Chairman of the Energy and Power Subcommittee of the House Committee on Energy and Commerce, "How Bush Made the Recession Worse," *Washington Post*, December 29, 1991, p. C7.

47. See Ruth Marcus, "FBI Told It Can Seize Fugitives Abroad," *Washington Post*, October 14, 1989, p. A15: and Associated Press, "Bush to Disobey Subpoena," *Montgomery Advertiser*, July 31, 1991, p. 3.

48. Elinor Randolph, "Cheney Cautions Congress on Debate on Gulf Policy," *Washington Post*, November 19, 1990, p. A22.

49. Frank J. Murray, "Bush: Vietnam 'Ghosts' Exorcised," *Washington Times*, March 18, 1991, p. A1.

14

WILLIAM P. KREML

Winning a Government: Reinvigorating the Political System

At the end of this book, as at the start, we must boldly confront the question: What do we win when we win? In previous chapters my co-authors have focused on the need for a Democratic party that can not only win office but win with policies, convictions, and intentions that will meet America's festering problems head on. That kind of Democratic party will deal with fundamental problems instead of advancing superficial remedies; will plan ahead instead of playing with expedient, short-run policies; will work steadily, persistently, comprehensively, to help realize the great American values of liberty, equality, justice.

But if the Democrats win office, win governmental power, what kind of government will they win? On countless occasions in the past, the Democrats have won elections, they have wanted to meet the needs of the populace, they have been committed to "making a difference," only to encounter the antimajoritarian breastworks in the American political system, to be trapped in the governmental maze, to be thwarted by endless "veto traps" and other checks and balances.

Hence, in my view, winning office—and even winning it with strong commitments to action—will be only the first step for the Democratic party. The party leadership, with the support of grassroots leaders, must take a long hard look at the political system they hope to make operative for the long haul. They will have to do what I undertake to do here: to analyze our fragmented system, to reassess the old balance of majority rule and "minority rights," to take an iconoclastic approach to the federalism, or division of national and state power, that so many Americans venerate, to look at "states' wrongs" as well as states' rights. And this will call for

Democrats to take the toughest step of all—to look at their own party and to ask whether it helps unite government or further fragments it, whether it can be an instrument for energizing government or enervating it; in short, whether it is part of the solution or part of the problem.

Governmental structures are never neutral. The framers of the Constitution, no less certainly than modern organizational theorists, knew that biases are inherent in all organizational arrangements. That is why the framers took all of the hot 1787 Philadelphia summer to devise the political system that they did. Their design, as Americans have been taught ever since, was purposefully centrifugal, spreading out the powers of government so as to blunt the potential of those majoritarian "factions" that might come together in a threatening way. Thus, structural centrifugality was linked to a check upon democracy from the beginning of the nation. If anything, the centrifugal nature of the government's institutions has increased over the last 200 years, and, almost unbelievably, conservative interests argue for more.

This centrifugally ensured check upon democracy was vigorously defended, of course, in *The Federalist*. Those essays of James Madison, Alexander Hamilton, and, more occasionally, John Jay meticulously described both the how and the why of the American political arrangements. The Antifederalists so vigorously opposed the Constitution that they made democracy, not the effectiveness or fairness of the new government, the central issue of the ratification debates. The writings of Richard Henry Lee, George Mason, Patrick Henry, and Elbridge Gerry, among others, were one large cry of "foul" directed toward constitutional limitations upon popular government. The Antifederalists' contribution, drafted ironically by Congressman James Madison in the first congressional session, was the Bill of Rights. Only the Bill of Rights, not the original seven articles, manifests the contribution of democratic interests, particularly in the states of New York and Virginia, where the ratification steamroller was slowed and the right of citizens to oppose their government was preserved.

Though neither well understood today by the public nor well taught in America's schools, the Bill of Rights is both philosophically and ideologically opposed to the Constitution's original articles. What is even less well understood, and less well taught, is the structurally centripetal nature of the Bill of Rights. Its principal purpose was, and still is, to preserve citizen-generated action through protection of free speech, a free press, and the like. These rights guaranteed the kind of public communication that necessarily precedes organized political opposition. Sadly, the Bill of Rights did not, and still does not, include specific reference to the greatest collective institution of modern democracy: the political party.

THE ORIGINAL FRAMEWORK

I will begin my discussion of America's all too checked and checkered democracy by outlining a brief but frankly theoretical perspective. The Philadelphia conventioneers, as well as those who have both formally amended and informally filled in the cracks of the Constitution over the last 200 years, rarely evaded the lessons of theory in their arguments. Those who would criticize the organization of the government should do no less.

A sound analysis of the American political system must necessarily be two-tiered. The grander tier would explain the differences among the ways that all institutions understand what they are dealing with. This analysis, in other words, should portray the different *forms* of understanding that various political institutions, depending upon their structures, impose upon everyday political problems. All institutions (like individuals) understand, process, and generate information. The forms, or structures, of that understanding, processing, and generating are no more neutral than are the forms, or structures, of government. Though the framers were 200 years ahead of organization theorists' more explicit study of such things, their intuition squares with any modern description of what they did.

At a second, more modest tier of explanation, I will offer an analysis of what I believe to be the key pre-constitutional balances in the private-to-public domains, legal-to-political domains, and antimajoritarian-to-majoritarian qualities of political influence upon the government. All three pre-constitutional balances, I suggest, impinge upon the centrifugal-to-centripetal imbalances that beset our governmental structures. They are central to the still-limited democracy that makes up American politics.

Following these brief framework descriptions, I shall apply both frameworks to three political arenas that should be significant to Progressive Democrats. The first is the local and state arena. Far too little has been written about the contribution of the structural imbalances within local and state governments to the larger inequities of American politics. The second is the formal constitutional arrangement. The design of America's principal public document, along with the additions and subtractions that have molded it further over the last two centuries, still check democracy as much as they ever did. Finally is the current status of America's "unwritten constitution." Sadly, the flexible, informal expansion and contraction of the institutions of the government that the formal Constitution allows has permitted those who have taken up residence within the nation's public institutions, particularly the Congress, to make the government even more centrifugal, and less democratic, than it has been in a long time. Any discussion of the undemocratic nature of the American government must detail what the Congress has done to itself, and to the nation, during the recent destructuring of its internal institutions.

A WAY OF KNOWING

As I have suggested, an inquiry into the democratic nature of governmental institutions must include an analysis of how different institutions understand, process, and generate political "raw material." This analysis, in turn, must rely upon a determination of whether or not certain political issues will be dealt with *at all* by relevant political institutions. Certain issues, by their very *form*, are inevitably either filtered in or out of any political discourse.[1] But the nature of this filtering, again, is best understood through an examination of the forms of understanding both of the political issues themselves and of the institutions that may or may not deal with them.

The old distinction between apples and apples, as opposed to apples and oranges, is useful to an understanding of the biases that characterize not only political structures but also the interactions between citizens and their governments. I find the terms "contractual" (apples and apples) and "aggregative" (apples and oranges) to be the best terms for describing the nature of citizen-to-government interaction. Contractual forms of citizen-to-government interaction are nearly always interactions that concern only two parties. They therefore almost necessarily *exclude consideration of any matter other than that expressed by the constituent and the governmental entity that is being accessed by the constituent.* In short, they include, exclusively, the quid pro quo of a service rendered for political support.

Aggregative forms of interaction, by contrast, *specifically include, or attempt to include, all of the relevant interests or considerations of the public good that might be affected by a governmental interaction.* In other words, aggregative forms include those considerations, and the concerns of those citizens, that are not represented by the immediate parties within a constituent-to-government negotiation. This explanatory framework suggests, of course, that the structural forms of all public institutions are significantly related to a corresponding preference for the forms of interaction that take place between constituencies and public institutions. Inasmuch as the structural biases of various institutional arrangements permit different considerations either to be or not be a part of the public agenda, different groupings of citizens realize better or lesser results from the government because of the *forms* of their needs and the "match" of those forms with the government's institutions. Those segments of the public who are best prepared to engage in a *contractual* form of interaction with the government fare better with a government whose lack of an aggregational capability in its decisionmaking favors the contractual form of governmental access. Those segments of the public who are unrepresented (usually because they are poor, unorganized, or unaware of where the levers of access to the government are) fare less well because the government is not constructed to entertain consideration of needs that are not presented in the contractual mode.

THREE CRITICAL BALANCES

In addition to the above framework for detecting the ideological bias of various political structures, a second, more modest framework exists that I believe complements the first.[2] This design, as I noted earlier, revolves around the balances that a political system maintains along three pre-constitutional continua. The first, the balance between private and public concerns, is as old as both political theory and the real world of politics. The United States, as a potential successor to the democratic evolution that originated in seventeenth- and eighteenth-century England, has traditionally insulated broad areas of concern from the reach of public authority.

If the balance of private-to-public domains in any political system is one of the keys to democratic governance, the cycles of America's politics clearly reveal a pattern of alternating conservative-to-liberal biases for private and public domains. The liberal bias toward the public domain was a significant part of Jefferson's Enlightenment-influenced political thought. The Declaration of Independence, in particular, shows the influence the Scottish Enlightenment and that strain of mildly communalist thought found in the writings of Francis Hutcheson.[3] Jefferson's Declaration is dedicated to the maintenance of the common weal, or the public domain.

The creators of the first seven articles of the Constitution, by contrast, were primarily concerned with the preservation of private rights. Their theoretical vision emphasized private property and limited government; and, if the Scottish Enlightenment was relevant for them at all, it was the more mechanistic skepticism of David Hume that influenced framers such as James Madison.[4] For the Federalists a free society was the society of a limited public sphere, because free men were deemed to be capable of managing an arena of unfettered private intercourse. A nation's political business, they argued, should never impinge upon that arena.

The pre-constitutional balance between political and legal domains is a cousin to the private-public balance. Though many of the conservatives of the constitutional period were lawyers, even the non-lawyers among the Federalists were more willing than the Antifederalists to extend common-law notions of property, contract, and tort into the interactive rules of America's yeoman farmers and tradesmen. Apart from the first three (institutional) articles of the Constitution, note that the fourth and sixth articles, respectively, include the full faith and credit clause, the "deliver up" clause for those who have run from their obligations, and the constitutional assurance that debts contracted during the Confederation would be owed after the Constitution's passage.

In contrast to the Federalist stance, and encouraged by a belief in the private law's rationality and the extension of that rationality to the public law, the Antifederalist position was weighted toward political rather than legal remedies. Spurred on by Edward Coke's very real seventeenth-century challenges to James I, and intellectually inspired by arguments such as the one Coke used to champion Dr. Bonham's freedom from conviction by those who would have benefited from his conviction, the Antifederalists opposed the Constitution because they thought it marked the reversal of an evolving democratic process. Legislated law in England and in the American states of Virginia, Massachusetts, and Rhode Island seemed to justify their confidence in democratic legislation.

It is in this connection, then, that the aforementioned misunderstanding of the Bill of Rights becomes important. The Bill of Rights protects individual rights only in the *legal* sense of protections that permit citizens to say or do certain things. But in a political context—that is, in the context of what the Bill of Rights is designed to encourage—four of the five First Amendment rights (religion being the exception) are meaningful only in terms of the gathering of others together to bring a public matter before the government. The exercise of such rights makes up the bedrock of democracy only when public institutions can respond to the claims upon them. And the democratic argument for these rights places their usage clearly within the public domain.

With regard to the third pre-constitutional balance, the balance of anti-majoritarian and majoritarian arrangements within any polity, the preferences of conservatives are as clear, both historically and theoretically, as they were in the previous two dichotomies. Given that the framers' fear of factions reflected precisely this angst about people conjoining that Madison spoke so frighteningly of in *The Federalist No. 10*, controlling the effects of such conjoining was the framers' purpose in the constitution. The writings of the Antifederalists, particularly Richard Henry Lee's *The Federal Farmer*,[5] attest to their distrust of the Constitution's antimajoritarian bias as well as to their distrust of the checks that kept the popularly elected assembly, the House of Representatives, from being what it could have been. Antimajoritarianism, too, would become part of the Federalist armor.

If the two-tiered philosophical framework outlined above properly illuminates not only the biases of the American political structure but also the reasons for which those biases still reside in the Constitution, we need not travel far to note that the private, legal, and antimajoritarian biases of America's framers, as well as their modern-day successors, led to the development of a political system that is as structurally centrifugal as it is unique. No other government in the world has developed such ingenious checks of one institution upon another within a governmental order. And certainly no other government links centrifugal structures to such a check upon democracy.

THE LOCAL AND STATE LEVEL

Both explanatory frameworks described above—that is, the perspective on the forms of understanding that make up America's representational style, as well as the perspective on the balances among the three pre-constitutional continua—prepare us to examine the specific institutional arenas that formed the core of the ideological imbalances of the American government.

The United States, of course, was a predominantly rural nation at the time of its founding. Five fledgling towns nestled along the Atlantic seaboard—Boston, New York, Philadelphia, Baltimore, and Charleston—were all striving for, but in only one case (New York) had reached, a population of 50,000 at the time of the writing of the Constitution. The absence of cities, both within the culture and in terms of the reality of the new nation-state, along with the clear political dominance of the vigilantly sovereign states, relegated cities to the subordinate political status that they continue to suffer. If even Jefferson, the greatest American Enlightenment figure of his time, could consider rural life to be more culturally "urbane" than city life, why should cities have enjoyed favorable political consideration from the Constitution-writing Federalists?

But the current condition of America's cities, particularly its largest cities, requires that we look at the status of the urban community in the context of the "states' wrongs" in which many states engaged at the opening of the twentieth century. Motivated largely by a desire to maintain their power in state legislatures over late-nineteenth-century, largely Catholic Southern and Eastern European immigrant populations, rural interests in state legislatures with large cities often acted in outright disregard of their own state constitutions by engaging in three patently anti-urban, and anti-democratic, actions. These actions still, to some degree, politically neuter America's largest cities.

First, large-city state legislatures radically restricted what had been an orderly pattern of annexation at the edges of their largest urban areas. The natural political aggregation that makes up a city, and that had naturally expanded America's cities beyond their original borders throughout the nineteenth century, was deliberately halted by changes in state laws that permitted some citizens (long before the oft-noted "white flight" phenomenon of the 1950s) to be a part of the larger metropolitan area without being politically a part of the city.

Not content with such restrictions upon city growth, large-city state legislatures, at the turn of the century as well, almost universally lowered requirements for municipal incorporation. To nobody's surprise, a collar of tiny but legally protected municipalities popped up on each city's borders, even though adequate education, fire, police, water, sewer, and other services were frequently lacking within these jejune pretenders to citydom. The noose was tightened further around the necks of America's great cities.

Eventually, many large-city state legislatures drove one last nail into their major cities' coffins. Ignoring their constitutions' admonitions requiring reapportionment after each decennial census, these states purposefully failed to reapportion their state legislatures. Most cities miraculously continued to grow; but though they should have exerted increasingly greater influence in their states (at least in the lower houses of their state legislatures), their voices were not fairly heard.

Coincidentally, it was a professional forerunner of one of the editors of this volume, Bill Crotty, namely Northwestern University political science professor Kenneth Colegrove, who first valiantly appealed to the courts in an effort to bring fair representation to America's cities. He was turned down in 1946. And although the *Baker* v. *Carr* to *Reynolds* v. *Sims* line of cases of the 1960s eventually ensured equitable representation in state governments, even adding a landmark insistence on upper-house popular apportionment, the horse was already well out of the barn. Now, although nearly 80 percent of America's population lives in metropolitan areas of the country, its core cities suffer from predictable declines in population and tax base, along with equally predictable increases in crime, housing deterioration, unemployment, and other maladies. The truth is that no other country in the world has balkanized its municipal regions to the extent that America has. Nor does any other country in the developed world suffer the degradation within its urban regions that now besets America's cities. The two phenomena are, of course, related.

The disaggregation of any citizenry—particularly one that separates the better-off from those who are forced to be more dependent upon their government; or a disaggregation that separates one race from another, or those within their earning ages from those who are too young or too old to work—means that the representative form of America's political system has itself predictably been altered, to the detriment of those who can least afford it. But the problem here extends beyond the fact that the poorest among us have become the most politically isolated. It extends even beyond the state-government biases that left these citizens outnumbered early in the century. Indeed, the real problem is that America's highly contractual *form* of representation, a form that responds overwhelmingly to the bargains that discrete groups make with discrete members of the government, discriminates against city dwellers whose claims upon the government require coordinated, comprehensive attention. Even the more self-sustaining members of the population cannot utilize an aggregative form of representation that would include them in governmental considerations.

Having an office that records the needs of those among the middle class who move into and out of privately owned homes is a public function of a fundamentally different *form* than having measles shots available for children of a single parent family at the same place and time that prenatal care is made available to that single parent, at the same place and time that job retraining is also made available to that parent—all of which matters only if physical security is available in a public housing complex that is overwhelmed by drug dealers. The difference between these kinds of needs is not a function of the degree of governmental action that is necessary. The real difference is that the middle-class citizen, or more likely the attorney who represents that citizen, need take but one discrete need before one institution of government and fulfill that need in an essentially contractual way. By contrast, the citizen who lives at the core of this nation's metropolitan centers evidences such a constellation of needs that no contractual form of meeting those needs, and *certainly no contractual form of petitioning the government so that the government will provide those needs in the first place*, is of any real value. For those interests that have little that they can bargain with politically, or for those interests that suffer from an inability to access a relevant bargaining point within the contractual mode of America's politics, America's political structures, in form as well as in substance, are deeply biased.

Moreover, as the current crisis of our cities shows, the separations between city and suburb are such that those who need a vital *public* sector increasingly have no governmental access at all. Whereas the suburban citizen has no need for government in the locating of a home, the wholesale decline and recent defunding of the public sector have made even more difficult the public allocation of adequate housing, which is essential to the less fortunate residents of the core city.

Similarly, whereas suburban residents can rely upon purely legal procedures to buy homes, redress grievances regarding the condition of their housing, or protect the private real property that now more rarely exists within a blighted city's core, the urban poor, who do not have access to the legal avenues that lead to the redress of wrongs either in a contractual or a tort-based (injury) action, cannot utilize *political*—that is governmentally directed—action to redress their grievances.

Finally, with regard to the majoritarian-to-antimajoritarian balance that is necessary for democracy, the balkanization of the cities, both by states and by the federal government, means that now-century-old discriminations against the cities render far less likely the creation of a majoritarian political strategy that would assist what Madison described as the debtor class. Apart from considering what the political impact of cities would have been within state governments had there been fair apportionment all along, think what the political impact of cities would be if 80 percent of the members of the House of Representatives were from entire, fairly delineated urban areas. Even controlling for the influence of medium-sized metropolitan areas within the urban political mix, would not the similarity of many of the problems of the cities across all of the regions of the country ensure a political alliance among cities that would constitute a "faction" so powerful that even Madison's structural protections would have to yield?

In sum, any thoughtful consideration of the biases of structure in the American political system cannot ignore—in fact, I think it must begin with—an analysis of the state-contrived arrangements of America's urban areas as well as the federal complicity involved in both ignoring cities in the Constitution and ignoring what the states have done to their largest cities over the past century. What happened to America's cities during this time was neither accidental nor unpredictable. What happened to them, in fact, happened well within the provisions, and the omissions, of the federal constitutional order. What has put cities where they are today is the biased, contractual form of America's party-weak and less than aggregative representation; along with the imbalances of America's private-to-public sectors, its legal-to-political sectors, and its antimajoritarian-to-majoritarian qualities of citizen aggregation; along with the convenient linkage of these imbalances with the centrifugal-to-centripetal structures of the national government.

THE CONSTITUTIONAL ORDER

Having reviewed the essence of the entire American constitutional arrangement, let me now focus upon a few characteristics of the constitutional order that I think best illustrate the linkages between our government's structural biases and the ideological biases of America's politics. Today, if not at the time of the constitutional ratification, the absence of any mention of political parties in the Constitution is as significant an omission as the absence of any mention of cities. As the aggregators of both political ideology and political activity, parties are what infuse the representative form of the apples-and-oranges, noncontractual form of understanding issues into a government that must take into account the needs of all its citizens, or at least those of a majoritarian segment of that citizenry. Parties do this by deciding upon the priorities of revenue raising and expenditure—quite simply, both *among* and *between* categories of political claims. The ability to prescribe the number of dollars that should be spent on education relative to the number that should be spent on national defense is absolutely necessary for judging among the political claims of the most disparate of political claimants. That ability rests upon the existence of an intermediate, filtering agent in the government that sifts together the claims of the defense industry with the representatives' own notions of the general good.

All organizations require some balance in their ability to know features of both the apples and apples form and the apples and oranges form. But the American political structure is out of balance in that its extreme separation between the legislative and executive branches encourages a form of representation that allows powerful private interests to promote their wellbeing in hidden corners of the government at the same time that it obstructs the consideration of the public good.

The textbooks dutifully report that the American government is a government of obstruction. True enough, but what they need to add is that America's governmental obstructions do not obstruct governance evenly. The American political system makes the obstruction of governance much easier when the public issue is, at least potentially, one of the apples and oranges form. As I suggested earlier, this is the form that not only attempts to aggregate public policy for the good of the whole but also, from the standpoint of equity, attempts to address aggregative issues such as those surrounding public health, public education, and public housing, all of which are important to citizens that are not well represented in the contractual mode.

Also, from the explanatory perspective of the three pre-constitutional balances outlined earlier, it should be evident that the structural centrifugality of the American constitutional arrangement deeply favors the private, legal, and antimajoritarian sides of the continuum. Whereas Coke and the early-seventeenth-century anti-Stuarts transformed the reasoning of the private and legal sectors of their day into the emerging democracy of public and political sectors, the American conservative today delightfully works to reverse Coke's democratic progress. Private interests dominate public governance, while expensive and too often unavailable legal means of redress crowd out the availability of public means of governmental redress. Finally, owing to the absence of strong political parties, particularly a strong Democratic party, majoritarian alliances among groups that need to bridge the categories of race, wealth, region, religion, and the like are less likely in American politics today. Majoritarian perspectives on gun control, the right to choose whether or not to have an abortion, and other long-running public issues are constantly thwarted from achieving their just and final democratic results.

To better understand these mid-range biases, particularly in terms of their impact on majoritarian politics, it may be helpful to look to America's great political cycles and to the structural nature of the cycles of American political history. From the Progressive Democratic perspective, four great Democratic presidents—Jefferson, Jackson, Wilson, and Franklin Roosevelt—believed in, and used, a Democratic party that bridged the legislative and executive branches in order to implement well-aggregated public policy. Jefferson's original conceptualization of the Democratic party; Jackson's reaching out for popular support and his building of post-caucus, convention-based nominating structures as well as a spoils system; Wilson's bringing of progressivism to the Democratic party with three constitutional amendments and unwritten constitutional changes in antitrust and banking regulation; and, finally, Roosevelt's creation of a novel coalition of politically activated citizens and the New Deal legislation that grew out of the strength of that coalition—all were testaments to institution-bridging party influence. The form of New Deal politics—that is, the willingness to address a mixed, disparate combination of public issues and constituencies and then to articulate political positions that grow out of a comprehensive sense of the common weal—was a necessary part of the politics that these Progressive Democrats championed.

In glaring contrast, if one thing is clear about the four conservative periods in American political history, it is that the time of the Federalists, of the National Republicans and John Quincy Adams, of the late-nineteenth-century robber barons, and of the irresponsible 1920s evidenced an absence of aggregative, constituency, and institution-transcending politics. The constitutional separation between the executive and the legislative branches was purposefully not overcome during these periods, the Federalist, Whig, and Republican parties having been delighted with the separation. Also, as the four periods of progressive politics marked a greater use of public, political, and majoritarian politics, wrapped within that centripetal vision of the constitutional order, the conservative periods marked the ascendance of private, legal, and antimajoritarian politics—all well protected by that centrifugal governmental structure.

I close these brief comments on the formal Constitution by pointing out that although it has been amended but twenty-six times, it is, in my view, about to become a battleground once again. Building upon a recent period of government and politics that has decidedly favored the conservative position, the Republican party is currently advocating both a constitutional limitation on congressional terms and a presidential line-item veto. The Democratic party, almost unbelievably, offers no counterproposals for constitutional reform; and some members of the party, notably Senator Edward Kennedy of Massachusetts, have even endorsed the line-item veto. Placing the executive branch in an even more superior position vis-à-vis the Congress than it presently is would only bring about a serious reduction in the representational power of the Congress; at the same time, a restriction on congressional terms would seriously weaken the public sector in favor of powerful private interests as well as the lawyer-lobbyists and congressional staffs who service those interests rather than the public good.

Thus, if the Constitution is to be a political battleground again, it is certainly time for the Democratic party to respond to the predictably disaggregative proposals of Republican conservatives and to develop some proposals of its own. An amendment that would formally place political parties into the Constitution, along with an amendment that would recognize America's cities for what they truly are today, should top any list of constitutional proposals for Progressive Democrats and the Democratic party. Other ideas, such as lengthening the congressional term to four years so that powerful interests are less able to dominate legislative elections, and allowing members of Congress to serve within the executive branch so as to permit greater cooperation among the branches, would serve the progressive agenda as well. James MacGregor Burns' notion of encouraging "team ticket" voting whereby the executive and legislative offices would have a single lever on state voting machines also warrants serious consideration. The sad fact is that American politics will only generate a cycle of progressive politics if those political candidates who call themselves progressive today acknowledge the linkage of substantive political outcomes with the biases of America's political structures, and recommend structural changes similar to those noted above as part of their campaigns.

THE UNWRITTEN CONSTITUTION

If ideological cycles have been important within the constitutional history of American politics, then they have also been important to the arena of structural concern that falls under the "unwritten constitution." During all four of the cyclical periods of progressivism that I identified above, formal constitutional change was rarer, and usually less important, than changes that occurred within the internal arrangements of America's political institutions.

In the case of Thomas Jefferson, it was not the substance of the Louisiana Purchase but the innovative cross-institutional bond of the Democratic Republicans that permitted a novel usage of governmental powers that should stick in the American progressive's conscience.

In the case of Andrew Jackson, it is the *way* that he became president—given Martin Van Buren's engagement of modern political aggregations and newly enfranchised citizenries, along with the innovative state and national conventions that aggregated those citizenries—that constitutes his legacy of progressivism for today.

Woodrow Wilson, building upon the intellectual ballast of the writings of Herbert Croly[6] and others, redefined electoral coalitions in a way that ensured the passage of child and women's labor protection and the antitrust and banking regulations mentioned above.

For Franklin D. Roosevelt, not only was the constitutional order strengthened by the new brand of party-led linkages between the Congress and the presidency, but the burden of strong party leadership was transmitted to the Congress so effectively that Social Security, the minimum wage, the Wagner Act protection for union organizing, and other landmark pieces of legislation were all enacted.

In view of the significant relationship of internal congressional structures to public policy, what has occurred within the internal structures of the United States Congress in recent years is every bit as perplexing as it is dangerous. These changes, propagated in the context of what their proponents, mostly Democrats, labeled during the 1960s and 1970s as political "reform," have in fact only accelerated the centrifugal nature of the government as a whole and crippled the government in terms of performance of its public function.

During this "reform" period, House and Senate staffs grew out of control, subcommittees exploded in number and authority, the three-day work week became routine, travel allotments soared, franking privileges grew enormously, and campaign funding rocketed to the point where none but the most well connected or personally wealthy of Americans could and did run for office. With these changes, the U.S. Congress engaged in the almost complete destruction of the integrity of its own internal, party-led leadership. In its place, it ensured its members not only an unimpeded, contractual form of relationship with their most powerful constituents but also the near certainty of reelection regardless of their inattention to broad public concerns.

A few facts are worth noting. Between 1967 and 1985 congressional staffs grew from 1,749 members in the Senate and 4,055 in the House to over 4,000 in the Senate and 7,900 in the House. Subcommittee staffs grew to such an extent that the House of Representatives now has fully 195 committees and subcommittees, all of which have their own staffs. The franking privilege grew from 170 million pieces of mail in 1970 to 750 million pieces in 1980. Recesses, of which none were taken in 1965 and few existed in other years, grew to 82 days by 1987. And, most important, 1971 and 1974 campaign reform legislation excluded political parties as the principal source of electoral funding and replaced them with interest-dominated Political Action Committees (PACs)[7].

Though volumes have been written on these structural, staffing, travel, and electoral funding changes, they are best seen not as changes in the amounts of money that are now needed for congressional travel, staff, and electioneering, or even as changes that greatly retarded the legislative efficiency of the Congress. Rather, they should be seen as absolutely fundamental changes in the *form* of America's legislative representation. They should also be seen, in the apples-to-apples versus apples-to-oranges context as well as along the three continua of my mid-range framework, as significant alterations in the structure of the American government. What is so tragic about all of this, particularly at a time when the progressive part of a grand political cycle in America was coming to a close and the Democratic members of Congress were feigning deep concern over a number of troublesome domestic problems in the 1960s, is that these Democrats engineered changes in their own institution that did nothing less than prevent them, and their institution, from dealing with problems that could not come to them in a contractual way.

It was this generation of Democrats in the Congress who violated all of the history and all of the ideological potency of their aggregative, centripetal heritage concerning the structure of the American government itself. It was these Democrats who almost guaranteed that consideration of the overall good of the nation, as well as consideration of any interest that was less able to represent its political needs before the Congress, would be impeded in favor of powerful specific interests. Private, legal, and antimajoritarian arenas and qualities of doing the public's business triumphed, thanks to the current generation of congressional Democrats, over the traditional Democratic commitment to public, political, and majoritarian arenas and qualities of governing.

As a result of these radical changes in the unwritten constitution, the apples-to-apples form of transaction—that nearly exclusive mode of direct favor given for direct favor received—grew to dominate American politics far more than it had at any time, certainly, since the 1920s. "Residual" issues, issues that concerned the problems of the cities, the problems of the poor, and the problems of the environment, education, health care, and the like, were increasingly ignored. And they were ignored because these issues were not *directly represented by a contracting agent that could bargain with a public officeholder in a contractual mode, as that mode was now mandated by the new structure of Congress.*

If many unforgivable things have already resulted because of the Congress's betrayal of its historical preference for the centripetal over the centrifugal institutional form, let us not forget that the entire distribution of wealth in the United States has changed dramatically in recent years. Though the redistributional burdens of the public sector had already begun to weaken by the 1970s (during which, incidently, both a Democratic president and a Democratic Congress were in power), the American distributional pyramid became a glaring example of "Robin Hood in reverse" when the Reagan tax bill passed in 1981—with the support of Democratic members of the House and Senate. In the decade since that passage, the upper 1 percent of Americans have seen their incomes increase by 122 percent, whereas the bottom 10 percent have lost nearly 15 percent of their income. For the first time since 1934, the top 20 percent of American wage earners now have an income that is larger than the bottom 80 percent. And, please remember, the distribution of income is still much less distorted than the distribution of wealth.

Yet it is still fair to say that if economic distribution is one sure mark of a nation's democratic nature, it is at best only an indirect mark. It is not, and never will be, the mark of democracy that the competitiveness of the election process itself surely is. Unfortunately, the recent changes within the structure of Congress, and the recent changes in the political process by which members of Congress are elected, have led to such imbalances in America's representational form that the very nature of American democracy is now threatened by the almost automatic return of incumbents to their seats in the Congress. In the last three elections, competitive election rates have fallen such that 98 percent, 98 percent, and 96 percent of incumbent House members won reelection. Similarly, 35 of 36 seats in the Senate were returned to their original holders in 1990.

The average Senatorial race now costs well over $1 million, the average House race costs well over $300,000, and by the first six months of 1991 over $33 million had already been collected for the 1992 races by Senators alone[8]: Such are the dramatic unwritten constitutional changes that have taken place within the American political system. But, again, it is not the amount of money that warns us of dangers to our democracy. The money comes from someplace. Surely, it no longer comes from parties; nor does it come from any aggregative grouping that would want America's worsening problems to be considered in a comprehensive and courageous way. On the contrary, Americans know that the significant money for political campaigns comes increasingly from individual interests alone. Apart from the charges of "influence buying" and "Congress for sale" that have all too frequently been documented, the further ascendance of the centrifugal form within the government solidifies the contractual nature of these campaign contributions. Do not forget, too, that these campaign funding changes, like the institutional changes, were brought about by a Democratically controlled Congress.

The Democratic position, which would be the proper heir to the traditional positions carved out by Jefferson's and Jackson's ideals of representative government, has been abandoned. Structures are no less neutral now than they were at this nation's founding. And not only are America's structures more centrifugal than ever, after these ill-considered and selfish reforms; they were made more centrifugal by Democrats, not Republicans.

CONCLUSION

What I recommend with regard to sub-constitutional reform, much like what I recommended with regard to constitutional reform, should be obvious. First, there is a need to return to a traditional organizational structure within that most important institution of our government, the Congress; hence committees, personal staffs, travel allotments, and the like must be returned to roughly the same status they possessed before the great "reforms." And, second, campaign financing must be revamped in such a way as to reinstate party control over who receives support on the basis of cooperation with the parties' governmental or oppositional policies. The foundation for the Democratic party's structural argument is therefore clear, in terms of both the party's ideological history and its traditional stance with regard to the structure of government. Unlike what is being offered by the candidates of the 1992 election, this structural argument should be placed at the top of the list of topics to be discussed by candidates as they campaign.

NOTES

1. William P. Kreml, *Psychology, Relativism, and Politics* (New York: NYU Press, 1991).

2. Kreml, *Losing Balance: The De-Democratization of American Politics* (Armonk, N.Y.: M. E. Sharpe, 1991).

3. Garry Wills, *Inventing America: Jefferson's Declaration of Independence* (Garden City, N.Y.: Doubleday, 1978).

4. Wills, *Explaining America: The Federalist* (Garden City, N.Y.: Doubleday, 1981).

5. Richard Henry Lee, *Letters from a Federal Farmer* (Englewood Cliffs, N.J.: Prentice-Hall, 1962).

6. Herbert Croly, *The Promise of American Life* (New York: Macmillan, 1909).

7. Barbara Sinclair, *Majority Leadership in the House* (Baltimore: Johns Hopkins University Press, 1983); Sinclair, *The Transformation of the U.S. Senate* (Baltimore: Johns Hopkins University Press, 1989).

8. Federal Election Commission, *1992 Campaigns Spend over $10 Million* (Washington, D.C.: FEC, 1991).

About the Book

All over the world, political parties are being born and political pluralism is being fostered. Ironically, here in the United States, the parties are blurring together ideologically, and the political process is suffering. One of the messages of this book is that a vital two-party system is essential to America's political health. The last thing this country needs, the authors argue, is two Republican parties. At this critical moment in history, the Democratic party has the opportunity to offer the nation a real political choice, a sense of direction, and a program to address the needs of Americans in a changing world. It is time, they say, for a change—a change that only the Democrats can provide.

As recounted here, a generation of Republican administrations have had their chance. The results have not been happy: deepening social divisions, heightened inequalities in income distribution, a decaying educational system, environmental exploitation, an insensitivity to the concerns of the less powerful, the largest public debt in history, and a foreign policy based on force. Recurring constitutional crises have also erupted, as epitomized by the Iran-Contra affair. The record is a sorry one.

Alternatives exist, and the best ones rest with the Democratic party. *The Democrats must lead.* It is their responsibility to offer a new vision of the future and the means for achieving it—to provide a program that is compassionate, just, and inclusive of all. The politics of greed, exploitation, self-promotion, and militarism must be put behind us.

Such are the themes of this extraordinary book. Leading academicians, each an expert in his or her area, emphasize the need for new leadership, propose contributions that a progressive Democratic party could make, and suggest what this party should stand for as well as how it can win in 1992. They urge the Democrats to be both brave and principled—brave in defying the conventional wisdom that Democrats must be moderate to win, and principled in sticking to progressive ideals.

The book provides analysis of such areas as the political impact of an issue-oriented, liberal party; the campaign and media choices required to get a progressive message across; the role and concerns of women, blacks, Hispanics, and other underrepresented groups; electoral and legislative strategies for success; and the substance of what a progressive policy agenda should contain.

Challenging and thought-provoking, these essays will help reshape political thinking during this critical period in the nation's history. Their objective is creation of a society that represents and responds to human needs, and the authors indicate the way to achieve these goals through an invigorated, forward-looking Democratic party.

About the Editors & Contributors

Samuel Bowles teaches economics at the University of Massachusetts at Amherst and at the Center for Popular Economics. Before moving to the University of Massachusetts, he was a member of the faculty of economics at Harvard University. He is the author, with David M. Gordon and Thomas Weisskopf, of *After the Waste Land: Toward a Democratic Economics for the Year 2000*; with Herbert Gintis, of *Democracy and Capitalism*; and with Richard Edward, of *Understanding Capitalism: Competition, Command, and Change in the U.S. Economy*.

James MacGregor Burns is Woodrow Wilson Professor of Government Emeritus at Williams College and is currently on the faculty at the Jepson School of Leadership Studies at the University of Richmond. A Pulitzer Prize-winning historian, he has published widely in the area of American government and politics and is the founder of Political Scientists for a Progressive Democratic Party.

William Crotty is professor of political science at Northwestern University. He is the author of a number of books on political parties and elections, including *The Party Game, Party Reform, Political Reform and the American Experiment*, and *Decision for the Democrats*, and editor and co-editor of several other works including *Political Parties in Local Areas, Political Participation and American Democracy*, and the four-volume *Political Science: Looking to the Future*. He has served as president of the Midwest Political Science Association, the Policy Studies Organization, and the Political Organizations and Parties Section of the American Political Science Association from which he received the Samuel J. Eldersveld Lifetime Achievement Award in 1991. He is presently co-chair of Political Scientists for a Progressive Democratic Party.

Lois Lovelace Duke is associate professor of political science at Clemson University and co-chair of Political Scientists for a Progressive Democratic Party. She is author of many pieces on media and politics and on women and politics, including the forthcoming *Women and Politics: Have the Outsiders Become Insiders?*

Betty Glad is professor of government and international studies at the University of South Carolina and previously taught at the University of Illinois. She has been a National Endowment for the Humanities Senior Fellow, a guest scholar at the

Brookings Institution, president of the Presidency Research Group of the American Political Science Association, and a vice-president of the International Society for Political Psychology. She prepared the "Election of 1976" segment of the *History of Presidential Elections 1789-1984* and has written many articles on the psychological aspects of the American presidency. Her books include *Jimmy Carter: In Search of the Great White House*; *The Psychological Dimensions of War*; *Key Pittman: The Tragedy of a Senate Insider*; and *Charles Evans and the Illusions of Innocence*.

David M. Gordon is professor of economics in the graduate faculty of the New School for Social Research. He is co-author of many works, including *Segmented Work*; *Divided Workers: The Historical Transformation of Labor in the United States*; *After the Waste Land*; and *What's Wrong with the U.S. Economy?* He is also a member of the Board of Economists of the *Los Angeles Times*. He received his Ph.D. in economics from Harvard University and lives in New York City with his wife, Diana R. Gordon.

Charles V. Hamilton has been the Wallace S. Sayre Professor of Government at Columbia University since 1969. He previously taught at Tuskegee Institute, Lincoln University (Pennsylvania), and Roosevelt University. His publications include *Black Politics: The Politics of Liberation* (with Stokely Carmichael); *The Black Experience in American Politics*; *Bench and the Ballot: Southern Federal Judges and the Right to Vote*; and, most recently, *Adam Clayton Powell, Jr.: The Political Biography of an American Dilemma*.

Mary Lou Kendrigan is assistant professor in the social science department at Lansing Community College in Lansing, Michigan. She is the author of *Political Equality in a Democratic Society: Women in the United States; Gender Differences: Their Impact on Public Policy*; and the forthcoming *Political Equality, Women, and the Military*. She is actively involved in the Michigan Democratic party and is a past president of the Midwest Women's Caucus for Political Science. She also has the distinction of being the first state board member of the Wisconsin Women's Political Caucus.

William P. Kreml, a professor in the department of government and international studies at the University of South Carolina, has researched and written extensively in the area of political philosophy. He is also the creator of psychological relativism, an original political philosophy. His most recent book is *Losing Balance: The De-Democratization of America*. He has been active in the constitutional reform movement and was a candidate for the U.S. Senate in the South Carolina Democratic primary in 1980.

Kay Lawson is professor of political science at San Francisco State University. Her many publications reflect her extensive research into American political parties and include a comparative study of political parties. She has edited the volume *When Parties Fail*, and her most recent book in this subject area is *How Political Parties Work: Perspectives from Within*. An active member of the Committee for Party Renewal, she has served on this group's executive committee for six years. She is also a former president of the national Women's Caucus for Political Science and a former member of the executive council of the American Political Science Association.

Lawrence D. Longley, professor of government at Lawrence University in Appleton, Wisconsin, is the author of more than seventy articles, papers, and books on American politics and political institutions, including *Bicameral Politics* (on Congress), *The People's President* (on the American presidency), and his forthcoming *Changing the System* (on U.S. and British electoral reform). A long-time grassroots Democratic party activist in Wisconsin, he served five terms as a county political party chairman and has been elected to the State Party Administrative (Central) Committee since 1971. Currently a member of the Democratic National Committee, Professor Longley will be an automatic, unpledged, and determinedly uncommitted delegate to the 1992 Democratic National Convention in New York City.

Jerome M. Mileur is professor of political science at the University of Massachusetts at Amherst. A specialist in American political parties, he is co-editor of *Challenges to Party Government* and former executive director of the Committee for Party Renewal. He has also chaired the town Democratic party committee in Amherst, Massachusetts, and has been a member of the party's state central committee.

Carlos Muñoz, Jr., is professor of Chicano and ethnic studies at the University of California at Berkeley. He holds a Ph.D. in government from the Claremont Graduate School and is the author of numerous pioneering works on the Mexican American experience and American urban politics. He also served as a key adviser to the 1988 Jesse Jackson Presidential Campaign. His most recent book, *Youth, Identity, Power: The Chicano Movement*, won the 1992 Gustavus Myers Book Award for "outstanding scholarship in the study of human rights in the United States."

James A. Nathan is presently Khalid bin Sultan Eminent Scholar at Auburn University at Montgomery in Alabama. A former professor of political science at the University of Delaware, he has authored several books on U.S. foreign policy and U.S. naval policy, and is currently at work on a history of the structure of international society. More than sixty of his articles have appeared in such publications as *World Politics, Foreign Policy, Virginia Quarterly*, and the *New York Times*. He is a former Foreign Service officer and has held senior appointments at the Navy War College and the Army War College.

Samuel C. Patterson is professor of political science at Ohio State University. His numerous publications in the fields of legislative politics and political parties include *The Legislative Process in the United States* and *Political Leadership in Democratic Societies*. From 1985 to 1991 he was managing editor of the *American Political Science Review*, published by the American Political Science Association. He was a Guggenheim fellow in 1984-1985, served as Roy J. Carver Distinguished Professor at the University of Iowa in 1985-1986, and won a Distinguished Scholar Award at Ohio State University in 1990.

Richard Santillan is a professor in the ethnic and women's studies department at California State Polytechnic University in Pomona. He has written and edited several articles and books on Latino politics in the United States, including *Rosita the Riveter: Midwest Mexican American Women in Defense Work, 1941-1945*; *Latino Political Development in the Southwest and the Midwest Region: A Comparative Overview, 1915-1989*; and *Latino Participation in Republican Party Politics in California*. Still under way is a book on Latino politics in the Midwest. Professor Santillan has been active in electoral politics since 1968, when he was involved in the "Viva Bobby Kennedy" campaign in California. Currently he is a senior consultant on state and local government with the Rose Institute of the Claremont Colleges.

Thomas Weisskopf is professor of economics at the University of Michigan at Ann Arbor; he is also a member of the Union for Radical Political Economic and the Democratic Socialists of America. He received his Ph.D. in economics from MIT in 1966 and taught at the Indian Statistical Institute and at Harvard University before joining the University of Michigan in 1972. He is co-author, with Richard Edwards and Michael Reich, of *The Capitalist System* and, with Samuel Bowles and David M. Gordon, of *After the Waste Land*. He has also published numerous articles in journals, periodicals, and reviews dealing with political and economic issues.

Index